APPROACHES TO INTENT.

APPROACHES
TO
INTENTIONALITY

WILLIAM LYONS

CLARENDON PRESS · OXFORD

Oxford University Press, Great Clarendon Street, Oxford OX2 6DP

Oxford New York

Athens Auckland Bangkok Bogota Bombay
Buenos Aires Calcutta Cape Town Dar es Salaam
Delhi Florence Hong Kong Istanbul Karachi
Kuala Lumpur Madras Madrid Melbourne
Mexico City Nairobi Paris Singapore
Taipei Tokyo Toronto Warsaw

and associated companies in
Berlin Ibadan

Oxford is a trade mark of Oxford University Press

Published in the United States by
Oxford University Press Inc., New York

First published 1995
First issued in paperback 1998

British Library Cataloguing in Publication Data
Data available

Library of Congress Cataloging in Publication Data
Lyons, William E.
Approaches to intentionality / William Lyons.
Includes bibliographical references.
1. Intentionality (Philosophy)   I. Title.
B105.I56L86   1995   128'.2—dc20   95–20275
ISBN 0–19–823526–7
ISBN 0–19–875222–9 (Pbk.)

Printed in Great Britain by
Biddles Ltd, Guildford and King's Lynn

To
Annie, la mia metà

PREFACE

Approaches to Intentionality is divided into two parts. The first and longer of the two parts, 'Modern Approaches', is devoted to critical accounts, which are also, I hope, fair and sympathetic accounts of the leading theories about intentionality in contemporary analytic philosophy of mind. I have singled out five theories for examination. I chose those theories which seem to me both to focus in a deliberate way upon intentionality and to be original and salient. I have also tried to describe those theories against their more general philosophical background. Others, admittedly, might see things differently and produce a different selection. I apologize, therefore, to anyone who feels left out.

This mapping of current theorizing about intentionality seems to me a worthwhile task in itself because the current discussions about intentionality have become increasingly more specialized and complex. Even to display the conceptual geography clearly would be a distinct gain.

In the second part of this book, 'A Different Approach', I have delineated another approach to intentionality, my own. This approach has been influenced considerably by work in developmental psychology and neurophysiology. On the other hand, above all, it owes an enormous debt to those that have gone before, especially to those whose tracks I have traced in Part I.

In both parts of the book I have tried to write in a clear, direct, and lively style. I have done this in the hope that it will prove accessible not merely to my professional colleagues but also to undergraduate philosophy students and even to interested 'outsiders'.

ACKNOWLEDGEMENTS

I have worked on this book for seven years or more, writing for months and then like some confused philosophical weaver unravelling it all and starting again. During those years, however, I have been sustained by the generous help and advice of many philosophical Rumpelstiltskins. Sometimes this help and advice has taken the form of correspondence or discussion about specific points, or the provision of reading material; at other times it has taken the form of a critical reading of a chapter or more. The list of such helpers and advisers is quite lengthy: Roger Anwyl, Roderick Chisholm, Martin Davies, Vincent Denard, Daniel Dennett, Fred Dretske, Jim Edwards, Jerry Fodor, John Gaskin, Sheila Greene, John Haldane, Robert Kirk, Brian Loar, Gregory McCulloch, Alan Millar, Ruth Garrett Millikan, David Novitz, Alan Slater, John Smythies.

However, I owe a special debt of gratitude to the Department of Philosophy at the University of Canterbury at Christchurch, New Zealand, who did me the great honour of inviting me to their department as an Erskine Visiting Fellow in 1994. This invitation enabled me to present the whole of Part II of this book to the departmental research colloquium as a trilogy of seminars. I profited immensely from the ensuing, very lively, discussions. In particular I was spurred on by the penetrating critique and warm encouragement of Jack Copeland. While in New Zealand I was also greatly honoured by the invitation to present a paper about my views on intentionality to the Department of Philosophy at the University of Otago at Dunedin.

Of course I must acknowledge my debt to my own academic household, Trinity College Dublin. My own department has always been a most generous and kindly source of both critical advice and encouragement, though at times they must have despaired of my ever finishing the book. My academic faculty, the Faculty of Arts Humanities, supported me with a generous grant from the Arts and Social Sciences Benefaction Fund and the College Board allowed me sabbatical leave on two occasions.

I would also like to thank Peter Momtchiloff of the Oxford University Press, and his reviewers and editors, for their generous and very positive help in preparing the manuscript for printing and then in bringing it to press. As regards the preparation of the manuscript from this end, in my tussles with my Macintosh Classic I have had invaluable help from my colleague Paul O'Grady.

Finally I would like to thank very warmly Professor John Rust for accepting for publication in his journal, *Philosophical Psychology*, a series of papers on intentionality over the years 1990, 1991, and 1992. For these papers amounted to my first public steps into the difficult terrain called theories of intentionality. With his permission I have made use of those papers, in heavily revised form, in Part I of this book.

CONTENTS

Introduction: The Etymology, Definition, Theory, and Problem of Intentionality

I have called this book *Approaches to Intentionality* because it sets out, in Part I, to discuss the most important contemporary approaches to or theories about the nature of intentionality and, in Part II, to reconnoitre a new approach to intentionality. So it is important here, at the outset, that I make clear what it is that theories of intentionality are about.

In my experience it is necessary, first, to defuse a not uncommon point of confusion. Intentionality has little or nothing to do with intentions in the sense of someone having an intention to do something or the road to hell being paved with good intentions. Intentionality in philosophy of mind has a different, technical sense. The etymology of the term might be the best place to start.

Etymologically the word 'intentionality' arises out of the medieval discussions of intentionality. Part of one well-known medieval account of intentionality involved making a distinction between *esse naturale* (natural existence, such as that of a tree or a rabbit) and *esse intentionale* (intentional or mental existence, such as that of a thought or mental image). In turn, the word 'intentionale' in the phrase 'esse intentionale' was derived from the Latin word *intentio*, which meant, roughly, 'having an idea' or 'the directing of attention in thought'.[1] The Latin root leads naturally into a short *definition* of intentionality as that concept is used in philosophy. Intentionality covers *those characteristics of mental activities on account of which those activities are said both to have a content that contains information about something beyond the content and the activity, and to involve a particular sort of attitude towards that content. Moreover, it is a peculiarity of mental content that it is necessarily 'perspectival'.* Let me try to make clear what exactly is involved in this definition.

---

[1] See e.g. Aquinas (1970: 1a, Q. 54, art. 4 ad 2; 1a, Q. 79, art. 1–4, 8, 10; 1a, Q. 84, art. 4 ad 3, 6, 7; 1a, Q. 85, art. 1, 2; and 1a, Q. 86, art. 1). For an overview, see Marenbon (1987, ch. 8).

Our life involves many activities; some of these are non-mental activities, some are mental activities. An example of a non-mental activity is kicking a football. An example of a mental activity is thinking about kicking a football. The shape or basic characteristics of mental activities seem to be fundamentally different from those of non-mental activities. Most, though not all, non-mental activities seem to have the linear shape of cause–effect processes. I kick the football by moving my leg which in turn makes contact with the object, the football, and moves the football off in the same direction in which my foot moved forward. That is, 'kicking the football' is a description of a physical causal process whereby a leg movement gave rise to an effect on an object, a football movement. On the other hand, when I think about kicking the football, I do not move my foot at all and there need be no football about. Indeed there need be no foot about. Owing to some great misfortune both of my feet may have been amputated. In my act of thinking, the foot and the football and the kicking exist only in so far as they are the content of my activity of thinking. To be part of the act of thinking the contents need have no existence outside of the act of thinking. They need not exist as objects or events in the world.

Mental acts, such as those of thinking or deciding, must involve a subject-matter or content. You cannot think or decide unless you have some content to think about or decide upon. I cannot say I am simply thinking but not thinking about anything. The act of thinking may have some effect, and in that sense also be part of a causal process, but it need not have any such effect in order to be an act of thinking of any kind. My deciding to go home may lead me to take the seven o'clock bus to Rathmines. But in order to be a mental act, my deciding need not have that effect.

Mental contents are said to be 'perspectival' because the information they contain is necessarily slanted or 'from one perspective rather than another'. If my beach bucket contains the football, then it contains it in a simple and straightforward way. The whole of the football, rather than some aspect of it or perspective upon it, is contained in my bucket. However, if I think about the football, only a certain perspective on or view about the football will be in my thoughts. If I am only 2 or 3 years old, then, because of the limitations of my knowledge, I may only be able to think of the football as 'thing to be kicked that my brother got as a Christmas present'. If someone asked me whether I had just been kicking a football, I might sincerely deny that I had. For, while I had indeed been kicking a football, I was only able to think about that activity under the one and only aspect or description I knew, namely kicking the funny thing my brother got as a Christmas present. This perspectival or aspectual parameter of intentionality is also true of all thinking, whether of an adult or a child. No matter how much I know about something, it is still limited to certain descriptions or perspectives or slants or aspects. I might think of Camus whenever someone mentions 'the author of *L'Étranger*' or 'French novelist born in Algiers in 1913' or 'the first editor of *Combat* after the liberation of Paris at the end of the Second World War' or 'the winner of the Nobel Prize for Literature in 1957' but not think of him when someone mentions 'the author of *Le Premier Homme*'.

The basic structure of paradigm mental acts, then, seems to be an attitude which operates over contents which contain information about something beyond themselves in a perspectival way. At least this is the case prima facie, that is, as presented in our ordinary psychological expressions of the most important of these mental acts. For we ordinarily express our beliefs, desires, wants, needs, decisions, expectations, and all the other kindred mental attitudes, in the form of a mental activity verb operating over a proposition introduced by the word 'that' or by the word 'to' or by some present participle. Thus we say 'I believe that today is Monday' or 'She hopes to go to Bologna for her holidays' or 'He dreads going back to school'.

From this point on, however, matters become more controversial. That is why I set out to write this book. *Theories* of intentionality have been with us as long as philosophy has been with us, though such theories have not always been emphasized by being given the title 'theory of intentionality'. On the other hand, in certain periods, questions about the nature of intentionality have been raised very explicitly. This was so in the Middle Ages, and again, with Brentano and Husserl and others, in the nineteenth century. However, it is fair to say that, in the second half of the twentieth century, in the world of English-speaking analytic philosophy of mind, a simply prodigious amount of time and energy has been devoted to discussing intentionality.

What contemporary philosophers have been trying to do is to put forward an adequate theory about what they believe are the underlying facts of intentionality. They want to look behind or below the linguistic expressions of our paradigm mental acts, the intentional attitudes, and see and say what is really going on. As we shall see, most often this has involved contemporary philosophers of mind in trying to give an up-to-date and 'tough-minded' account which they feel is consonant with the findings in the relevant sciences that deal with the mind. One significant upshot is that contemporary theories have concentrated on the notion of information-bearing content and its processing. In comparison, other aspects of intentionality have been seen as far less important. So another upshot is that, in contrast with the theorizing of Brentano and Husserl, consciousness or attention have no longer been seen as essential to intentionality. On the other hand, this modern bypassing of consciousness could be construed as a return to the more objective approach of the medieval theorists of intentionality.

So, in this post-Darwinian era, some philosophers have tried to give an account of intentionality which they believe is in keeping with the view that our mental capacities are evolved biological capacities and so, ultimately, must be nothing but a complex configuration and functioning of some physico-chemical bits and pieces. Others, more influenced by our computer technology, have tried to give accounts in terms of modern information-processing systems or quasi-linguistic representational systems. Still others have felt that we have been misled about the true nature of our mental capacities by adhering too literally to the surface structure of our linguistic expressions of those capacities. Still others have limited intentionality to these surface, ordinary language expressions. The detail of such theorizing is the material of this book.

Most of the proposals which have emerged in the course of the ingenious contemporary attempts to give an adequate and scientifically respectable account or theory of intentionality are themselves the subject of further intense discussion. Thus, to take just one example, there is an intense debate about representational theories of intentionality which centres on the following questions. Must an adequate account of intentionality involve the postulate that inside human heads there is an innate language or other form of symbolic system for representing the incoming sensory information? How else, other than via some form of representational system, could a human organism contain information as a content over which it could operate or 'attitudinize'? If so, how can we give an explanation of how such representations were formed? Then how can we explain how such representations are interpreted or understood? Or should we even talk about inner representations as being interpreted or understood by the human physiological 'system' which houses them?

Contemporary philosophers have sometimes approached intentionality as if they were seeking a solution to a *problem* rather than searching for an adequate theory. For the most intractable aspect of theorizing about intentionality has been how to reconcile talking about mental acts and mental contents (or 'holding information in one's mind and thinking about it in some way') with the view that our mind is nothing more than some aspect or other of the brain and, perhaps, some other neurophysiological bits and pieces. To put this problem in another way, in this post-Darwinian age any sensible person, contemporary philosophers would say, should admit that we humans are part of the natural biological evolution of species, just as much as cats and frogs and dogs are. Ontologically speaking, we are nothing more than physical, biological beings. There are no souls or pure mental substances inside us. This being so, there arises a genuine problem about how one can separate non-mental activities from mental activities. For if mental acts are just certain sorts of activities of certain sorts of brains, then a mental act seems to be a physical act of much the same sort as is kicking a football. Or, in short, there is a genuine problem about how and whether these new post-Darwinian reductive approaches to mind can convincingly 'naturalize' intentionality.

As I said above, these contemporary discussions are the material of this book. Even Part II, where I dip my own spoon into the pot and do my own stirring, is to a certain extent a matter of taking down some packet soup marked 'contemporary debates about the nature of intentionality'. However, the *inspecteur gastronomique* might consider a soup that involves removing many ingredients that seem to be past their best and bringing in a number of fresh ingredients, all served in an unusual form, to be a genuine *potage à la maison*. At any rate, it is time now to begin laying out the ingredients of this modern debate. In the first chapter in particular, and for each of the chapters in Part I, I will try to lead the reader into the debate in a gentle way. I will do this by beginning with a historical preamble which sets the scene. In addition I have tried to order the chapters chronologically, though there is a certain amount of artificiality in this because many of the theories and the debates run parallel with one another. The story is not a simple one of one theory being displaced by another and this in turn being displaced by yet another. The true picture is much messier. I tidy it up for reasons of clarity and utility.

I
Modern Approaches

I

The Instrumentalist Approach

To suggest as one might be tempted to, that the new reductive approaches to intentionality, reconnoitred in the early part of this century, were simply the result of the behaviourist victories over Cartesianism in both philosophy and psychology would be an oversimplification. Matters were much more complex. At least as important as the rise of behaviourism was the retooling of nineteenth-century positivism by the Logical Positivists of the Vienna Circle and the consequent reshaping of the style and content of a great deal of modern philosophy. For the positivistic philosophers produced, or at least aimed to produce, a 'scientific philosophy' which would lay bare the logical and conceptual bases of the natural sciences. In fact what happened was that, by and large, they became fixated on discussions about the nature of language itself. However, it was also true that, in the course of their scrutiny of the language of psychology, and in pursuit of their aim of reducing the language of psychology to the language of more fundamental natural sciences, the Logical Positivists very often found common cause both with mainstream behaviourism and with physicalism. But to make sense of all this I need to go back, at least briefly, to the beginning of this revolutionary period.

It was the now distinctly unfashionable nineteenth-century philosopher Auguste Comte, who (along with his mentor, Saint-Simon) coined the name 'positivism' and began the movement which was to lead eventually to Logical Positivism. For Comte believed that each area of human knowledge evolved over time from a theological standpoint, via a metaphysical one, to a culmination in a positive scientific approach where the explanations were to be sought and found in terms of causal laws based on observation and experiment. Via such diverse figures as John Stuart Mill, Herbert Spencer, Ernst Haeckel, and Ernst Mach, positivism was elaborated into the fairly stable doctrine that the only genuine knowledge was scientific knowledge; that the only genuine method for gaining knowledge, including knowledge about all aspects of human life, was the scientific method of producing and testing causal hypotheses by reference to observation and experiment; that the whole of science could, in principle, be reduced to one fundamental science, wherein the basic observed elements were faithfully described and tabulated, and in consequence that the bases of all our knowledge were the sense experiences resulting from these basic observations.

Positivism was thus a hymn to natural science, extolling it as the sole repository of real, factual, or positive knowledge. At the same time positivism deprecated metaphysics and all its works. The most obvious ancestors of the positivists were the British empiricists; their most vociferous offspring were the Logical Positivists of the Vienna Circle and, later on, the analytic philosophers of the English-speaking world. In effect the Logical Positivists combined the analytical-cum-logical work of Frege and Russell and Wittgenstein with the aspirations of the nineteenth-century positivists. Thus, in typical fashion, the Logical Positivists sometimes expressed their anti-metaphysical stance in terms of a clear and austere logico-linguistic principle, called a 'verification principle'. A simple version of a verification principle claims that a statement (or sentence) is literally meaningful (or significant) if and only if it is either empirically verifiable (or falsifiable) or it can be seen, or shown, to be true (or self-contradictory) simply by means of the analysis of the conventional meanings of the signs or symbols used in the statement.[1] The meaning of all terms or phrases is thus anchored to checkable facts about either language or the world. The particular statements and general laws of the mainstream natural sciences were grouped under the 'empirically verifiable' label, and the indispensable statements of logic and mathematics were grouped under the 'verifiable by the analysis of their conventional meanings' label. So all that was worth preserving was shown to be meaningful. The rest could be consigned to the bonfire of the inanities.

An important part of what was new to this logical version of positivism was its belief that logic was the chief tool of philosophy as mathematics was of science, and its belief that the task of philosophy was to work on the logical and conceptual foundations of

---

[1] I attribute this particular version of a verification principle to no one in particular, but similar versions are to be found in Carnap (1963: 76) and Ayer (1946: 35).

science. This latter task in turn was held to comprise, at least in part, the reduction of the language of the human sciences to the language of the physical sciences. As regards psychology, this task was often described in terms of the translation of psychological language into physical language, initially into neurophysiological or behavioural language but with the hope and belief that ultimately it would be possible to translate neurophysiological statements and statements about behaviour into statements couched in the language of physics. One of the central figures involved in this latter task, and one who has exerted a major influence on subsequent reductive theories of intentionality, is Rudolf Carnap.

Carnap joined the Vienna Circle soon after its inception at the invitation of its central figure, Moritz Schlick, and found its doctrines very congenial.[2] In November 1930, while teaching at the University of Vienna, Carnap was invited to Warsaw to deliver three lectures to the Warsaw Philosophical Society (which included Tarski and Leśniewski). The three lectures were on formulating psychology in physical language, on the elimination of metaphysics, and on the tautological character of logical inference. In short the lectures were on three of the central concerns of the Logical Positivists. The first lecture was published two years later in *Erkenntnis*, the house journal of the Vienna Circle, under the title 'Psychologie in physikalischer Sprache' ('Psychology in Physical Language').

In 'Psychology in Physical Language', one of Carnap's background doctrines is that *any* true science must ultimately be expressible in physical language for only a language made up of terms for observable objects, properties, and events will be truly universal and intersubjective, and so truly scientific. Besides, strictly speaking, there are only physical events, and so only statements about physical events could be literally true statements about the world. In the context of psychology this means, so Carnap argued, that in the absence of a mature neurophysiology, we must fall back on a behaviouristic physical language for psychology. As Carnap so tersely put it, 'All sentences of psychology describe physical occurrences, namely, the physical behaviour of humans and other animals'(1959a: 165). The 'sentences' referred to are not the sentences psychologists themselves may employ, for they may be unredeemed Cartesian

---

[2] In Carnap (1963: 20) the author remarks that 'my interests and my basic philosophical views were more in accord with those of the Circle than with any group I ever found'.

introspectionists or associationists or whatever, but the sentences into which, Carnap believed, any meaningful sentences employed by psychologists could and should be translated. In due course, these sentences describing the physical behaviour of humans would be retranslated into statements in the language of physics, the fundamental science. Thus, said Carnap, 'Now it is proposed that psychology, which has hitherto been robed in majesty as the theory of spiritual events, be downgraded to the status of a part of physics' (1959*a*: 168).

When he came to the task of delineating the details, Carnap admitted that at present one could not go much further than a translation of, say, 'He is excited' into something like 'His body (especially his central nervous system) is characterized by a high pulse rate, and respiration rate, by the occurrence of agitated movements, by vehement and factually unsatisfactory answers to questions, etc.'[3] In short, Carnap was under no illusion about what sort of 'translation' work was possible. In regard to psychology, he realized that his translations had advanced no farther than those of the psychological behaviourists (1959*a*: 181). What he believed was important in his way of getting to this point was in seeing the task as one of translating one language (strictly speaking, one vocabulary) into another. Given his distinction between the language which is the object of investigation (i.e. the 'object language') and the language in which the 'logical syntax' (or 'metalogic') of the object language is formulated (i.e. the 'metalanguage'), then Carnap believed that he was making clear that the task of *philosophical* psychology was to produce a metalanguage for psychology. For in producing such a metalanguage, one would lay bare the metalogic or logical syntax of psychological language, that is the correct account of the signs occurring in psychological language. This in turn would enable, at least eventually, the translation of the signs in the psychological object language into the signs of the physical object language.

More widely viewed, Carnap was setting an agenda for philosophical psychology in which only questions of language would and should be featured. Viewed through an even more widely angled lens, Carnap (1937: 4, 325, 332–3) was suggesting that traditional philosophy should be replaced by the study of the syntax of the

---

[3] At this point I am adapting material from Carnap (1959*a*: 170–3).

language of science.[4] Philosophy was not so much untying knots in our thinking as decoding signs in our language.

QUINE AND THE INTENSIONAL VOCABULARY OF PSYCHOLOGY

While it is true that Carnap did not leave us any account of intentionality as such, it is also true that his account of how philosophical psychology ought to proceed did influence the modern discussion of intentionality which by and large was shaped and carried out in American universities. One who was influenced by Carnap, even before Carnap settled in America, was W. V. O. Quine.

After finishing his Ph.D. at Harvard—his dissertation was on some aspects of Russell and Whitehead's *Principia Mathematica*—Quine was awarded a Sheldon Travelling Fellowship, which he decided to spend making contact with recent European philosophy. He spent five months in Vienna, which included attending meetings of the Vienna Circle and listening to Schlick's lectures at the University of Vienna. Carnap had just moved from Vienna to Prague, and Quine followed him there. For a period of six weeks he attended Carnap's lectures, had discussions with him, and read *The Logical Syntax of Language* as it emerged from Mrs Carnap's typewriter. Quine next spent six weeks in Warsaw where, among others, he met and had discussions with Tarski. Quine describes these two periods, in Prague and Warsaw, as 'the most intellectually rewarding months I have known' (1986: 12).

While Quine has never embraced (though he may be said to have flirted with) the Logical Positivism of Carnap, and in his celebrated article 'Two Dogmas of Empiricism' (Quine 1961) has expressly repudiated the analytic–synthetic distinction embedded in the Logical Positivists' Verification Principle,[5] Quine's view of psychology is surprisingly close to that of Carnap.

For Quine, like Carnap, physics is the fundamental natural science and only what is sanctioned by physics is part of the true and ultimate structure of reality. Quine argues that his ontology—what

---

[4] In Carnap (1937) the author was still using the term 'syntax-language' for 'metalanguage'. I felt that his later term, 'metalanguage', was more apt and revealing.

[5] The article 'Two Dogmas of Empiricism' first appeared in the *Philosophical Review* (1951).

he takes to be bedrock reality in the universe—precludes mental or intentional items and events, such as beliefs and desires. Of course we may find it useful in our everyday lives, even indispensable in practice, to talk in terms of beliefs, desires, hopes, intentions, thoughts, and the rest, but we should not be misled by the usefulness of intentional language in daily linguistic commerce into thinking that it describes what is really there. Quine holds that there is no nor can there be any science of intentionality which reveals the nature of real mental events. What autonomy psychology has is merely a pragmatic one. We humans find it useful to describe ourselves and others in intentional terms, and so to set to one side and refine the vocabulary used in such descriptions. As Quine himself puts it in *Word and Object*.[6]

One may accept the Brentano thesis [that you cannot explain the meaning of intentional idioms by means of any non-intentional vocabulary] either as showing the indispensability of intentional idioms and the importance of an autonomous science of intention, or as showing the baselessness of intentional idioms and the emptiness of a science of intention. My attitude, unlike Brentano's, is the second . . . Not that I would forswear daily use of intentional idioms, or maintain that they are practically dispensable. (1960: 221)

Quine sometimes puts his views about psychology, and in general talk about the mental, in terms of a distinction between extensional and intensional language. Though not easy to define in an exact way, this distinction, or something very like it, has been in use since at least the era of medieval philosophy.[7] The *extension* of a term is whatever real thing or object or property or relation, or in general what fact of the matter, if any, is usually (that is, conventionally) picked out or referred to or individuated or selected by the use of a sign or symbol in the language, code, or calculus in question. On the other hand the *intension* of a term is its meaning or sense or significance for any user of the term, or how such a person would be expected to understand the term.

Thus, for Quine, the correct language or notation for fundamental natural science is extensional, because an extensional language homes

[6] *Word and Object*, incidentally, is dedicated 'to Rudolf Carnap, Teacher and Friend'.

[7] What I have in mind is the significatio–suppositio distinction of medieval logic. (Later on there was the comprehension–extension distinction of the Port Royal school.)

in directly on what is real without recourse to any subjective under-standing or 'slant'. Thus a truly scientific language, being extensional, fits well with orthodox propositional and predicate logic, that is with the logic of objects, properties, and events. Psychology, at least when couched in the language of belief, desire, and other intentional terms, is basically intensional, and so such psychological terms do not latch on to real items and events which physics has isolated but merely mirror our common-sense or 'folk' understanding of the sources of human behaviour. Psychological terms, even when they are used as referring terms, are rich in intensionality but short on extension.[8]

Seeing Quine's account of psychology and psychological lan-guage in this way makes it clear why he departs quite sharply from Carnap in one very important respect. He does not believe that we can translate psychological language into physical language as you cannot translate a basically intensional vocabulary into a basically extensional one. To attempt to do so would be a bit like first learn-ing that General Gordon fought like a lion at the Battle of Khar-toum, but then being surprised to discover that in fact he did not have a tail, sharp claws, big incisors, and a mighty roar. As Quine himself puts it:

It is only our somewhat regimented and sophisticated language of science that has evolved in such a way as really to raise ontological questions. It is an object-oriented idiom. Any idiom purports to tell the truth, but this idiom purports, more specifically, to tell about objects. (1979: 160)

It [my approach to physicalism] is not a reductionist doctrine of the sort sometimes imagined. It is not a utopian dream of our being able to specify all mental events in physiological or microbiological terms. It is not a claim that such correlations even exist, in general, to be discovered; the group-ings of events in mentalistic terms need not stand in any systematic relation to biological groupings.[9] (1979: 163)

On the other hand, Quine, like Carnap, favours a behaviouristic vocabulary for psychology, at least till we have something better,

---

[8] Quine's dim view of intensional language in general also leads him to have a dim view of modal logic; see e.g. essays 12–14 in Quine (1981), where, at one point, he says 'in thus writing off modal logic I find little to regret' (1981: 121).

[9] On the other hand, such a passage should be set beside a passage like the following: 'Our three levels [mind, behaviour, neurophysiological states] thus are levels of reduction: mind consists in dispositions to behaviour, and these are physi-ological states' (1975a: 94). An ordinary chap could easily get confused.

such as a language based on a mature neurophysiology. But he is not suggesting a translation from the former to the latter. They are both extensional vocabularies and one may turn out preferable to the other, but this would be because one has greater predictive value, not because one is better as a language in some sense than the other. It is likely that the generalizations of a mature neurophysiology would predict better the future behaviour of humans than do our currently available behaviouristic ones. The ultimate reason for this greater predictive power of neurophysiology in comparison with behaviourism, Quine would suggest, would be because neurophysiology is closer to the real physical facts of the matter than is behaviouristic psychology. In the meantime, however, the explanations of behaviourism might be the best we can find.[10]

DENNETT AND THE INTENTIONAL STANCE

It is arguable that the fullest and clearest version of an instrumentalist account of intentionality in this Carnapian-cum-Quinean mode is that of Daniel Dennett. Dennett's first book, *Content and Consciousness*, which grew out of his doctoral thesis at Oxford (submitted in 1965), contains the following passage:

So, one can only ascribe content to a neural event, state or structure when it is a link in a demonstrably appropriate chain between the afferent and the efferent. The content one ascribes to an event, state or structure is not, then, an extra feature that one *discovers* in it, a feature which, along with its other, extensionally characterized features, allows one to make predictions. Rather, the relation between Intentional descriptions of events, states or structures (as signals that carry messages or memory traces with certain contents) and extensional descriptions of them is one of *further interpretation*. If we relegate vitalist and interactionist hypotheses to the limbo of last, desperate resorts, and proceed on the assumption that human and animal behavioural control systems are only very complicated denizens of

---

[10] Quine (1975*a*: 87) writes that 'in all we may distinguish three levels of purported explanation, three degrees of depth: the mental, the behavioural, and the physiological. The mental is the most superficial of these, scarcely deserving the name of explanation. The physiological is the deepest and most ambitious, and it is the place for causal explanations. The behavioural level, in between, is what we must settle for in our descriptions of language, in our formulations of language rules, and in our explications of semantical terms.' He might have added, 'and in our explication of the language of the propositional attitudes'.

the physical universe, it follows that the events within them, characterized extensionally in the terms of physics or physiology, should be susceptible to explanation and prediction without any recourse to content, meaning, or Intentionality. (1986: 78)

With the addition of a few appropriate stylistic changes I can easily imagine that either Carnap or Quine might have written that paragraph. For Dennett is telling us that what is really there, bed-rock reality, the facts, can be captured fully by an extensional vo-cabulary. Any employment of an intensional vocabulary—such as occurs in talk of propositional attitudes[11] or, in general, of mental events—is employment of a vocabulary that arises in answer to some felt need for interpretation or heuristic overlay of some kind upon the facts. For example, for ordinary everyday purposes, even if neurophysiologically well informed, one would want to interpret the physiological events in the brain in the light of the perceptual input into the brain, which stimulated those physiological events, and in the light of the behaviour which resulted from those same events (plus additional events) occurring in the brain. For everyday purposes one is interested in having available an easy-to-apply, macro or 'writ large', picture of the agency of one's fellow humans. One is interested in a language that depicts them as rational and purpose-ful agents who are conscious of and react to their environment.

A neat way of interpreting a particular example of this complex causal chain of physical events (perceptual input, brain events, and subsequent behavioural output) might be to say 'Mary ran very fast and merged with the crowd at the bus stop because she believed the man in the raincoat was following her'. The constituent or at least implied sentences 'Mary ran very fast and merged with the crowd

---

[11] A *propositional attitude* is a mental event or brain event, or at least a linguistic event (exactly what sort of event it is is a matter of dispute), which involves taking up an attitude, such as of believing or desiring or hoping or fearing, to something where this something is readily expressible in propositional form. Thus a belief will normally be expressed, or at least expressible, as '*X* believed that so-and-so' and a hope as '*Y* hoped that such-and-such'. The attitude operates over or governs the propositional content, which is linguistically identified by the that-clause following the verb. This attitude amounts to a distinct and peculiar mode of 'entertaining' the content in question, and so in turn it is what differentiates the different propositional attitudes. In this way of talking most but not all mental events are held to be expressible in propositional form and so legitimately called 'propositional attitudes'. However, some mental events—such as certain feelings, like pain, for example—are considered to be inexpressible in propositional form and so not rightly called 'propositional attitudes'.

at the bus stop' and 'Not far behind Mary, moving in the same direction, was a man in a raincoat' amount to an observer's extensional description of a complex group of physical events. This description is interpreted or explained in a certain way by adding a further clause which attributes to Mary a propositional attitude (an intentional event) with its appropriate content, namely 'because Mary believed that the man in the raincoat was following her'. This propositional-attitude clause does not add to an observer's current knowledge of the real causes or real events associated with Mary's run to the bus stop, that is it does not add to an observer's knowledge of real physical causes and real physical events. However, it does add to our understanding, in the sense that it fits the observer's account into a conventional and well-known account in terms of reasons and motives. It also alludes to the fact that some central (brain) states must be cited in any complete causal and scientific picture of the events in question, for even in the conventional account there is the implication that events inside Mary's head played some part in the outward observable events. As Dennett himself explains: 'The ideal picture, then, is of content being ascribed to structures, events and states in the brain on the basis of a determination of origins in stimulation and eventual appropriate behavioural effects, such ascriptions being essentially a heuristic overlay on the extensional theory rather than intervening variables of the theory' (1986: 80).

Dennett began to develop this account of intentionality in his book *Brainstorms*, first published in 1979. In this book Dennett explicitly embraced functionalism,[12] though, as we shall see, he did so in a rather idiosyncratic 'instrumentalist' fashion. Functionalism, of the more regular sort, is the view, as it is sometimes encapsulated, that the mind is to the brain as a computer's software or program is to a computer's hardware or physical structure and organization. The computer's program lists the functions which the computer is running through, or will run through when a suitable

---

[12] Though not a classical functionalist, Dennett could be said to have helped develop certain aspects of functionalism in philosophy and psychology. He certainly would not want to claim that he began it. If one wants to play the difficult and not very useful game of 'Who began ———?', then, as regards functionalism, the honour probably goes to Kenneth Craik's *The Nature of Explanation*. As regards subsequent development of the theory, one would have to include quite a large number of names besides those of Dennett: Putnam, Fodor, Block, Cummins, and Stich, to name but a few.

opportunity arises, and so is the computer described functionally. For example, the computer might be programmed to list all the students in the department in alphabetical order, and then to extract all those names beginning with the letter M. While the computer is carrying out these functions, the computer's hardware is in operation. A very knowledgeable electronics engineer (given that the computer is in fact an electronic one) might be able to list all the electronic or physical processes which incarnate in the machine all the functionally described processes of listing in alphabetical order and extracting names beginning with the letter M. Functional talk and structural-cum-process talk are two different ways of talking about something.

On the other hand, Dennett is also careful to distance himself from any rigid or narrow use of the computer analogy. Because of our very different nature and nurture, he does not believe that we humans could all be said to share the same evolutionarily produced program. Think of an inhabitant of the Ifaluk Atoll in the Western Caroline Islands in the Pacific Ocean and a native of Los Angeles. What 'program' are they likely to share?

Dennett's functionalism is driven by much more pragmatic considerations. In a way which produces useful predictions about how humans will behave in given circumstances, we can *attribute* internal functional states to humans. In doing this we should resist any inclination to think that thereby we are picking out or individuating real detectable brain states or processes, and *a fortiori* real detectable mental states and processes. In addition, while acknowledging that brain states or processes are all that are really there inside our head, we should not be misled into thinking that our functionally described states and processes must really exist at some other level or in some other place. The most we can say is that when, for the purpose of explanation, understanding, or prediction, we attribute a particular functional state or process to a particular person, say Mary, then, if we are quick about it, and open up her cranium immediately, of course we will find *some* brain state or process going on there in Mary's brain. Thus there will always be the possibility of token–token identities, that is the possibility that a token or particular sample of our functional description of some person (for example, the descriptive sentence 'Mary believes that the man in the raincoat is following her') can be hooked up to or be grounded in some particular or token brain state or process (or more likely some neural network being activated in a certain way) which is going on at that time in the relevant person's brain and is centrally implicated in causing the events which make the token functionally descriptive sentence a useful description of that person. However, Dennett would emphasize, we must be careful not to use the phrase 'refer to' here, for strictly speaking a sentence like 'Mary believes that the man in the raincoat is following her' is not a referring expression, or at least not a successful one, in regard to Mary's brain. For tomorrow, even if we have grounds for attributing the exact same belief to Mary, we might find, after opening up and peering into her head, or after hooking up her brain to some sophisticated scanning device, that a different network in her brain is active, or that the same network is active but in a way that is significantly different from the way it was active today.

A fortiori we are missing the point of Dennett's *instrumentalism* or *heuristically ascriptivist functionalism* if we expect that attributing similar beliefs to two or more persons—say we make the claim that both Mary and Susan believe that the man in the raincoat is following her—would thereby lead to our finding similar brain states or processes operative in the persons concerned. For we attribute functional states to some person, not on the basis of any neurophysiological knowledge, which anyway ordinary people do not have, but on the basis of an observation of how that person behaved (including linguistically) in the light of what she can be supposed to have perceived in her environment. In the light of perceptual input and behavioural output we project upon that person certain central (in the head) functions for that is *how* our ordinary, everyday psychological explanations operate. Thus we can be said to attribute an in-the-head or centralist function to some person neither as a result of actually peering into his or her head nor as a result of correctly inferring real internal 'intervening' processes. Rather we make such attributions as a result of guessing what part, when speaking in a special 'intentional function' way, the brain and central nervous system would have played in the complex production line of perceptual input, central processing, and behavioural output, *if* it were an 'intentional engine'.

For the language we use of humans when attributing to them central functional states is intentional language. For better or worse, over many centuries, or more likely over many millennia, we have developed a very neat and sophisticated vocabulary for giving functional explanations of the in-the-head sources of human behaviour. We attribute to humans current perceptual input (perceptual information about their immediate environment) which combines with an existing central deposit of knowledge or beliefs, and which in turn links up with a network of desires, needs, wishes, wants, aims, hopes, and the like, to produce appropriate output (usually behaviour of some sort). Thus our ordinary, everyday intentional language is a language where the operating items are information-loaded or contentful ones. We say, for example, that Mary perceived that such-and-such and, since she already believed that so-and-so and desired to such-and-such, then that was why she behaved in the way she did.

In turn this intentional description can be seen to be the expression of a particular sort of attitude or stance, the *intentional stance*, which humans take up to their fellow humans, to other animals, and even at times to machines. We deliberately view our fellow humans, or the dog next door, or at times our car, or the lift, as functioning in terms of a belief–desire system. We say Mary *wants* or *desires* the protection of the crowd at the bus stop because she *believes* she is being followed by a man whom she *believes* might be dangerous. It is a useful and economical way of understanding humans to view them as functioning in terms of maps or pictures of the world (i.e. knowledge, belief, guesses, expectations, and so on, about the world) which, combined with aims or plans of action in the world (i.e. wants, wishes, desires, hopes, and suchlike), lead to action in the world (i.e. to bring about the fulfilment of the aim or plan of action).

More importantly, to take up the intentional stance—particularly if one then proceeds to stiffen it up into a more rigorous psychological system—is also a useful and economical way of predicting human actions. As Dennett himself put it at the beginning of chapter 1 of *Brainstorms*: 'I wish to examine the concept of a system whose behaviour can be—at least sometimes—explained and predicted by relying on ascriptions to the system of beliefs and desires (and hopes, fears, intentions, hunches . . .). I will call such systems *intentional systems*, and such explanations and predictions intentional explanations and predictions, in virtue of the intentionality of the idioms of belief and desire (and hope, fear, intention, hunch . . .)' (1978: 3).

If I know that someone is afraid of something, I will expect that they will seek to avoid the danger by escaping from it, or fighting

it off, or enlisting help. If I think that someone is in love with John
(that is, I believe that she thinks John is physically or mentally
attractive, or both, so that she desires to be in his company, to
cherish him, defend him from attack, and so on) then I will expect
or predict that most probably she will accept his invitation to lunch
tomorrow and not write a scathing review of his latest novel.

The intentional stance also works in regard to animals. If I am a
wildlife photographer and I am trying to creep up on a pride of lions
resting under an acacia tree, then when I see a lioness suddenly
stand up and sniff the air, I might express her action as 'She knows
I'm in the vicinity'. I might go on to predict that 'The pride will
move on in a minute'. On the other hand, if I also attribute to the
lioness certain needs or desires ('She is very hungry and has cubs
to feed'), and note that the situation is favourable to her satisfying
those needs or desires ('It is almost dusk and I'm the only game
about'), then I might reasonably predict that 'The lioness is quite
likely to attack me at any moment', and so take appropriate action.

In general, one takes up the intentional stance in order to explain
and predict and so plan or take action. That is, we should be clear
once again that Dennett's functionalism differs from more 'regular'
functionalism (such as, as we shall see in due course, that of Fodor
or Loar) by its emphasis on the heuristic basis for ascribing functional states. As Dennett makes clear, 'the definition of intentional
systems I have given does not say that intentional systems *really*
have beliefs and desires, but that one can explain and predict their
behaviour by *ascribing* beliefs and desires to them' (1978: 7). Or,
put even more bluntly, 'The decision to adopt the [intentional]
strategy is pragmatic' (ibid.). Dennett points out that there are other
stances, besides the intentional, which we take up to things. We
might consider a machine, for example, from the point of view of
its design, that is we might take up the *design stance*. We might
know that the car is designed with a maximum speed of 120 miles
per hour, or that the lift is designed to carry not more than twenty
persons at a time, and so be able to predict what will happen if
someone attempts to push the car to a speed of 140 miles per hour
or if thirty people are squeezed into the lift. We can consider humans
also from the design stance. We know that humans are not designed
to fly unaided or to remember on average more than seven nonsense
words on first reading, and so might make predictions on the basis
of such design knowledge.

While the design stance is also, at least in part, a functional stance, for in taking up this stance one is considering something from the point of view of what it has been designed to do or not do, it is not an intentional stance. One is not attributing any network of content-loaded or propositional attitudes to humans or animals or machines, but real abilities or capacities, which are built into their structure and organization. Thus another important way in which the intentional stance and the design stance differ is that while the intentional stance is a purely pragmatic and ultimately make-believe point of view, the design stance is not. The design stance seeks the real design blueprint as a basis for making predictions about how the machine or animal or human will behave, or as a basis for giving explanations of why something has behaved in the way it did.

A third stance is the *physical stance*. To take up this attitude or stance is to consider something only in so far as it is made of a certain material or of certain types of material which have certain properties. To take up the physical stance to, say, a calculator is to investigate or discuss the calculator's electronics (given, of course, that it is an electronic calculator). To take up the physical stance to humans is to investigate their physiology or, at a more basic level, their physics and chemistry.

In any sort of psychology we want to understand the sources of human behaviour to the extent, at least eventually, that we can predict human behaviour on the basis of our knowledge of its sources, in particular on the basis of our knowledge of how humans function inside their heads. In ordinary social intercourse we also want to understand the inside-the-head sources of human behaviour to an extent that enables us to predict what humans will do. If we could not do this reasonably well, we would be constantly surprised by the actions of our fellow humans. We would be more or less continually in the dark as to what someone would do if we said or did such-and-such. Life would be unbearably unpredictable and tense and unpleasant. Coming into the department each day would be a bit like meeting each day a new tribe of people who had never before been in contact with anyone outside their own tribe. I say 'a bit like'; in fact matters would be much worse. For each individual in the tribe would also be a stranger to each other individual in the tribe. So it would be more like meeting each day a very tense and nervous and suspicious and touchy new tribe of people, who didn't get on among themselves, and who had never before been in contact with strangers.

Even in professional psychology the functional description of humans is still basically in terms of our intentional story about humans, that is in terms of human beliefs, desires, and so on. The reason for this is that, at present, the intentional stance works best. Eventually we may be able to replace this intentional account by a non-intentional account, perhaps by some account expressed in terms of a purely extensional mechanistic vocabulary. But this gradual adoption of an explanation or theory in terms of a lower-level extensional vocabulary may only be possible if first, at an intermediary stage, we take up a design stance which produces an account which mirrors reasonably closely human brain design selected by nature in the course of our evolution. At present we cannot do so but it is still an aim which professional psychologists should have. As Dennett puts it:

This migration from common-sense intentional explanations and predictions to more reliable design-stance explanations and predictions that is forced on us when we discover that our subjects are imperfectly rational is, independently of any such discovery, the proper direction for theory builders to take whenever possible. In the end, we want to be able to explain the intelligence of man, or beast, in terms of his design, and this in turn in terms of the natural selection of this design . . . (1978: 12)

With our feet firmly back on the ground, we realize that, in our ordinary, everyday social intercourse, as well as in our formal psychological enquiries, the functional description of ourselves and our fellow humans is still carried out more or less entirely in terms of our 'folk', or common-sense, intentional story. We may be tempted to believe that it will always be so. We may be tempted to believe that it will always be so because this story is so clear and concise, and so easy to understand and use. However, Dennett would want to remind us that, while our common-sense intentional talk is so very useful, we should not forget that it is just a story. It is not a description of the facts about what goes on inside our heads, so any professional psychology done in terms of this story cannot hope to be an account of the facts. A true account of the facts, an accurate description of human psychology, must wait at least upon a mature neurophysiology. So Dennett would also want to remind us that taking up the physical stance, and perhaps even the design stance, in regard to the sources of human behaviour, is a long way off.

Dennett describes a recent book, *The Intentional Stance*, as 'a series of post-*Brainstorms* essays in which I attempted to revise, re-express, and extend my view' (1987, p. ix). The result is a work with a markedly increased emphasis on the pragmatic and idealized nature of the intentional stance and on the claim that its value lies almost wholly in its power to predict behaviour. 'The perverse claim remains: *all there is* to being a true believer is being a system whose behaviour is reliably predictable via the intentional strategy, and hence *all there is* to really and truly believing that *p* (for any proposition *p*) is being an intentional system for which *p* occurs as a belief in the best (most predictive) interpretation' (1987: 29).

Dennett points out that, according to this more clearly defined and uncompromising view on intentionality, a thing can be said to have internal states or processes that represent only in the sense that, when we attribute information-carrying or content-containing intentional states and processes to them, these attributions enable us to predict very well what behaviour will be produced by such a system when it is operating in a known environment. For example, neither the internal states of thermostats nor those of humans literally carry information in an internally represented or encoded or depicted form. Rather, from the outside looking *on* but not *in*, we find that we can ascribe content-containing or information-carrying intentional descriptions to thermostats or humans, and thereby predict with regularity their reactions or behaviour. When we are said to believe that it is now raining, our heads do not contain states or processes that encapsulate or embed or encode or depict the sentence or proposition 'It is now raining', but we find it very useful to act as if they did. For if I attribute to you a belief that it is now raining, I can predict that very likely, before you go outside, you will put on a raincoat or take out your umbrella from the cupboard or do something to protect your new lambswool pullover from the rain.

Dennett maintains that there is no language of thought in the sense of an innate language of the brain. However, there is a language of thought in the sense that we find it very useful indeed to ascribe thoughts and cognate intentional states to ourselves and others, and to express these ascriptions in a propositional-attitude vocabulary. We find such ascriptions useful in the prediction of human behaviour precisely because, whether we realize it or not, we attribute a particular thought or belief or desire or hope to someone on the basis of what a human just like that person (with just such capacities, needs, and past biography) would be expected to do in just such circumstances. Putting on raincoats, raising umbrellas, or sheltering under something or other is just the sort of behaviour a rational human animal would exhibit in just such circumstances. So we can regularly attribute to a human in just such circumstances a state or process such as a belief or desire or both which readily yields the behavioural consequence of putting on a raincoat, raising an umbrella, or sheltering under an awning. We can do this because we have discovered that an idealized rational intentional system (of perceptual input, belief–desire central states, reasoning powers, and purposeful behavioural output) works well when applied to humans. So what reality beliefs and desires have, Dennett is emphasizing, is purely instrumentalist: 'people really do have beliefs and desires, on my version of folk psychology, just the way they really have centers of gravity and the earth has an Equator' (1987: 53).

In general, Dennett maintains, brains are not semantic engines but syntactic engines, though this latter phrase must be unpacked very carefully. Brains are not driven, causally driven, by meanings or intentional states or by representations of any sort but by physical states and processes with determinate but non-symbolic structures, organizations, properties, and relations. Of course these physical states and processes might be interpreted in the light of perceptual input and behavioural output as having meaning or intentional content or representational powers. On the other hand, in our folk psychology, we do not normally pin our propositional-attitude descriptions on to particular physical brain states, for the simple reason that we are completely ignorant of the latter. All we do, all we need to do, is pin these propositional attitudes on to particular humans, or at most on to their heads, as notional attitudes legitimized by the intentional stance. So, in saying this, Dennett is moving even further away from the original guiding analogy of 'regular' functionalism, the computer, for he is denying quite emphatically and clearly that human brains are symbolic systems like digital computers.

Given this account, the most we can say about human brains and representations is that they *tacitly* represent. As Dennett explains: 'For the whole point of tacit representation is that it is tacit! States of such a system get their semantic properties directly and only from their globally defined functional roles' (1987: 223). Thus we attribute representations to humans in exactly the same way as we attribute any semantic (or meaning-bearing) properties to them, that is by taking up the intentional stance or strategy in regard to them. Just as humans do not have real intentional states or propositional attitudes in their heads, so they do not have real representations in their heads. It just is the case, however, that it is very useful, in our folk psychology, to attribute intentional states to our fellow humans and, in our professional psychology, at least at present, to attribute internal representations to the brains of our fellow humans. But there is nothing more to intentionality than this.

From one point of view this positivistic approach to intentionality, culminating in the instrumentalist or pragmatic account of intentionality in the work of Daniel Dennett, is immensely attractive. For it solves the problem of intentionality at a stroke. For the blunt answer given by the positivists to the central question about intentionality, namely the question about how the mind or brain gives content to its states or processes, is that neither the mind nor the brain is intentional in any way. The mind has no intentionality for the simple reason that there is no mind, and the brain has no intentionality because it has neither states nor processes with content. Intentionality is merely a feature of a particular part of our language plus a strategy which generates that 'language game'. It just happens to be the case that, by a process of trial and error most likely, our ancestors evolved an intentional or propositional-attitude way of talking about one another which enabled them to predict human behaviour with success.

HAS DENNETT OVERSTATED THE PRAGMATIC NATURE OF INTENTIONAL TALK?

I suppose that the nagging doubt about this swingeing view arises because of its uncompromising emphasis on the purely pragmatic nature of our intentional talk. Time and again Dennett has reiterated that '*all there is* to being a true believer is being a system whose behaviour is reliably predictable via the intentional strategy' (1987: 29). That our intentional talk gets predictions right, though it is just a useful story with no hold on the real facts of the matter, seems just too lucky to be true. It seems just too fortuitous to be credible that the folk psychological account of the sources of human action is not merely neat and comparatively easy to understand and to use, but also possessed of immense predictive power, yet at the same time cannot be said to be a true, factual picture of anything.

When I say that Fred will go home now because he hates crowds and knows that there are only five minutes till the end of the base-ball match, and when, lo and behold, within a minute or two Fred stands up, leaves his seat, and then the stadium, this is an incredibly precise and true prediction that I have made. It must reflect psycho-logical *facts of some sort*, otherwise it looks as if I have made a true prediction in psychology on the basis of a false or 'make-believe' picture of the relevant facts. It looks as if I have made a successful prediction without any firm basis. If that were so, we would have to say that it was quite magical and mysterious how I ever did arrive at any true prediction by employing the intentional stance, and how humans ever did generate their intentional explanations and predictions.

To put this another way, if my predictions based upon the inten-tional stance were predictions based upon a picture which had no relation at all to the facts about why humans behave as they do, then my predictions ought to be about as useful and precise as an astrolo-ger's predictions. If I take up the astrological stance to you, then I might depict you as influenced by the constellation Virgo, as you were born on 6 September, and after noting that Virgo is in such-and-such a position in the sky this month, as seen from the northern hemisphere, and in such-and-such a relation to other star clusters, declare that such-and-such will befall you. But any predictions I made would be either so vague as to be useless or just plain wrong, or else a one-off piece of incredibly fortuitous guessing. This would be so because there is no causal connection between distant clusters of stars and individual human actions unless, like the wife of a recent president of the United States, one first believes in astrology and then decides to make decisions on the basis of what astrologers say.

It is no alleviation of our incredulity or dispersal of our mystifica-tion to say that the basis of our predictions made from the inten-tional stance is that in the past such predictions have turned out true, at least for the most part. For to say this is just to push the whole demand for an explanation of the extraordinary success of predic-tions made from the intentional stance back into the dim and distant past. It is to base a baseless prediction upon a preceding chain of baseless predictions in which each individual prediction in the chain depends for its procedural justification on the long chain of similar predictions standing behind it. In effect, to do this is to proffer an infinite regress of baseless but successful predictions as the explanation of the success of this most recent baseless prediction. It is a bit like the justification of induction by a process of induction.

Of course, Dennett is not justifying the intentional stance and its predictions in this way. In a sense Dennett himself gives the game away as to his real explanation, for part of his story about the intentional stance is that its success is a result of the trial and error of evolution.

We, the reason-representers, the self-representers, are a late and specialized product [of evolution]. What this representation of our reasons gives us is foresight: the real-time anticipatory power that Mother Nature wholly lacks. (1987: 317–18)

Or putting the point from a slightly different angle, he writes:

The first answer to the question of why the intentional strategy works is that evolution has designed human beings to be rational . . . The fact that we are products of a long and demanding evolutionary process guarantees that using the intentional strategy on us is a safe bet. (1987: 33)

That is, at this point Dennett seems to be admitting that trial and error-correction by evolution would not ultimately produce success for predictions derived from a particular stance unless evolution had also brought it about that this stance had some sort of connection to some of the facts which had some causal relation, proximate or distant, to the behaviour one is trying to predict. For no matter how many trials you make, and how many errors you try and adjust to, no variation on the astrological stance will ever predict that Fred will stand up and leave the stadium within the next two minutes (unless again you know that Fred believes in astrology and is standing next to an astrologer or some such). It is significant too that, with the intentional stance, the person whose behaviour is being predicted does not have to believe in the intentional stance. That person might be an inhabitant of a remote island in Oceania whose language has no intentional terms. Or the subject might be a 1-year-old child or a lioness. Yet in each of these cases the intentional stance can deliver useful and true predictions.

Of more significance is Dennett's admission that the intentional strategy works because 'evolution has designed human beings to be

rational'. In this context this would mean that evolution has designed humans with 'practical reason'. In turn this would mean that
humans are designed to say to themselves such things as 'I want to
avoid scurvy and if, as I believe, ensuring that I have an adequate
daily intake of vitamin C will ward off scurvy, then I want to have an
adequate daily intake of vitamin C'. But this looks as if humans are
designed to operate in terms of want–belief- (or belief–desire-)type
reasoning. But Dennett has told us that describing humans in terms
of beliefs and desires is just a heuristic 'make-believe' overlay upon
the real facts. Dennett might reply that there is no contradiction
here. Granting humans rationality does not imply that thereby they
must have real beliefs and desires or other propositional attitudes in
their heads. He might say that his position is merely that humans
have been designed to make use of 'make-believe' belief–desire-
type reasoning. Humans have evolved so as to be just the sort of
species that invents belief–desire-type reasoning as a heuristic overlay upon the real facts. If this were so, it would be hard to explain
why we humans evolved in just that way *without mentioning* some
intimate relation between the named beliefs and desires by which
we organize our own behaviour in a rational way and some real
facts about our psychology. Just as it would be hard to explain why
a rabbit has evolved so that it will run away when it sees a dog, but
'seeing a dog' is, for a rabbit, just a perceptual way of organizing
its behaviour which has no relation to the facts.

However, for other reasons as well, I do not think that Dennett
can maintain his position. For I do not think that Dennett's
instrumentalism can ultimately avoid the implication that human
heads must have real contents. For it is at least implicit in Dennett's
account that our 'intentional stance' talk (about humans or other
organisms, or about machines for that matter) is talk based not just
on the usual behavioural output of humans in given environmental
circumstances, but on the *presumed perceptual input* into them as
well. For when, via the intentional stance, we talk about someone
or some organism, what we do is attribute to the person or organism
a belief *that so-and-so*, and a desire *that such-and-such*. It is the
'so-and-so' and the 'such-and-such' which are the guts of our ordinary
intentional talk and ultimately that which give it predictive power.
To slip into an invented jargon for a moment, our folk psychological intentional talk, when it involves attributing a simple perceptual
belief to someone, could be seen as really just finding a substitute,

a simpler substitute, for an attribution to someone of a particular content or 'filling' for his or her presumed-perceptual-*information* input slot. Likewise, when our folk psychological intentional discourse involves an attribution to someone of a basic behavioural desire, then this could be taken as really just finding a simpler substitute for an attribution of a particular content or 'filling' for his or her likely-behaviour-given-that-*information* output slot.

But let me display this point by means of an example. Let us say that I am looking out of my office window and catch sight of a man in the street. I see the man approach the entrance to *Le Café en Seine*. He goes into the restaurant but reappears about a minute and a half later. He then stands outside the entrance, a little to the right of the door and back from the flow of pedestrian traffic along the pavement. After five minutes or so, he looks at his watch, then, dodging among the pedestrians, walks into the middle of the pavement and looks first up the street and then down it. Then the man returns to his place just to the right of the door of the restaurant. He looks at his watch again, purses his lips, stamps his feet, and slaps his gloved hands together. Soon after, he begins to pace backwards and forwards in front of the restaurant.

With some confidence I say to myself that the man in front of the restaurant is waiting for someone to join him for a meal in the restaurant. I am also confident that this man believes that the person who is to join him is not yet in the restaurant and is late. Moreover, I can see that the man is rather annoyed by this. I might say to a colleague who has just joined me at the window that this man wishes whoever it is that he is waiting for would arrive soon. Given his rather agitated and decidedly impatient behaviour, I might predict that he is not waiting for a lover whom he has just recently met or for his adored aunt but for his eldest son or his wife.

I have interpreted the man's behaviour in terms of what information he himself seems to have gathered by means of his senses (by looking in the restaurant, along the pavement, and at his watch) and the behavioural response that he has made to that information (his taking up a position near the entrance to the restaurant, his stamping of his feet, rubbing his hands together, and pacing about). And then I have made a prediction on the basis of that interpretation.

What interpretations we can make about some person and, in the light of such interpretations, what predictions we can make about what he will do or about what will happen to him will depend, initially, on our knowledge of *his information*. For our interpretations and predictions will depend on what we can learn about the perceptual information 'in his input slot' and his forward planning as revealed by his responses. In turn, both of these will depend in some measure on our background knowledge of what sort of information was in the possession of a person just like that, who exhibited just such behaviour in just such circumstances in the past.

Putting our folk psychological descriptions in this way should make us see that they imply acceptance of the claim *that the human brain is an information-processing or content-utilizing device*, though this implication is not made on the basis of any translation of our folk psychological account into an information-processing vocabulary, no matter how successful the translation. The point of my momentarily translating our folk psychological intentional terms 'belief' and 'desire' into a rebarbative jargon of 'presumed-perceptual-information input slots' and 'likely-behaviour-given-that-information output slots' is to force us to accept that folk psychology only works (makes successful predictions) because it links input and output *at an informational level*. Folk psychological explanations work, predictively work, because ordinary folk have got it right that between input and output we humans operate as information-processing devices, that we humans are indeed at least information-processing engines of some sort. Whether we operate as information-processing devices in just the way that our folk psychology describes or not is another matter. I myself would be greatly surprised if, in ignorance of neurophysiology, but by the exercise of serendipity alone, our folk psychology did give an accurate picture of just the sort of information-processing system we are. So it is not inconceivable that our current folk psychology and cognitive science are right to view the brain intentionally. But they may be wrong about the workings of the brain's intentional system. They may be right to claim that the brain is an information-processing device but wrong to suggest that the units of this system are interrelated by means of operating over contents, expressed as propositions, according to the rules of some intentional logic.

So far I have questioned that part of the instrumentalist account of intentionality which says that our intentional talk is purely pragmatic and has no connection with facts about what goes on inside our heads. I have argued that there is an important link between the explanations and predictions of the intentional stance and facts about human behaviour and the environment in which the behaviour is produced, which in turn lead us to facts about what is going on, informationally speaking, inside our heads. In the next section I want to prod and probe Dennett's anti-realism about intentionality.

DENNETT, REALISM AND ANTI-REALISM, AND PRAGMATISM

Rejecting the view that our intentional vocabulary gives us a reductively literal picture of the cognitive–appetitive activity of the brain will always draw some theorists, such as Dennett, into exploring the view that, in consequence, realism about the propositional attitudes should be rejected. But I think that there are lots of other ways of being a realist about intentionality without being 'reductively literal'.

Indeed, given that our ancestors, and most of us today, know nothing about neurophysiology, it would be very surprising if the intentional stance did carve nature at its neurophysiological joints, if it did pick out, in a literal one-to-one way, real brain states and processes. Dennett is surely right to be anti *that sort of realism*. After all, from the point of view of our evolution, including the evolution of our psychological thinking, it is not so long ago that we thought the brain was our body's refrigerator. It would be extraordinary then if we found ourselves, via our common-sense or 'folk' psychology, doing sophisticated neurophysiology. On the other hand, when our ancestors adopted or were adapted to the intentional stance, it must surely have been on the basis of its success. We would not have stuck with it, if it did not get things right much of the time, which, I have argued in the previous section, means 'right about human psychology' much of the time. But this success need not be explained in terms of facts at a neurophysiological level. This success might be explained through its connection with some equally real but 'higher-level' or macro facts about humans. For example, the success of our employment of our common-sense explanations and predictions in terms of the propositional attitudes might best be explained, at least initially, through its connection with some clearly observable *peripheral* facts about humans; that is, facts which they must have been able to discover fairly readily 'from the outside looking *on* but not *in*', so to speak. It might have been on the basis of facts about, say, observed human behaviour in observed environments, or about the observed human behaviour of observed human types with languages with observed types of linguistic categories in observed types of cultures. In turn, these *peripheral* facts might imply other, but not-directly-observable, *centralist* (or in-the-head) facts.

It may seem that, in our use of our common-sense psychology of the propositional attitudes, we speak as if beliefs and desires and hopes and wants and intentions are in human heads. When we ask someone whether he or she believes in God or not, such a person might take up a ruminative posture. He might close his eyes and ponder on the matter. Then he might open his eyes again and, after a minute or so, tell you what he thinks or believes. The person seems to be engaging in some inner search or at least engaging in some in-the-head processing. Nevertheless, it could be that, in taking up the intentional stance in regard to someone, such that we then ascribe or attribute a belief to that person, all we ('outsiders looking *on* but not *in*') could be doing is redescribing an interplay of certain peripheral facts in a *centralist*, or in-the-head, form. My suggestion is that we do so redescribe, but do so for good and legitimate reasons. We posit realities in our heads because we hold that the 'interplay of certain peripheral facts' must have an intimate and important connection with what goes on in our heads. Even so, 'in-the-head' realism can take many forms. Only one of these forms involves *reifying* (or, perhaps, *realifying*) *by reducing* things to neurophysiological or in-the-head physico-chemical objects and events.

We can satisfy this genuine hankering to relate beliefs and desires to realities 'in the head' yet, at the same time, avoid crude neurophysiological or physical reductionism. We might do this, as I have already suggested, in the following way. In the first instance our attributions of the propositional attitudes to ourselves and others may be on the basis of publicly observable facts about the environment (which have a causal influence on us) and facts about behaviour (upon which we have a causal influence). Only in an oblique way, after a consideration of the implications of these facts about behaviour and the environment, might we be led into positing certain facts about what must be going on inside our heads. It might be because these environmental-cum-behavioural facts imply that we humans must be engaging in some sort of 'information processing' that we are drawn into locating the realities underlying our neat summary terms for information processing and decision making— 'believing', 'desiring', 'hoping', 'intending'—in our heads. But they might be in our heads in a *macro* way, not a micro way. It might be the case that we should posit the realities in question at a higher level than the neurophysiological and, *a fortiori*, at a higher level than the physico-chemical. It might be the case that what we should be locating in our heads are real *functions*, without any commitment as to who or what is performing the functions, or even whether it is the same thing or things that perform the same function on different occasions. This, as we shall see (in subsequent chapters), has been the reply to Dennett by 'the realist arm' of functionalism in philosophy of mind.

Taking such a realist view of the propositional attitudes does not rule out pragmatism altogether. Dennett is quite right to latch on to the pragmatic aspect of our propositional-attitude talk. For it seems to be quite true that the form of our intentional talk has been dictated *to some extent* by pragmatic considerations. It seems to be true to say that our vocabulary and grammar of the propositional attitudes has been shaped by the necessity of making it concise and easy to use. The form may be said to be concise and easy to use because it puts complex facts (about, say, perceptual input and the rational processing of it, in complex cultural contexts) in simple form. It puts complex facts about humans and their motivation and behaviour in the form of information-containing and information-employing states and processes in the head. It is easier, for example, to say 'He believes it is going to rain' than to say that 'Against a background of a presumption that he is the sort of organism that seeks to avoid rain, he went outside, directed his eyes in a focused way at a group of clouds which would be described by an informed meteorologist as nimbus clouds, then took up an attentive attitude to the object of his focused gaze for such-and-such a time, then said to a passer-by "That looks threatening", then went back into the building and up the stairs to his office, and finally looked about in the cupboard in the corner where his umbrella would be if it were in his office', and so on. It is easier to say 'She wants a new pair of shoes' than to say 'Over the last few days she has been comparing unfavourably whatever pair of shoes she is wearing with whatever pair of shoes her interlocutor is wearing, has been constantly talking about the shoe sale in Switzer's, and saying to her husband such things as "I see Mrs McMahon has just bought herself a pair of Gucci shoes. I don't know how they can afford it. She's a waitress and he just drives a bus"', and so on.

In short, it is hard to deny that the form and style of our ordinary language vocabulary of the propositional attitudes, and their syntax and logical interrelations, is likely to be shaped by pragmatic-cum-cultural considerations. But to admit that is not to imply that their employment is purely pragmatic. After all, the employment of our vocabulary for some diseases (for example, ME or 'cot death' or neurosis) is to a large extent purely pragmatic, for the simple reason that we do not know about the realities underlying our use of such terms. On the other hand, we do not deny that there are realities underlying our use of such terms. It is just that we are still searching for them. So it may be that the pragmatic aspects of our talk about the propositional attitudes loom large because we are still more or less in the dark about the realities underlying such talk.

DENNETT AND A CURIOUS SORT OF REDUCTIVISM

In one sense Dennett's instrumentalist position is more reductivist than that of an *appellation contrôlée* reductivist. For Dennett has set about naturalizing our intentional attitudes by reducing them to mere talk about propositional attitudes. We find such talk useful, and perhaps indispensable, though Dennett seems inclined to believe that, in the fullness of time, we will want to try and dispense with our intentional stance and its explanations and predictions. In another sense Dennett's position is not reductivist at all. It is just dismissive. For it does not reduce the propositional attitudes downwards to some lower-level physical states or processes which are posited as the ultimate realities in this context. According to Dennett, in the fullness of time, one may be able to supplant and so to discard the intentional stance (and discard talk about the propositional attitudes) and jump down to the design stance or even to the physical stance. So while his instrumentalism involves a meta-thesis about the correct level of description for what, at present, we describe in terms of our propositional-attitude attributions, it is not a thesis about what our talk about these attitudes really picks out at a lower, real, physical level.

Firstly, let me voice the uneasiness (or is it open-eyed wonder?)

that tends to come over me when philosophers jump down or even talk of the possibility of jumping down, to the level of physics, or at least 'the physical'. And let me acknowledge the disquiet that comes over me when philosophers conclude that it makes obvious good sense that, in the fullness of time, we would or should want to be able to give a physical explanation (if not a physicist's explanation) of our mental capacities. Given our present physics, it is at least an open question whether human mental capacities could ever be 'accommodated within the framework of physical explanation, as presently conceived, or whether there are new principles, now unknown, that must be invoked'. I am, of course, quoting here from the last few pages of Noam Chomsky's *Language and Mind* (1968: 83), where he points out that such talk of reducing psychological explanations to physical explanations, or substituting the latter for the former, means that we must be using the term 'physical explanation' in a rather empty or trivial sense. For the physical explanation in question is more than likely to be one that, at least eventually, must call upon significantly different explanatory resources than those employed by our current physics. Of course, there is no reason to believe that some future neurophysiology will not be based on some future physics which will have expanded so as to embrace within its explanatory arms a convincing explanation of all human capacities including the mental ones. For after all, on different occasions, physics expanded so as to embrace concepts, categories, and principles which enabled it to give acceptable explanations of gravitation, electromagnetic force, and massless particles. But, in expanding so as to accommodate an explanation of human mental capacities, this future 'expanded neurophysiology', which in turn is underpinned by a future 'inflated physics', may not be readily identifiable with what we now call neurophysiology or physics. For a reductivist to give a physic*alist* explanation of intentionality does not, of course, mean that the explanation must be in terms of the concepts, categories, and principles of physics (though, sometimes, Dennett seems to be implying this), but it does mean that any acceptable explanation *must be consistent with* those concepts, categories, and principles. So what is being discussed here is whether it makes much sense to state here and now that, in the future, we will be able to give an account of our mental capacities which will be consistent with the concepts, categories, and principles of physics. But who could possibly answer that question *here and now*?

'Future science', whether it be 'future neurophysiology' or 'future physics', is always the reductivist's most widely used and most gilded calling-card.

Dennett seems to have followed Quine in holding that either you naturalize intentionality by a downward reduction of intentional psychology to, first, behaviourism, then neurophysiology, and finally physics, or you take the view that it will be impossible to succeed in this downward reduction so that all you are left with is the 'make-believe' of our intentional talk. As we shall see, some of Dennett's contemporaries have taken the first option and suggested a number of ingenious ways of explaining the relation between our explanations in terms of the propositional attitudes and a neuroscientist's explanations of what the brain is doing when it controls our actions and reactions in the light of input from the environment. Others, such as the eliminative materialists,[13] have taken the second option and out-Dennetted Dennett. They have said, in effect, that our talk about the propositional attitudes is indeed just talk, but have then gone on to say that it is not only dispensable but should be dispensed with as soon as possible. It should be shown the philosophical door because it is a trouble-maker. For our talk about the propositional attitudes is not merely misleading but downright false at least in the context of serious philosophy of mind or professional psychology. For a psychologist to persist in his or her use of the propositional attitudes in his explanations in professional psychology is no better than a physicist persisting in this day and age in talking about the ether or phlogiston.

In the next four chapters I will concentrate on those who oppose Dennett's anti-realism about intentionality and propose instead various ingenious ways of showing that one can be a realist about minds. Indeed they endeavour to show not merely that one can be a realist and a physicalist about minds, but also that one can satisfy any scientistic hankerings to naturalize intentionality. And, furthermore,

[13] As in the work, for example, of Paul Churchland (see 1979, 1984) and of Patricia Churchland (see 1986). The Churchlands are not denying that the brain may function in some representational way, but they are denying that its functioning mirrors in any respect the intentional choreography of the propositional attitudes in our folk psychology. Furthermore, they deny that our ordinary intentional folk psychology is of much, if any, use at all. It is, they suggest, just a bad theory with a poor predictive record. We are better rid of it altogether in much the same way as we are better rid of talk about phlogiston or the ether in physics as well as in the informed discourse of ordinary people.

all this can be achieved without any of the crudities of an identity theory whereby one says that the mind is nothing but the brain, and so types of mental state or process are to be literally identified with types of brain state or process.

I will concentrate on this realist approach because it has been the dominant approach. Excepting a return on the part of a few to a fairly orthodox Brentanian standpoint, wherein intentionality is said to be a feature of conscious or phenomenal states *alone*,[14] and, as I have just mentioned, a desire on the part of some for a complete elimination of the mental and all its works (including what they see as its remnants in our folk psychology), the main emphasis of recent work has been to argue for real intentionality in the head. In some quarters this realism has taken the form of a move to champion mental representation without the mental. It has amounted to a persistent attempt to put forward a physicalist theory of brain representation which would make clear how brain states and processes could contain within themselves contents which represent or, in general, can be said to be about things other than themselves.

This reaction against the anti-realism of Dennett or the dismissive eliminativism of the Churchlands[15] is not as large as it might appear at first glance. For these realists, perhaps best represented by the vigorous work of Jerry Fodor, are, like Dennett himself, unabashed physicalists. What is more, they usually accord language the central role in any theory of intentionality worth having. For Fodor the intentionality of the propositional-attitude vocabulary of our folk psychology is the outward expression of the inward intentionality of the language of the brain. This intentionality of the brain and its computations and thoughts is the original and true bearer of intentionality. It is ordinary, natural language which is the Johnny-come-lately, with only derived and secondary intentionality. Humans, with their brains, generated the marks and noises of natural language, and ordained them for a representational role. However, we should look at this view and its implications in detail in the next chapter.

---

[14] As in the work, for example, of Roderick Chisholm (see Chisholm and Sellars 1958) and, especially, John Searle (1983, 1992).
[15] See n. 13 above.

2

The Return to Representation

The instrumentalist account of intentionality, as exemplified in the work of Dennett, held that when we are said to believe that it is now raining, our heads do not contain states or processes that encapsulate or embed or encode or depict or represent in any way at all the sentence or proposition 'It is now raining'; we merely find it very useful to think and speak as if they did. Fodor, on the contrary, believes that when we believe that it is now raining, then, in a perfectly literal sense, our heads do contain the proposition 'It is now raining' encoded in the brain's language of thought. For Fodor holds that brains are semantic engines driven by intentional states. Intentional states are a natural kind, for they are a real kind of state that real brains have. But let us begin a little further back.

Fodor comes to the problem of intentionality via an intimate knowledge of linguistics and psychology. Though trained primarily in philosophy, his intellectual companions are more often to be found among workers in the fields of psycholinguistics, experimental psychology, and artificial intelligence than among those in philosophy. Moreover, his work seems to be influenced comparatively little by the history of philosophy, and if he can be said to have an intellectual mentor it is Noam Chomsky.

While being one of the masters of modern linguistics, Chomsky also makes it clear that he believes linguistics is best studied as part of a continuum with philosophy and psychology, and he does not shrink from drawing out the philosophical and psychological implications of his linguistic views. Chomsky has argued that different languages make use of the same, or at least very similar, formal operations in the generation of the well-formed or grammatical sentences of those languages. In this sense it can be said that all human languages are remarkably similar in structure, and so share a 'universal grammar' (or are circumscribed by the same 'general linguistic theory').

The study of universal grammar, so understood, is a study of the nature of human intellectual capacities. It tries to formulate the necessary and sufficient conditions that a system must meet to qualify as a potential human language, conditions that are not accidentally true of the existing human languages, but that are rather rooted in the human 'language capacity', and thus constitute the innate organization that determines what counts as linguistic experience and what knowledge of language arises on the basis of this experience. Universal grammar, then, constitutes an explanatory theory of a much deeper sort than particular grammar, although the particular grammar of a language can also be regarded as an explanatory theory. (Chomsky 1968: 24)

Chomsky suggests that the most plausible explanation for the universality of this universal grammar is that a child is genetically endowed with an innate capacity to engage in those formal operations which enable it to learn whatever natural language is spoken in the environment into which the child is born. The positing of such a universal grammar makes sense of the fact that children learn to speak a natural language in a reasonably grammatical way after even a comparatively brief exposure to spoken samples, of varying degrees of grammatical correctness, of their native language. Moreover, Chomsky would add, it seems reasonable to conclude from this that, in some sense, the universal grammar is 'wired in' to the human brain. The language capacity which this universal grammar makes possible is 'species-specific' (that is, specific to humans alone) and is more or less independent from human intellectual capacities (Chomsky 1968: 52–3, 68 ff.).[1] It can also be said to be a truly 'emergent' capacity in the sense that it cannot be seen as an evolutionary development from primate 'language' or animal communication of any sort (Chomsky 1968: 58–61).

Fodor, I think, would concur quite readily with almost all of these views of Chomsky, and if the Carnap–Quine–Dennett instrumentalist view of intentionality is seen as the culmination of the empiricist-cum-positivist line of thought, then the Chomsky–Fodor view of intentionality might be viewed as a natural extension of the rationalist tradition.[2] On the other hand, as we shall see, Fodor in particular adds a network of empiricist branch-lines.

---

[1] See also J. Lyons (1977, esp. ch. 10). At one point, Fodor says that 'Chomsky's demonstration that there is serious evidence for the innateness of what he calls "General Linguistic Theory" is *the* existence proof for the possibility of a cognitive science' (1981*b*: 258).

[2] Chomsky certainly sees it as such (1968: 25, 67, 76).

THE LANGUAGE OF THOUGHT

Fodor's best-known and seminal work is *The Language of Thought* (first published in 1975), which he describes as a work in speculative psychology rather than in philosophy of mind, because he is concerned to put forward an a posteriori theory which is constrained by facts from the empirical sciences, especially those of psychology and linguistics. For Fodor the mind is an aspect of the brain, for he is a physicalist. He is also a functionalist in the sense that he holds that, to describe humans as having beliefs or desires or hopes or wants or intentions or any of the other propositional attitudes is to describe the cognitive functions of humans. But for Fodor, unlike functionalists such as Dennett, these ascriptions of cognitive functions are to be taken literally. Humans really do function internally in just that way. Humans really do have beliefs and desires and hopes and wants, or at least something very like them, in their heads.[3] In a later work, *Representations* (1981*b*), he says that unless we limit our claims about individual mental functions to those cases 'where there exists a [computational] mechanism that can carry out the function' and 'where we have at least some idea of what such a mechanism must be like', we are likely to be dealing in functionalist 'pseudo-explanations'. After all, if there were no such checks from the direction of the brain and its computational mechanisms on our functionalist story-telling, then we may as well claim anything we like. We may as well claim that within our heads we have a 'universal question-answerer', for positing such a functional capacity fits neatly with the fact that most often humans produce an answer (output) whenever they are asked a question (input).[4]

In other words Fodor is an industrial-strength realist about intentionality and the propositional attitudes.[5] The guts of his theory of intentionality is that intentionality is primarily, originally, a real feature of our brains. Language is intentional only in a secondary sense, for it is intentional only in so far as some of the sentences

[3] Fodor cautions that 'the vindication of belief/desire explanation by RTM [the Representational Theory of Mind] does *not* require that every case [which] common sense counts as the tokening of an attitude should correspond to the tokening of a mental representation, or vice versa' (1987: 24).

[4] Fodor discourses on functionalism in general, and his version of it, at length in (1981*b*: 11 ff.).

[5] As Fodor has put it, 'I have pursued discussion in this book on the assumption that realism is a better philosophy of science than reductionism' (1976, p. ix).

which we utter in our natural languages describe real features of the minds of ourselves or others. It is this fact which leads us, in generating our natural languages, to generate within those languages a special vocabulary which involves verbs which are employed to operate over a propositionally encapsulated content. For example, if I said that Mary decided to stay at the bus stop rather than to make a run for it to the local police station because she believed certain things, had certain desires, connected the two in her mind, and came up with a certain evaluative decision, then I am describing a series of real processes in Mary's brain which involve computational operations over encoded propositional contents. Mary really has represented to herself (in her brain) the possible behavioural scenarios 'that I should stay at the bus stop' and 'that I should make a run for it to the local police station'. Also, most likely, at some time she has represented to herself a web of more general beliefs and desires, which she has connected up with these two behavioural scenarios and which make these behavioural scenarios relevant and plausible and sensible solutions to her problem. That is, most likely, she has also evaluated these behavioural scenarios in such a way that she can be said truly and literally to have decided on one of them for good reasons.

Now to do all this, in her head, Mary must be able to make use of some medium in terms of which she can represent the behavioural scenarios, beliefs, desires, evaluations, and decisions. Mary's brain must have a language of thought whereby the propositional contents of beliefs, desires, and the other propositional attitudes are first represented, and then operated on or processed in the individual ways which go to form the different propositional attitudes. For the same propositional content, for example 'that there will be rain', can be the information content of two different attitudes. One can believe that there will be rain and hope that there will be rain, or believe it but not hope for it, or hope for it but not believe it will turn out so. To put all this another way, because computation can take place only after information or content is encoded in computable form, then—as Fodor is never tired of reminding us—there can be no computation without representation (see 1976: 31, 34).[6]

Fodor is adamant that *any* psychological explanation of the sources

---

[6] Fodor defines 'a computation' as 'a transformation of representations which respect . . . [their] semantic relations' (1983*b*: 5).

of human behaviour must ultimately make reference to or at least presuppose a human's employment of an internal representational system of very considerable richness. Since, unlike Brentano and latter-day Brentanians, he does not believe that we have grounds for positing any mental substance independent of the brain, then this representational system must be not merely the language of thought but also a language of the brain. To put it bluntly, Fodor holds that there are brain states which represent and so have content. Intentionality, or the capacity to have informational content, is thus a feature of our brains.

In this respect Fodor departs significantly from Chomsky. For Chomsky the language of thought will be some natural language, the learning of which is made possible by our universal grammar. This universal grammar is a universal or near-universal capacity to learn natural languages, not a language for representing concepts or the contents of propositional attitudes or anything else. Fodor, on the other hand, believes that we must have a universal language of thought or 'language of the brain' in terms of which we really do our thinking (or do our mental computation). Only then, and only sometimes, might we publish the results of our thinking in some natural language expressions. Another way of putting this contrast is to say that Chomsky believes we have strong grounds, from empirical data about natural languages and how we come to learn them, for positing a universal grammar, or universal *capacity*, for generating our different, yet importantly similar, natural languages. Fodor, however, believes that we have strong empirical grounds for positing a real innate *language* or representational system *which is the basis for our universal capacity* to learn natural languages, acquire concepts, and even perceive in the full sense.

EVIDENCE FOR THE LANGUAGE OF THOUGHT: CONCEPT LEARNING, LANGUAGE LEARNING, AND PERCEPTION

Viewing all this from further back, Fodor is arguing for a Representational Theory of Mind. This theory is an empirical theory which makes a claim about how in fact our brains operate and so runs the risk of being falsified by future research. (See Fodor 1976: 47, 99; 1981*a*: 51; 1981*b*: 122–3.) Moreover, it is adopted chiefly for empirical reasons, for research in psychology into the nature of perception and learning, and in linguistics into the way natural languages are acquired, seems to supply us with compelling evidence that the human mind operates computationally and by means of a brain language which can be said to be the language of thought. (See Fodor 1976: 34.)

Let us first take concept learning. This, Fodor suggests, is essentially a process of hypothesis formation and confirmation. For example, to form the concept of a chair, a person has to extract what is common to all the things to which we intuitively grant the title 'chair'. Thus he or she will only gradually work out that a chair is something which we reserve for sitting on, and is usually designed with that in mind, and so is smaller than a bench but bigger than a footstool; however, unlike a stool it has a back on it; and so on. But for such a person to hold 'in place' in her head, for future confirmation or rejection or addition or amendment, a provisional model or representation is to make use of some medium of representation. Fodor goes so far as to claim that 'it is worth emphasising that no alternative view of concept learning has ever been proposed' (1976: 41).

Perhaps more controversially, Fodor claims that a similar story must be told in regard to perception. To see something is to interpret the nature of a distal (outside our head) object on the basis of myriad proximal (inside our head) stimulations via various sense organs. We form a hypothesis or best explanation on the basis of the swarms of micro stimulations that crowd the brain. At any one moment we richly interpret the world on the basis of fairly impoverished perceptual data, because our interpretation is like a hypothesis built up over many such moments. If we could not or did not learn in this way from previous perceptions, we would find our way round the world today far less quickly and assuredly than we in fact do, for we would have to act on each occasion *de novo* and without benefit of past perceptions. Each day our world would be like the world of a newborn child.

These perceptual hypotheses that we form are not concepts, as they are not definable in linguistic terms. The 'deliberations' of perceptual hypothesis formation are not accessible to us (our consciousness) in the way that our conceptual deliberations frequently are. Moreover, the formation of such perceptual hypotheses are equally a capacity of human and non-human animals. Thus, besides humans, cats and dogs and maybe even bumble-bees must be credited with a representational system in which to represent and store the working models or hypotheses which are at the basis of their perceptual interpretation of the world outside their epidermis. Furthermore, this sharing of the brain's representational system by both human and non-human animals will lessen any tendency we might have to view the brain's language as just an internalized version of some natural language.

Because both human and non-human animals possess the brain language which is the basis of perception, but only humans possess the brain language which is the basis of concept formation proper, it is probably the case that a human's brain language is not monolithic but comprises more than one system (Fodor 1976: 157–8). There must be, besides the language of thought, the language of perception, and there may well be others. Whether we should call the language of thought and the language of perception two languages or two parts of one language or two subsystems of one large language system is probably neither decidable nor important. However, it does follow that the term 'language' will apply more strictly to some parts of our brain language than to others, for the similarities between a particular brain language and natural languages will be greater or less depending on the language or subsystem in question. But what should by now be clear is that what is common to all parts or subsystems is that they are all representational.

In his book *The Modularity of Mind* (1983*b*), Fodor develops this aspect of his general Representational Theory of Mind in the direction of suggesting that the mind-cum-brain is not merely representational and computational but also functions most probably by means of a series of interconnected 'modular systems' or '*special purpose* computational mechanisms' (1983*b*: 120). Thus the human brain is likely to include in its architecture, for example, on the one hand a comparatively simple system that engages in the analysis of perceptual input, and on the other a rather more complex one that generates and 'fixes' our beliefs, and then the interconnections between the two systems. However, as this aspect of Fodor's general theory is not our concern here, I shall not pursue it further.

So to return to the question of whether there is a language of the brain, Fodor believes that there are other grounds for holding that there is, whose source is linguistics rather than psychology.[7] For

---

[7] At one point, Fodor squares his shoulders and challenges the opposition to 'try doing linguistics without recourse to mental representations' (1981*b*: 29).

example, says Fodor, there are compelling reasons derived from linguistics for asserting that 'one cannot learn a language unless one has a language' (1976: 64).[8] For learning a natural public language must involve a prior capacity to grasp the basic items and operations which a person needs in order to speak or write any natural language. For example, it can be demonstrated, Fodor claims, that a person could not employ correctly any predicate of any natural language unless in some way she could represent to herself, in a language that stands behind and is developmentally prior to the natural language, what would satisfy the conditions for the correct application of that predicate. This point might be seen more clearly by being put in the following way. Unless she can first represent to herself in some way what her very first predicate, her very first ascription of what '. . . is an x', amounts to, she could never recognize the occasion for correctly employing the predicate '. . . is an x'. Since a predicate operates, so to speak, as a marker on things that fall under the extension of that predicate, it follows that in order to know which things she can put the marker on, she must have had some way of representing to herself what the extension of the predicate was. She must have had some system for representing or depicting that extension prior to her first use of her first natural language predicate.

If we reflect for a moment upon the nature of our ubiquitous companion the computer, says Fodor, we will experience less resistance to this whole notion of a brain language, for a digital computer computes in one language but communicates with the programmer in another. The computer's internal machine language is (usually) unknown to the programmer, and so in that sense private to the computer. The programming language on the other hand is the medium of discourse between programmer and machine, and is what appears on printouts for the use of others, and so in that sense it is a fully public language. The two languages, the private machine language and the public programming language, are connected in the machine by means of an 'innate' compiler. In that sense our brains are like digital computers, for it is in our brains that the internal representational system (or systems), which is the language of perception and thought, is 'compiled with' or connected up to our public spoken natural languages. (See Fodor 1976: 66 ff.; 1981*b*: 11 ff.)

---

[8] Wittgenstein (1958, §32) attributes a similar view to Augustine (1983: 1. 8).

SOME A PRIORI REASONS FOR ADOPTING THE LANGUAGE OF THOUGHT HYPOTHESIS

I may have given the impression that Fodor's arguments for a language of thought and, more generally, for a Representational Theory of Mind, are entirely of a linguistic-cum-psychological sort. This is not so. In his paper 'Propositional Attitudes' (first published in 1978), Fodor argued that there are 'a number of a priori conditions which . . . a theory of propositional attitudes (PAs) ought to meet. I'll argue that, considered together, these conditions pretty clearly demand a treatment of PAs as relations between organisms and internal representations; precisely the view that the psychologists have independently arrived at' (1981*a*: 45). That is, Fodor is suggesting that there are philosophical arguments, of an a priori sort, for holding a Representational Theory of Mind and, in particular, for holding a language of thought hypothesis. The 'logic' of such arguments is that an inference to the best explanation of our folk psychological beliefs about propositional attitudes and our folk psychological practice of propositional-attitude attribution points to there being real representations of a linguistic or quasi-linguistic kind in our heads.

Fodor argues that any worthwhile theory of the propositional attitudes must explain why our ordinary language expressions of those attitudes (or at least those in English and many other languages) take the form they do. That is, any worthwhile theory should explain why such expressions take the form of a subject and verb with a relation to a *content expressed as a that-clause*, where the that-clause possesses quite definite logical features. Fodor suggests that only a theory which has in its explanatory armoury a hypothesis of a real language of thought can explain these logical features. For these logical features stem from the *sentence-like structure of the internal contents* of our propositional-attitude expressions. Thus only a hypothesis which proposes that we have real sentences inscribed in our brain can make sense of these features, in the context, at least, of wanting to produce a 'naturalized', physical account of the propositional attitudes.

Let me take just one example to make Fodor's argument clearer. He says that one important and ineradicable feature of our propositional-attitude expressions is what he calls 'Frege's condition', or their 'opacity'. This feature is perhaps best explained in terms of a simple example. Let us say that I have a belief that my cousin is coming to stay next week. My having this belief does not imply that, since the cousin is in fact a girl called Louise McNabb, I thereby have a belief that Louise McNabb is coming to stay next week. For I may not know or believe that my cousin's name is Louise McNabb. All I believe is that my cousin is coming to stay, for that was all I was told and so believe. Thus if someone says to me, 'I hear that Louise McNabb is coming to stay', I might deny it, quite sincerely.

The point of the example, from Fodor's point of view at least, is that the content of our beliefs and other propositional attitudes clearly operates *under a definite description*. What I believe (or my belief) has causal force, including motivational force in regard to my actions, and explanatory force, including making sense of my actions to myself, only under this one description. It is, as Fodor points out, as if I really have inside me, *inscribed in me*, a single operative description of Louise McNabb, a description of her as 'my cousin who is coming to stay', and no other operative description of her. So, says Fodor, it clearly makes the best sense to hypothesize that, when we believe (or desire or hope or intend etc.), this must involve our having a real sentence inscribed in our brains. In turn, this must mean we have a real language of the brain or language of thought in which to do the inscribing. Thus, when I believe that so-and-so, this must involve some part of my brain operating over some sentence (in my brain language) which expresses 'that so-and-so'.

INTENTIONALITY AND THE REPRESENTATIONAL THEORY OF MIND

As regards intentionality, the Representational Theory of Mind entails that any propositional attitude, such as a belief that so-and-so or a desire that such-and-such, is literally a computational relation between an organism and some formula in the internal code of that organism. The formula is the object of the propositional attitude in question. In turn this internal formula is a piece of information represented, in the case of humans, in the brain's language of thought. As Fodor puts this, in his book *Psychosemantics* (1987), 'To believe that such and such is to have a mental symbol that means that such and such tokened in your head in a certain way; it's to have such a token "in your belief box," as I'll sometimes say' (1987: 17). Moreover, it is in virtue of this system for representing and process-ing information that mental states are related causally to one an-other. Intentional attitudes are related causally and informationally (i.e. semantically) at the same time, and the former relation holds in virtue of the latter. (See Fodor 1976: 198 ff.; 1981*a*: 49; 1981*b*: 114.) Thus when she says to you, 'You intend to go to America because you believe that what you need is an environment sympathetic to your political viewpoint, and believe that only in America will you find such an environment', then her folk psychological intentional account of your decision and how it came about is, if correct, at one and the same time both an account in terms of your reasons for your decision and a literal account of the causal interplay of the propositional attitudes at work in your brain. The latter causal account follows the same paths as the former in-tentional account because the brain, like a digital computer, is a computational or intentionally operated engine.

In *Psychosemantics*, Fodor develops at some length his account of how in fact the brain, in pursuing its purely mental activities, operates both causally and intentionally at the same time, and in such a way that the causal path of the brain processes is the path dictated by the rational interplay of the contents represented by those brain processes. The way to develop this account, Fodor sug-gests, is again to look to the computer analogy.

Here, in barest outline, is how the new story is supposed to go: You connect the causal properties of a symbol with its semantic properties *via its syntax*. The syntax of a symbol is one of its higher-order physical properties. To a metaphorical first approximation, we can think of the syntactic structure of a symbol as an abstract feature of its shape . . . It's easy, that is to say, to imagine symbol tokens interacting causally *in virtue of* their syntactic structures. The syntax of a symbol might determine the causes and effects of its tokenings in much the way that the geometry of a key determines which locks it will open. (1987: 18–19)

A better example for illustrating how the syntax of the symbol is the bridge between its meaning and its causal influence might be the punched cards of the Jacquard looms. In the early nineteenth cen-tury Joseph Marie Jacquard invented a weaving machine in which each set of threads that moved in unison was tied to a particular rod. Which set of threads was to be moved and which was to remain in position, so as to create the desired pattern, was controlled mechanically by the holes in punched cards tied together in strings and smoothly moved forward over a drum. When one of the cards was positioned opposite and pressed against the complete set of rods, those threads on rods whose ends lay opposite a hole in the card remained at rest, while the other threads were moved. Thus the pattern of the holes both caused the picture or pattern on the woven cloth and, in the 'language' of holes on a card, could be said to represent it. Charles Babbage, the nineteenth-century inventor of the first completely automatic universal or general-purpose computer, intended to use Jacquard's punched cards for controlling his Analytic Engine, which is what he called his universal computer, though in fact the computer was never built. Babbage was so impressed by Jacquard's invention that he kept on the wall of his drawing-room in Cambridge a portrait of Jacquard woven on Jacquard's own looms at Lyons (Hollingdale and Tootill 1975: 41–8).

Given this story, Fodor might say, mental representations are the mind's punched cards. The patterning on them, in terms equivalent to holes and unpunched spaces, is the syntax of these mental representations, and this syntax is produced by both our genes and the input of perceptual stimulations from the world outside. The content or representational power of this syntax only exists in so far as the syntax functions causally as part of our mental loom.

Fodor points out that an important general consequence of adopting the Representational Theory of Mind is the preservation of the autonomy of psychology. For if the Representational Theory gives us an accurate picture of how the brain works, then the desired and proper explanations in psychology will be computational ones in terms of the interplay of the propositional attitudes. In turn the interplay of the propositional attitudes will be explained in terms of the interplay of various ways of processing contents which are represented in the language of thought. At both these levels the psychological explanation is produced in intentional terms, though, in its canonical scientific form, it may not employ much of our ordinary folk psychological intentional vocabulary, not because the latter is inaccurate but because it is not sufficiently detailed. It would follow, therefore, that psychological explanation could never be reduced to the non-intentional explanations of neurophysiology or to the even more basic ones of physics and chemistry (Fodor 1981*b*: 24 ff.). Fodor himself believes that 'the functional organization of the nervous system cross-cuts its neurological organization' (1981*b*: 144), for the reason that, while psychology is interested in natural kinds (i.e. the natural kinds which are mental states and processes), not all natural kinds correspond to physical kinds. Sciences of which this is true, such as psychology, are thus 'special sciences' rather than basic sciences like physics and chemistry (1981*b*, ch. 5) and preserve their autonomy in relation to the basic sciences. As Fodor puts it:

Quite possibly there never will be a state of science which [when?] we can, as it were, do neurology *instead of* psychology because, quite possibly, it will never be possible to express in the vocabulary of neurology those generalizations about relations of content that computational psychological theories articulate. Psychologists have lots of things to worry about, but technological unemployment is not likely to be one of them. (1981*b*: 165)

The Representational Theory of Mind also bestows on mental states and processes themselves a sort of autonomy, namely an autonomy in the sense that they can be and should be investigated in isolation from and so without reference to the context which may have given rise to them and to the behavioural output which they in turn might produce. In this sense Brentano and Husserl were right about psychology. Psychology can be and should be carried out by means of a sort of methodical and single-minded isolation. Where Fodor would not follow Brentano and Husserl is in advocating any form of or employment for any type of Cartesian or phenomenological introspection. What Fodor has in mind, as the correct approach to psychological investigation, is what he calls 'methodological solipsism' (1981*b*, ch. 9).[9] This amounts to the claim that mental states (or processes) are wholly individuated by reference to items internal to the organism whose mental states they are, and that psychological investigation of mental states (or processes) should reflect this fact. A belief or a desire, for example, can be and should be individuated, as that sort of propositional attitude rather than some other, firstly by reference to its propositional content and secondly by reference to the way the content is processed or governed (1981*b*: 226). There is neither need nor justification for any investigation into the

[9] Fodor (1981*b*, ch. 9) points out that the phrase 'methodological solipsism' was coined by Hilary Putnam (1975*a*). Fodor contrasts 'methodological solipsism' and 'methodological individualism' in (1987: 42–3).

environmental causes or behavioural effects of the belief or desire in question. To think otherwise is to fall back into behaviourism.[10]

Perhaps I should conclude this account of Fodor's Representational Theory of Mind, with its inherent realist view of intentionality, by quoting his vigorous advocacy of intentional psychology in general and our common-sense 'folk' version of it in particular. Our common-sense belief–desire explanations of human behaviour are, he says, not merely 'pretty close to being true' but it should be acknowledged that they explain 'vastly more of the facts about behaviour than any of the alternative theories available' (Fodor 1987, p. x). It follows, then, that any stiffened-up version, such as the 'rigorous and explicit intentional psychology that is our scientific goal' (1987, p. xii), can only do better, if that is possible. Seen in reverse, any attempt to give up the firm basis of psychological explanation in our common-sense belief–desire accounts would be 'beyond comparison, the greatest intellectual catastrophe in the history of our species' (ibid.).

THE REPRESENTATIONAL THEORY OF MIND AND FOLK PSYCHOLOGY

Is this the good news delivered con brio by the philosopher as he descends from the holy mountain, or the impersonated high spirits of the whistler left out on a lonely mountain road late at night? It is this we must look into now.

To accept the Representational Theory of Mind is to accept that mental representations are very like the internal representational states of a digital computer, and that mental acts are very like the internal operations of a digital computer. To accept the Representational Theory of Mind, in Fodor's version at any rate, is to accept that mental representations represent in no stronger sense than the punched cards of a Jacquard loom represent. Further, to understand a symbol or representation at the level of the brain is merely to employ something in a causal sequence so as to bring about the

---

[10] Fodor has always been particularly scathing about 'the failure of behaviouristic psychology to provide even a first approximation to a plausible theory of cognition' (1976: 8) and about 'the fatuity' of the behaviourist account of verbal behaviour (see 1981*b*: 251–2). On this latter point, as one might expect, he is a great admirer of Chomsky's 'polemic against Skinner' in his review of Skinner (1957).

result that the sequence is designed to produce. Even to say this is not quite right, for there is no employer, no humunculus who understands what the punched card is doing. The Jacquard loom 'understands' the pattern on the punched card only in so far as, and in the sense that, via the mechanistic movements of its rods and threads and other physical bits and pieces, and with the power from some power source, it reproduces a pattern on the woven thread which the punched card is apt for reproducing.

But in accepting an account like this it is not at all clear to me that one has accepted thereby a 'special science' of psychology which amounts to a stiffened-up, or more 'rigorous and explicit', version of our folk psychology, and so shares in the glory we accord our folk psychological account of the human mind because of the clarity, concision, and explanatory and predictive power of that folk account. In fact, I shall argue, the Representational Theory of Mind does not so much stiffen up and make rigorous our folk psychological explanations in terms of beliefs and desires as involve itself in a task which is quite different from that performed by our folk psychology.

What I am saying is that Fodor's claim, that his Representational Theory of Mind, including his hypothesis about the language of thought, is a lower-level, stiffened-up, professionalized, and so more rigorous version of our folk psychological explanations in terms of the propositional attitudes, is misplaced. Unlike, say, Brian Loar, who (among the tasks he sets himself, as we shall see in Chapter 5) does set out to produce a tidied-up and more rigorous version of our folk psychological explanations, Fodor is concerned with a quite different and distinct task. Fodor is really concerned with an investigation into how one can produce a realist and physicalist account of the propositional attitudes, where such realism involves placing the propositional attitudes firmly 'in the head'. That is, he is concerned with producing a realist and physicalist account of 'narrow content' (i.e. wholly in-the-head) content. Unlike Loar, we find in Fodor no account of what a new special science or more rigorous intentional explanation of some human action would look like. We find no new, more rigorous account of the necessary and sufficient conditions for attributing a belief or a desire or an intention to someone. We find no new, more rigorous logic which sets out in a formal way the conditions for when, say, a belief that x and a desire that y should lead to an intention that z. And we find no new, more rigorous account of the truth conditions for beliefs or the satisfaction conditions for desires or the fulfilment conditions for intentions.

Fodor has not given us a new special science of psychological explanation based on our folk psychological explanations in terms of beliefs, desires, and the other propositional attitudes. Rather he has given us a brain's-eye-view of the propositional attitudes. He has told us what he believes must be the case if propositional attitudes are really in the head. He has told us that we must have in our heads a representational system which is more like a natural language than any other representational system. That is, Fodor has put forward a Representational Theory of Mind plus a hypothesis about the language of thought.

I do not think that Fodor can step aside from this charge by saying that in investigating the real nature of the language of thought he is thereby producing a stiffened-up version of our folk psychology. For he has busied himself investigating what must be *the nature of the internal mechanisms* underlying our overt intentional descriptions and explanations not *the form a more rigorous set of intentional computations*, and so ultimately a more rigorous set of intentional explanations, should take. Fodor might object that neither he nor anyone else can set out the form of a more rigorous set of intentional computations till someone has first made clear what the in-the-head bits and pieces are upon which the computations are actually computed. He might say that he is merely engaged in the preliminaries to a new 'special science' of psychology which is based on the propositional attitudes.

To me it seems that Fodor has taken our folk psychological explanations in terms of the propositional attitudes as more or less gloriously successful and then said, 'What does that entail if we *naturalize* the propositional attitudes by placing them inside our head?' That is, he has not sought to make our folk psychology even better, by making it more *rigorous*; rather he has set out to depict what an industrial-strength *realism* about our folk psychology would amount to. If this is a fair account of what he is really doing, then Fodor has no grounds for saying that his Representational Theory of the Mind must share in, and indeed have an enhanced share in, the glory of our folk psychology, just as a particular physicist has no right to say that his particular theory of gravity, merely because it is more realist as an account, thereby must share in the continued success of the folk wisdom that objects thrown up into the air must fall back down to earth.

Fodor's Representational Theory of Mind, when seen in full computational mechanistic detail, is closer to the behaviourist theory of mind, which he so despises, than to our folk psychology. For on Fodor's account, Mary's belief has become an internal structure apt for producing a certain sort of response, because *content* has become the shape or structure of some brain state or process (or grouping of them), and *attitude* has become some other brain state or process (or grouping) causally interacting, electrochemically, with the former brain state or process so as to render it apt for producing certain sorts of behaviour. Skinner would feel quite at home with this account. He would suggest only that you add that the internal states are usually mobilized into action, at least ultimately, by an environmental input, and that any ensuing behavioural response will be shaped in part by stored feedback from the further effects (or consequences) of previous responses in just such circumstances. There is a difference in emphasis, certainly, in that, like Chomsky, Fodor would emphasize the extent to which the internal states are innate and shaped by evolution, while Skinner would emphasize the part played by the environmental input and the consequences of the behavioural output. Admittedly, the differences run a little more deeply than that. For Skinner would also say that psychology need only attend to environmental input and behavioural output and its consequences. Fodor would reply that surely 'real psychology' only begins when you begin to tell the story of what is going on, inside the human head, between environmental input and behavioural output. For that is where our cognitive-appetitive life is.

Folk psychology, however, is not a theory about the nature of the mind at all but a system for explaining behaviour. Certainly such a system entails certain things about the nature of mind (such as that the mind includes mental acts of believing and desiring). However, if this aspect of our folk psychology were to seek a mentor in the world of academic philosophy and psychology, it would do best to look in the direction of Brentano's account of mental acts. For here we have a post-Cartesian account of conscious grasps, in the sense of understandings, of content, where no time or space in the explanation is given over to talk about shape or structure or syntax as the driving force of mental acts.

Finally it might be said that this implicit folk psychological account of mind (as does Brentano's) depicts humans as, above all, *conscious* beings. It explains the propositional attitudes as conscious processes whereby the human in question takes up a conscious attitude to something he or she *understands*, where 'understands' means 'grasp the *meaning* of' or 'makes sense of' or some such.

This latter sort of objection—that the Representational Theory of Mind seems to leave out consciousness—probably would not trouble Fodor overmuch. Fodor could simply reply that a theory of the propositional attitudes is prior to any theory of consciousness in regard to those attitudes. This is so because, presumably, any belief that so-and-so or desire that such-and-such can be either conscious or non-conscious. So to make any headway into an account of the propositional attitudes as conscious processes, one must first make headway into an account of the propositional attitudes themselves. To do the latter involves first and foremost making headway in regard to a theory of content. That, Fodor might say, is exactly what I have been up to.

A CLOSER LOOK AT LANGUAGE LEARNING AND THE LANGUAGE OF THOUGHT

In adducing empirical evidence for his innate language of thought, Fodor relied on two sources, linguistics and psychology. His most widely known and discussed argument as regards the linguistic basis of the language of thought was presented in terms of the bold claim that 'one cannot learn a language unless one has a language', where 'has' means 'innately possesses' and 'having a language' means 'possessing the brain's language of thought'. Then Fodor proceeded to explain that, in order to learn any natural language, one needed an innate capacity to run through the formulae or set of rules which a person would need to follow in order to learn and employ correctly the words and sentences of any natural language. In detail, by way of an example, Fodor argued that a person could not employ any predicate of any natural language unless she (or he) had some way of representing the extension of the predicate, that is, some way of representing to herself when and to what she should apply the term. If the predicative expression 'is a chair' is to be learned and correctly applied, then the learner must have (innately) the capacity to represent to herself the fact that 'is a chair' applies (to keep the example simple) to material objects made for sitting on and having a backrest. Now if a person, say Petra, already knows a natural language fairly well but does not yet know the expression 'is a chair', then there is no difficulty. Someone says to Petra, say in English, 'You know what a material object is, don't you? And what "sitting on something" means, and what a backrest is? Well, "chair" means "a material object which is made for sitting on and has a backrest".' Petra learns in English the meaning of 'is a chair'.[11]

Fodor's argument, however, amounts to his saying, 'Now consider the case of the very *first* predicate or predicative expression someone learns, that is, the first predicate learned by someone who does not yet have any natural language vocabulary. How can she ever have learned this first predicate unless we accept that innately she possesses a language of thought?' For the sake of illustrating this point, let us say that we try and teach Petra's 7-month-old son, Fred, a first English expression. Rather foolishly, most probably, we choose the expression 'is a chair' rather than 'Mum' or 'Dad' or 'Eat up'. Now we might start by pointing to a chair and saying 'chair', and trying to get Fred to point to the same chair and say 'chair' at the same time. Maybe we even succeed in getting Fred to say 'chair' every time he crawls into the kitchen and looks in the direction of his red high chair with the Donald Duck transfer on it. But, Fodor would say, Fred has not even begun to use the English expression 'chair' correctly, because when taken into the lounge or bedroom, Fred fails to point and say 'chair' in regard to any of the chairs in those rooms. Fred would only begin to convince us that he understands and so has truly acquired the use of the term 'chair' when he can pick out and put the label 'chair' on the majority of chairs he comes across or at least on all the conventionally shaped ones. This, Fodor would maintain, could only take place if and when Fred has succeeded in representing to himself, in the language of thought, that anything which is a material object designed for sitting on and possessing a backrest merits the predicative expression 'is a chair'.

Let us grant that, after nearly two months and a great deal of persistence on the part of a group of patient researchers from MIT, whom we have had to call in to help us, Fred does learn, as his first

---

[11] I should acknowledge some debt, in regard to the discussion in this section, to Simon Blackburn (1984: 51–7).

English words, to employ the phrase 'is a chair' correctly. He goes around the house, boring the pants off his parents and brothers and sisters by gleefully saying 'is a chair' in regard to the lounge chair, the high chair, the bentwood kitchen chair, the rocking-chair, and so on. However, it is at just this point, say those who disagree with Fodor, that the Fodor story about language learning meets its first real problem. Let us grant that, in acquiring his understanding of the predicate 'is a chair', Fred represented to himself in the language of thought the fact that this short chain of sounds was to be applied to, and only to, material objects which are made for sitting on and have a backrest. What could 'represented to himself' amount to in this context? 'Represent' in regard to natural languages means learning to correlate a sound or written mark with something observable or with some description expressed in some natural language one already has, and thereby giving significance to the sound or written mark. But, *ex hypothesi*, the language of thought is innate, and so it cannot have been built up by correlating its marks or sounds with something else. Fred cannot have correlated 'is a material object' (encoded in the language of thought) with any observations of things in the kitchen or bedroom or lounge, for observed or empirical data are acquired data. If Fred himself cannot have made the connection between the inner mark in his brain and something else, so that the inner mark becomes thereby a representation or symbol for this other thing, who can have done so and how? Must we humans, like the slave boy in Plato's *Meno*, be said to have acquired knowledge in a previous life? Any such move, whether of a fanciful or unfanciful sort, will not do. For information acquired in any previous life or mode is still acquired, and so cannot be part of any explanation of how innate representations can occur. Besides, any such *Meno* move looks like explaining how one learns the first words of a natural language by reference to the possession of another natural language acquired in another time and another place. To do this is merely to invite the asking of the original question (as to how the marks of the language became representations) of this second-order language. In turn this looks like the first step backwards of an infinite retreat from the present battleground.

Fodor, I think, would want to block this retreat and, in general, to derail the objection that threatened to lead to it, by admitting that the sense of 'representation' as applied to the language of thought must differ substantially from that which applies to the words of natural languages. For after all, he might remind us, he has made no secret of the fact that the language of thought is more like a digital computer's machine language than any natural language.

Still the difficulty will persist. For in the case of a machine language (in a computer whose printout is in some natural language) it was some human who made sure that the mechanistic processes of the computer are correlated, via a compiler, with some natural language. Indeed the mechanistic processes only gain meaning or representational power by such a hook-up. A particular process in my calculator only represents the number 5 in so far as it is linked electronically with the LCD display of a simple line drawing which conventionally is taken to represent the number 5 in arabic notation for simple whole numbers.

Next week I might take my calculator back to the factory to have that same mechanistic electronic process hooked up to an LCD or surface display of the Queen of Hearts, for I might be converting my calculator into a poker-playing electronic game. Now if the brain's language of thought is more like a machine language than a natural language, then how can it be that we humans could be born with an inner machine language (the language of thought) which can be said to represent yet could not have been linked by any sort of compiler with any natural language, and could not yet have been hooked up by anyone to any other sort of surface display? In short, how can we be born with inner processes that represent, in the way the symbols of a machine language do, yet *ex hypothesi* we cannot have gone through any procedure whereby those inner processes were linked either to any object in the world or to any conventional sign or symbol in any existing language, code, or calculus?

If Fodor retreats further and says that all he means is that we are born with a brain that has the capacity during its maturation period to make the link-ups and correlations whereby the inner processes come to represent, then it looks as if he can no longer say that we are born with a *language* of thought (even in the sense of 'language' that is embedded in the phrase 'machine language'). He can only say (along with Chomsky) that we, but not cats and dogs and snakes, have a brain that is so constructed, and 'wired up', that we can readily learn natural languages. For we have the capacity in our lifetime to make links between sounds or marks, and produce a whole dynamic network or grammar for the ensuing representations.

If this is Fodor's position on the brain's innate language of thought, then it is a bit like someone's saying, not that we are born with the ability to walk, but that we are born with the ability to learn to walk. But who would dispute this? Who would dispute the fact that we need innate brain capacity in order to walk? For, of course, if the neural connections in the brain, and between brain and legs, are wrongly connected or damaged, then we will never be able to walk. Strictly speaking, we cannot even say that we are born with a primitive language of proprioceptive feelings, which enables us to walk by enabling us to feel when we are balanced and to keep our balance when we are moving forward or backward. We have to acquire—though for the most part we are not aware of the process—first the feelings and then the correlations between the inner feelings of our own muscles and the disposition of our body in space, and the correlation between the feeling of the pressure of the floor or footpath on the soles of our feet and our remaining upright. We succeed only after considerable time and difficulty. Learning to walk is a great step for mankind that is achieved only after a long and turbulent routine of crawling, standing, staggering, bumping into things, and slipping, falling, and sobbing. In general, as regards any human knowledge or skill, it does not make sense to say of it that it is purely innate. Everything is a mixture of the innate and acquired. Language and thought are no exceptions.

Be all that as it may, Fodor might reply, there are still the a priori grounds for holding that there must be an innate language of thought. That is, how else can we explain that the contents of our propositional attitudes behave like sentences except by positing that there must be a language of thought with sentence-like structures? There does not seem to be an acceptable alternative explanation. Therefore, in this context, an inference to the best explanation is an inference to the language of thought.

This, as we have seen, seems especially to be the case if we consider what Fodor calls 'Frege's condition'. For how otherwise could we explain the sort of blindness or opacity exhibited by our mental acts of believing and desiring, which in turn seems to stem from the opacity of the contents of our beliefs and desires? We seem, in short, to believe or desire *under a definite description* of the content or object of our beliefs and desires. This chosen or privileged description is then opaque or blind or impervious to other descriptions of the same thing or state of affairs or event captured by the privileged description. Therefore, it seems that what we believe, the content, must somehow be inscribed in us in the form of one particular sentence-like expression.

My puzzlement here can be expressed by asking why we need to jump from the *opacity* of our beliefs and desires to a *linguistic* version of that opacity. Why should we infer from this opacity that there must be sentences or sentence-like structures in the head? Every contact between any two things in the universe must be 'privileged' or 'aspectual' or 'from a particular point of view'. When one billiard-ball bumps into another, the first ball hits or scratches or at least bumps into just one side of the other billiard-ball. When we first catch sight of a friend in the street, we see the front or side or back of her. So it should be no surprise that when we find our way in the world or act in regard to the world or make plans in regard to the world or at least make plans of it, then all these activities will be aspectual. So it should be no surprise that when we believe or desire something, then we do so in an aspectual way, or with a limited point of view.

I think that a positive case can be made out that something's being aspectual, and so blind or opaque to other aspects, is not *ipso facto* grounds for saying that it must involve sentence-like structures. For sentences are only one sort of thing which is aspectual. Other aspectual things are pictures, imprints, and moulds. These things, at least arguably, are all 'informational', if, perhaps, not fully representational. However, there are other aspectual things which are clearly not representational at all. Things such as grasps of and contacts with. Though I shall go into this at considerable length later on in this book (in Chapter 6 in particular), a little bit more should be said here. There do seem to be information carriers which are not representational in any normal use of the word 'representational'. Being information carriers, they are *ipso facto* carriers of bits or aspects of information about something. Being non-representational, there is no necessity to posit sentence-like structures in their explanation. To give just one example here, the effects in the interior of a plant of the action of sunlight on its periphery are information-carrying effects. For these inner effects register in a causally covariant or analogue way certain features of the action of the sunlight upon the exterior of the plant. It could be that our brains, which of course have a causal role to play in our capacity to express our beliefs in the form of propositional-attitude expressions, act in a way which is closer to the innards of a plant than to the innards of a digital computer. Thus our innards might be non-sentential but give rise to the sentential, just as the innards of a sausage machine might be non-sausage-like but give rise to sausages. But I shall leave the matter like that for the present.

EXAMINING FODOR'S ACCOUNT OF CONCEPT FORMATION

Let us now turn to Fodor's argument that any plausible theory of concepts and concept-formation needs to postulate an innate language of thought. Because a concept is an intentional item with an intentional content, Fodor argues, then for a person to have a concept, it must be the case that this person 'houses' (in her or his head) some content. To house a content is to represent some information in some language, code, or calculus. To house a content non-consciously in the head is to represent it in the brain's language of thought. Moreover, Fodor continues, the development or learning of a concept must involve dummy runs as regards these intentional contents. For example, to learn and so eventually to be said to have acquired the concept chair, a child might try storing the information 'has four legs and toys on it' but, after corrections from her mother, she will have to discard the 'having toys on it' segment. By trial on her part and error-correction on the part of her mother, the child might replace the discarded segment with 'is for sitting on', or some such. The point is that the trial-and-error process must have been carried out via a subroutine that involves representing in one's head the parts or segments of the putative or would-be concepts. Or, to put it another way, concept acquisition involves the formation of hypotheses. To put this in terms of a Fodor-like axiom, 'No conceptualization without hypothesis formation (and so representation)'.

Fodor's account of concept acquisition, as a process of hypothesis formation via the representation of the hypothesis, together with subsequent proving trials for the hypothesis, may well be correct for someone who already possesses some natural language vocabulary. But in such a case there seems to be no need to go beyond the natural language as the medium in which the hypotheses are tested. The child with some English surmises out loud or to herself that a chair is for sitting on and always has a toy on it. Her mother, say, is the other part of the process of concept acquisition, for she corrects

Modern Approaches

either the child's linguistic formulation (in English) of her hypothesis that a chair is for sitting on and always has a toy on it, or else she corrects the child's attempts behaviourally to discriminate (pick out) chairs on the basis of the formulation. So Fodor's grounds for postulating a language of thought as the necessary medium for all concept acquisition must be based on the necessity of hypothesis-forming procedures when a prelinguistic child sets out to gain her *first* concepts of, say, her mother or her chair, and so sets out to acquire her first words, 'Mummy' and 'chair'. So let us look at the case of the prelinguistic child.

One response to Fodor might be to say that, if concepts are not merely representation-dependent but also *hypothesis-loaded*, as he alleges, then we should say that a prelinguistic child could not have any concepts at all. In other words concept acquisition must be a quite sophisticated and late phase in a child's cognitive development, and must come after the acquisition of some earlier, non-conceptual, natural language vocabulary rather than pre-date it as its foundation.

However, neither Fodor nor I would be happy with that response. I would not want to endorse it, partly because I find little to commend in any view which seems to imply a sharp cut-off between the state of possessing concepts and language and the preconceptual state. Now you have a concept, a minute ago you had none. I am inclined to think that a prelinguistic child does have some primitive precursor of the philosopher's and linguist's idea of a concept, because a prelinguistic child can discriminate objects and events quite accurately, and retain and employ such capacities to discriminate. However, and this is where I do differ sharply from Fodor, I do not see the need to explain the acquisition of these proto-concepts in terms of an innate language of thought and, *a fortiori*, innate concepts of a linguistic or representational sort. On the other hand, I would agree that these proto-concepts will depend upon *something innate*, for all acquired capacities must, somewhere along the causal line, trace their origin back to something innate. This is best seen in the context of our basic capacities to make perceptual discriminations. As Peter Carruthers puts it, in terms of his distinction between three levels of concepts, in his *Human Knowledge and Human Nature*,

Armed now with the distinction between these three different notions of concept possession [as discriminatory capacity, as part of the content of beliefs and other propositional attitudes, and as items of conscious linguistic thought], we can see immediately that our basic repertoire of discriminatory-capacity concepts must be innate. If we could not, in the first place, respond differently to stimuli of different colours or temperatures, or to lines and boundaries within our visual field, then we could never learn anything else. These elemental capacities for discrimination must be built into the very structures of our perceptual apparatuses. (1992: 97–8)

Non-human animals also recognize both particular objects and types of objects.[12] The digger wasp recognizes its own burrow-nest solely by means of visual cues from the environment surrounding the nest, but recognizes its prey, the honey-bee, by means of a combination of sight and smell. If the digger wasp can be said to have something like a proto-concept of its nest and prey, then the vehicle for achieving this is perceptual. Perhaps we should call the proto-concept a 'perceptual discriminator' (or 'discriminator' for short) in order to obviate any tendency to postulate any sort of linguistic or quasi-linguistic processing. At any rate, in recognizing its own nest, the wasp seems to note how the objects around the entrance to its ground nest (the stones, plants, and so on) are arranged, and to store this arrangement in memory. So its discrimination of its own nest is in the 'language' of percepts, and this, presumably, at least as regards what goes on 'underneath' or in the brain, is in part an innate one. But, as will become clearer in the discussions of Part II (especially Chapter 6), there are good reasons for believing that the underlying innate basis for perceptual memory and perceptual discrimination is an analogue system not a symbolic or representational system. The information is carried by causal impresses or imprints, like foot-prints, rather than by rule-governed expressions or representations or inscriptions, like sentences.

Perhaps a prelinguistic child learns to recognize her mother, teddy bear, and high chair in the corner in much the same way as the digger wasp did its nest, via visual discrimination.[13] Or, in the

---

[12] Readers will recognize a brief allusion in the example provided to the work of Tinbergen (1951, 1972).

[13] Besides acknowledging a debt to Carruthers (1992), I should acknowledge some inspiration from Andrew Woodfield (1987). In this paper Woodfield suggests that it may be wrong 'to describe any of the child's representations as "concepts" until they form an inferentially integrated network like our own' (1987: 26). Till then we should call them 'proto-concepts'. Likewise, he suggests, Fodor should concede that a child forms these 'proto-concepts' (which are representations of some sort) 'before the time when he can represent hypotheses. The sort of representations wanted are *recognition-schemas*' (ibid.).

case of recognizing her mother, most likely the discrimination is by means of a combination of visual, tactual, auditory, and olfactory discriminations. The child's conscious, combined 'perceptual blue-print'[14] might be sufficiently complex that it could only fit one person, her mother. When the child is older, she may develop a sophistic-ated perceptual discriminator for chairs as a type, and use the sat-isfaction of the conditions embodied in the discriminator as licence for the use of the noise 'chair' as a label for the objects so discrimin-ated. In short, the first powers of discrimination of objects, both particular and general, which a child develops, may be exercised by the employment of quite raw percepts. In turn, as I shall endeavour to make clear later on (in Part II), there are good reasons for *not* explaining our perceptual powers, at the level of the brain, in terms of a language or language-like system.

So then it does seem possible to outline an alternative to the Fodorian rationalist account. That is, it does seem possible to give an account of proto-concept formation which does not depend on any innate language of thought or system of representation or sys-tem of innate concepts, but only on perception (or the capacity for rudimentary perceptual discrimination), which in turn, at the level of brain functioning, seems to involve information without repre-sentation. Given the viability of this alternative to the language of thought hypothesis, it does not seem implausible to say that full-blown concepts—linguistically formed and defined concepts—*must* arise at a later date, namely when the first vocabulary a child has, which is formed on the basis of the primitive perceptual discrim-inators,[15] becomes thickened to include a second-level vocabulary built up out of this first-level one.

But Fodor also argues that we need to postulate some innate concepts, and so in turn a language of thought in which to express these concepts, on some other grounds besides those associated with the learning of concepts (see especially 1981*b*, ch. 10). One of these arguments, unsurprisingly, is that no non-rationalist view, that is, any version of empiricism, works. Since I have been addressing the

---

[14] Carruthers (1992: 104–10) uses the term 'prototype' at this point, and refers the reader to psychological research supporting this usage; namely to Lakoff (1987).

[15] On one reading, Fodor himself allows for such non-linguistic 'concepts' in his explanation of the hypothesis formation that goes on in the context of perception by infants and animals (see the earlier section 'Evidence for the Language of Thought' in this chapter).

possibility of an alternative, non-rationalist, non-Fodorian view throughout this chapter, and throughout this section, and will do so again in Part II of this book, I will not do so again at this juncture. Another argument put forward by Fodor is the Kantian one that certain concepts—such as those of space and time and causality—are so universal and so indispensable that they must be innate. This, of course, is not a good argument, for universality and indispensability can be associated with something acquired. For we may first acquire and then use something, and the use become more or less universal, and then none of us may be able to do without it. It may become universal and indispensable. Electricity may now be indispensable for any culture that has acquired it. Maybe our concepts of space and time are now indispensable, but nevertheless they may have been acquired. To take a long, evolutionary view of acquisition —and why not?—*Homo habilis* may not have had such concepts.

Fodor also puts forward a Chomskyan argument for the innateness of certain basic concepts of our culture. Fodor suggests that, as with language in general, children pick up certain basic concepts, such as those of space and time, so easily and after so little exposure to their employment by adults and, often, after exposure to as many degenerate or deviant uses as correct uses of such concepts, that they must be innate. This is a better argument, but it should not trouble an empiricist. For no one is denying that basic human capacities, such as those of language learning and visual discrimination and walking, depend on *something innate*. What is at issue is *what exactly* must be innate. Why should the capacity to acquire basic concepts demand innate *concepts*? The capacity to walk is based, among other things, on the prior capacity to have proprioceptive feelings, that is, in this context, sensations of our own muscle tone and limb movements. The final 'output' or macro capacity is the complex one of walking, but what is prior and innate and micro is not inner walkings or inner limb movements or inner muscle movements, and inner concepts of them, but an inner capacity for certain forms of movement or sensory discrimination. If our legs are anaesthetized, we cannot walk. For we cannot feel the way it should feel if we are both balanced and mobile at the same time. We acquire this 'feel of the way it should feel' only after a long process of *learning* to walk. But there seem to be no grounds for positing a theory of learning to walk which involves *concepts*. If this is so, then such non-conceptual learning might also be the model for our learning such things as spatial awareness and a sense of time passing. Such a model certainly cannot be ruled out a priori.

Some general points about *learning* are in order here (see Carruthers 1992: 100–1). Whenever Fodor finds himself talking about learning, at least in the context of perception or language or concepts, he seems immediately to slip into an account in terms of hypothesis formation and hypothesis testing. This model of learning, it seems to me, is just one form of learning, a form suited to certain complex and sophisticated capacities but not to others. It is probably the right model to apply to our *knowledge that* or propositional-cum-conceptual knowledge; for example, to our propositional-cum-conceptual knowledge that a cat is a sort of animal, or to our propositional-cum-conceptual knowledge that this object is to be called 'a chair', or to our propositional-cum-conceptual knowledge that Canberra is the capital of Australia. But we humans, and other animals, have *knowledge how* and *knowledge of* as well. Examples of *knowledge how* are knowing how to swim or walk or ride a bicycle (and not being able to say how we can swim or walk or ride a bicycle). Examples of *knowledge of*, or memory-based recognitional knowledge, are an infant's recognition of its mother's face, and my recognizing that this is a photograph of Athens, and your recognizing that this is the smell you experienced in hospital last year (without having the capacity to say why in each case). Now the rudimentary capacity for perceptual discrimination (the capacity of even a newborn infant to make certain visual or auditory or olfactory discriminations, for example) seems more like *knowledge of* or *knowledge how* than *knowledge that*, and if so there seems little pressure to say that what is innate in regard to this capacity must be representational or linguistic in nature. In turn, if our first real concepts are based on perceptual proto-concepts (or basic perceptual discriminators), then we have a story about the beginnings of our conceptual life without the invocation of a language of thought. There may be a language of percepts, in the sense of perceptual models or templates or patterns of sensations, and some innate underlying analogue basis in the networks of the brain, but that is a different matter and not something Fodor's empiricist rivals would or should want to deny.

How, in detail, a child gets from these perceptual proto-concepts, or discriminators, to an adult's richer, linguistically based, concepts is also another matter. I do not have a well-grounded theory—though

some ideas—about the 'cross-over' from simple, percept-based behaviour to sophisticated concept-based actions. However, for my
present purposes, I do not need one.[16]

CONNECTIONISM VERSUS THE REPRESENTATIONAL
THEORY OF MIND

Fodor has made no secret of the fact that he conceives of the Representational Theory of Mind as an empirical theory which will
stand or fall according to whether, in the future, our knowledge of
how the brain works confirms or undermines the theory. As he
himself puts it:

Speculative psychology, so conceived, is fraught with fallibility. For one
thing, since it seeks, fundamentally, to extrapolate from the available scientific theories, it is in jeopardy of those theories proving to be false. It
may, after all, turn out that the whole information-processing approach to
psychology is somehow a bad idea. If it is, then such theories of the mind
as it suggests are hardly likely to be true. (1976, p. ix)

Recently there has been some suggestion that connectionism in
artificial intelligence provides such a plausible alternative to the
information-processing approach, so that we would have to say that
it gives us (or looks well placed to provide us in the future with) a
better account of how the human brain might enable humans to
know, believe, desire, and so on.[17] Roughly speaking, at the present
time connectionism is an account of how artificial networks of nodes,
which interconnect electrically, can perform certain cognitive tasks
such as word recognition, concept learning, and inference drawing.

In a little more detail a connectionist system is a neural-like,
electrically driven, interconnecting network. In turn any layer in
such a network consists in a collection of neuron-like nodes. The
word 'connectionism' derives from the fact that each node in any
particular layer is usually connected to a group of nodes, or possibly
every node, in the two layers between which it is sandwiched.
Sometimes a node will also be connected with other nodes in its

---

[16] But see Carruthers (1992: 104 ff.) for a plausible empiricist version of how it
might be construed.

[17] As regards connectionism, I have depended very much on Tienson (1987),
Cummins (1989), Crick (1989), Bechtel (1987), and P. S. Churchland (1986, ch. 10).

own layer. Furthermore, the system's layers are organized, roughly, into an input layer or layers, which receive electrical impulses from outside the system, and internal processing layers which are connected both to these input layers and to the output layer or layers. These latter deliver resulting electrical impulses to the surface of the system or outside the system.

A node itself has an afferent and an efferent pathway for the electrical currents. In other words it can receive an electrical impulse as well as transmit one. The node can be turned on or off, or, more usually in such systems, it will have a threshold such that, when an electrical impulse higher than the threshold is received by the node, then the node will transmit an electrical impulse. Below this threshold, while still active in the sense that it is 'on duty' and receiving, it will not send on any electrical impulse. Furthermore, when it does send on an electrical impulse, this can have the result of being either excitatory or inhibitory in relation to that part of the system to which it is connected.

There is a further complication. The transmission of an impulse from one node to another will also be a function, in part, of the 'strength' of the connecting wire between the two nodes. The strength, or 'weight' as it is more usually called in this context, will vary inversely to the strength of the resistance in the wire or connection. The higher the resistance, the lower the strength of the impulse 'allowed' along the connection, and vice versa. Thus weight of electrical impulse is often expressed in terms of resistance. While there are no limitations on the way the nodes can be interconnected, a typical, if simple, system is one in which input impulses advance forward through the system from input, via central processing layers, to exit at the output layer or layers. However, in addition, there may be a feedback or 'back propagation' mechanism which will be able to alter parts of the main forward movements of the internal processing layers. For example, the back propagation mechanism may be able to alter parts of the internal processing interconnections until the desired output is in fact the upshot of the original input impulse.

One way in which connectionist systems differ from classical computer architecture is in their having no program, and so no central processing unit of an executive kind which oversees and administers the program. In that sense, in regard to connectionist systems, there are no sets of rules fed in and so no rule-following.

Rather the system is driven by trial and error. You operate the system by setting it to get a desired output from a known input. It 'learns' to do this by 'correcting' the internal processing layers' connections and weight of connections, until the system is in fact delivering the desired output for the known or given input. It is a bit like tuning a car engine. The desired output is a smooth-running engine—an engine which drives the car with a steady purr, no misfiring, no waste of fuel, and which does not emit heavy noxious fumes from its exhaust-pipe. The input is the ordinary petrol from the gas station. The internal processor is the car's engine. The processing that goes on is the tuning or tinkering on the engine by the mechanic, in response to feedback from the engine to his experienced ear and eye, and the engine's own internal combustion processes, until the desired output is achieved. In response to information fed back through his ears, eyes, and hands, the mechanic adjusts the timing of the spark-plugs by adjusting the distance which the spark must travel between the plug's firing terminals, and adjusts the flow of petrol to the carburettor or fuel mixer by adjusting the fuel injection needle, and so on. If the engine tuned itself, by means of some built-in feedback mechanism, so that by gradual adjustment and readjustment the actual output matched some template or model of a desired output (a smooth-running engine), then the engine might be said to have 'learned' by trial and error to run smoothly.

A connectionist system will sometimes be soft or plastic in the sense that it will be made in such a way that it will deliver the desired output in response to an input that merely resembles the paradigm input rather than strictly duplicates it. If the input is, say, a human voice saying 'London from Crook Crossing', and the desired output is the best route to London from Crook Crossing in Northumberland, and if you want to sell your system to foreigners as well as to orthodox English speakers with a south-east of England accent, then you will want the system to respond to the input 'Loondoon', 'Larndarn', and 'Loerndoern', as well as 'London'. A connectionist system will be plastic in this way if it can be triggered when a sufficient number of the input nodes is activated to the right level such that a sufficient number of connections to other layers is made and so the desired output produced. Thus there might be, to continue this example, input nodes that respond to electrically interpreted accounts of the sounds 'Lun', 'Loon', 'Larn', and 'Loern', and nodes for 'dun', 'doon', 'darn', 'doern', and maybe 'din', 'dan', and 'den' as well. The system may work if any of these nodes are activated in the right way. When plastic in this way, a connectionist system is said to resemble the human brain, for we humans can understand and respond correctly to all manner of pronunciation of the word 'London'.

Now Fodor, or at least a supporter of the Representational Theory of Mind, may respond to the suggestion that connectionism provides a viable alternative to the Representational Theory of Mind by making the following points. Firstly, Fodor or a Representationalist might say that in fact there is no good reason to believe that connectionism accurately mirrors the way our brains operate, and in consequence there is no good reason to accept connectionism as a viable alternative account to the Representational Theory of Mind. For example, unlike the neural-like networks of connectionism, the brain does not seem to operate any back propagation mechanism. As Francis Crick has explained,

It is also extremely difficult to see how neurons would implement the back-prop [back propagation] algorithm. Taken at its face value this seems to require the rapid transmission of information backwards along the axon [or the long nerve fibre which carries electrical impulses away from the body of a neuron or nerve], that is, antidromically from each of its synapses [i.e. against the usual and natural direction of electrochemical flow in the nerve fibre]. It seems highly unlikely that this actually happens in the brain. (1989: 130)

There is, of course, no let or hindrance to the possibility that later connectionist systems will do without 'back-prop' so that Crick's criticisms of connectionist systems on this account would no longer have a target. Indeed there are grounds for saying that this is already the state of affairs in regard to connectionism.

Crick adds another criticism, namely that the brain does not seem to possess anything like the special error-detecting neurons which would be needed to direct the brain's error-detection-and-feedback operation by sending precise signals to particular neurons or nodes (1989: 131). If this is so, then what we would have to say is that connectionism is an interesting exercise in artificial intelligence, and in the future most probably a very useful one as well, but not grounds for saying that the brain is not an information-processing device of the type suggested by the Representational Theory of Mind. On the other hand, it is rather too early to speak definitively of what connectionist systems are and are not capable of.

Even so Fodor and the Representationalists might counter-attack by saying that anyway, if looked at closely, connectionism will be seen to be a form of representationalism. (See e.g. Tienson 1987, sect. 4; Cummins 1989, sect. 4.) After all, any form of inbuilt 'teaching device' that helps the network system 'to learn' by correcting its errors must send quite precise signals or information to a node if it is to effect a change in that node. It must say something like 'Alter your weight (or strength) by so many units' or 'Raise your threshold to such-and-such' or 'Disconnect yourself' and so on. It follows then that the electrical impulse sent from the teaching device to the errant node or nodes is sending information *represented* by the electrical impulse. Besides it could be argued that the network as a whole is constantly representing things, or at least that the network does so when the trial-and-error process is complete and the system as a whole has settled down to producing the desired output. Let us say that the input is 'Crook Crossing to London' (i.e. a request for the best route from Crook Crossing to London) and the correct output is 'Join the B6343 route due south of Netherwitton and then . . .' and so on. The network's stable pattern of electrical activity, which regularly produces 'Join the B6343 due south of . . .' etc. as output for the 'Crook Crossing to London' input, can be said to represent 'Join the B6343 due south of . . .' and so on. What may be true is that the system does not deal in concepts or sentences or propositions or other language-like modules at all when it is computing the correct output. In fact the term 'computing' may not readily reflect the true nature of its trial-and-error processing (Cummins 1989, sect. 5). But Representationalists might say simply, 'Well, it wasn't we who suggested that connectionism was a good model of the way the human brain represents'.

Equally, of course, the Representationalists cannot declare a priori that the brain will turn out to be either a representational system or *a fortiori* a representational system which is also an intentional system based on computations over propositional contents. We shall just have to wait and see.

Before leaving behind this discussion of Fodor, I should make it clear that, somewhat artificially, I have focused on Fodor's earlier language of thought accounts of intentionality. Like any good philosopher, Fodor expands and subtly revises his accounts. In recent years, such as in his book *A Theory of Content and Other Essays* (1990), Fodor has developed his accounts of information processing, representations, and the relations between folk psychology and the 'special science' of psychology, in directions which are closer to those taken by Fred Dretske or Brian Loar than to his own earlier views. However, at the risk of failing to do him justice, I shall discuss these developments in later chapters, as they arise in the work of Dretske and Loar themselves.

3

The Appeal to Teleology

MILLIKAN AND PSYCHOLOGY AS BIOLOGY

In the second half of the 1980s, roughly speaking, there emerged a reasonably clearly delineated contemporary position on intentionality which diverges quite radically from the accounts we have explored so far. For part of the impetus behind this position seems to be a belief that neither the view of intentionality as just a feature of our common-sense way of talking about the mind, nor the view that intentionality is a real feature of the language of our brains and of what we do in our heads with the propositions expressed in that language, captures the real nature of intentionality. This new position or theory is associated especially with the work of Ruth Garrett Millikan and was expounded initially in her book *Language, Thought, and Other Biological Categories*, published in 1984, and subsequently in a series of articles extending and defending the theory (Millikan 1986, 1989*a*,*b*,*c*,*d*, 1990, 1991).

Of the three contemporary theories of intentionality which I have discussed so far, this seems to me the most original, at least in the sense that, while one can find hints and suggestions in the work of others, such as Darwin (1972; see also Millikan 1991), Wittgenstein (1958), and Sellars (1956, 1963),[1] there is no obvious precursor for Millikan's own work in the way that Chomsky is to Fodor, or Carnap and Quine are to Dennett. Arguably, and somewhat paradoxically, her main source of inspiration is what she calls 'meaning rationalism' (see 1984, epilogue), for it is against this rather general standpoint that, above all else, she seems to be reacting. Meaning rationalism is that theory, initiated by Descartes, that sees the world through the 'veil of ideas'. Meanings, thoughts, and ideas are the main denizens of the mind, and the mind is known first-hand and in a privileged way by self-consciousness and by introspection. We are certain in our knowledge of these inhabitants of our own minds but the rest, including things in the external world, are problematic.

[1] It is worth mentioning that one reviewer (Godfrey-Smith 1988) believes that Millikan's account of 'proper functions' is related to the work of Larry Wright (1973).

On the other hand, with equal vehemence Millikan wants to reject the usual modern alternative to Cartesian rationalism, namely the suggestion that we give up any hope of finding a firm foundation for our knowledge and embrace some version of pragmatism or relativism. The best we can do, a pragmatist or relativist might put it, is to admit to ourselves that there are no foundations for our knowledge and beliefs. A claim that my belief is true is just a claim that my belief coheres with most of those held by the other members of my community or a claim that my belief will enable me to function adequately in my environment. Millikan rejects such views for she believes we can do better. We can find a firm foundation for our knowledge, not by any inner peering into the mind as Descartes would have us do, nor, for that matter, by any outer straining of the senses in an attempt to achieve immediate, direct, and irrefutable observations of the world, as the empiricists would have us do, but by reference to the biology of belief.

Millikan wants to demonstrate also that intentionality is an objective natural feature of humans and not a subjective Cartesian or Brentanian one. Moreover, it is not objective by being a real feature of our way of talking or, in general, of language whether of the brain or elsewhere. It is a real feature of the world in the way that other human bits and pieces are, such as arms and legs, or hearts and lungs.[2] Intentionality is a real, non-linguistic, biological feature. It has been produced in humans by evolution just as surely as their arms and legs and hearts and lungs have. Thus the subtitle for her book is 'New Foundations for Realism'. It could equally have been 'A New Way to Naturalize Intentionality'. In her difficult, but rewarding, work *Language, Thought, and Other Biological Categories*, Millikan begins by quoting (rather, misquoting) a passage from Wittgenstein's *Philosophical Investigations*: 'Think of the tools in a tool box: there is a hammer, pliers, a saw, a screwdriver, [a rule,] a glue-pot, [glue,] nails and screws.—The functions of words are as diverse as the functions of these objects' (Millikan 84: 1). She then goes on to suggest that, while a tool such as a screwdriver has a proper function, namely to screw in (or out) screws, it could be used to poke holes in walls or prize up the lids of paint tins. In much the same way, a bodily organ or member has its proper function but,

---

[2] A title of one of her articles, expounding and extending her theory, is 'Biosemantics' (Millikan 1989*a*). Cf. a title of one of Fodor's recent books, *Psychosemantics* (Fodor 1987).

through misuse or damage, it may fail to perform it. The proper function of a human hand is to grasp things (to keep matters simple) but it could be used, in a clenched form, as a hammer to drive corks into bottles. Sometimes the proper function may involve the co-operation of other things. Thus, while a key does have a proper function, this proper function cannot be explained fully without mention of the lock into which it fits. A key functions properly as a key in so far as it opens or closes a specific lock, the lock whose key it is. So, in general, we need to look to the *effects* a device is *designed* to have in order to understand its *proper function*.

In the case of organisms, including the human organism, the design in question will be that which has been brought about by evolution in terms of natural selection. The proper function of a screwdriver is to drive in (or out) screws, because that was the effect for which the inventor of screwdrivers designed the screwdriver. The proper function of the human heart is the reasonably stable function of pumping blood throughout the body, for this contributed and still contributes to the nourishment and so survival of humans, and in that sense has been 'designed' for just such an effect by the processes of random genetic mutation and recombination and the 'selection' pressures of the natural environment. The proper function of the dance of the male stickleback is to arouse the mating response of the female stickleback because that is the response for which natural selection has selected the peculiar movements of the male stickleback.[3] Put strictly, the human heart and the dance of the male stickleback have not been 'designed' by evolution, but their design has been brought about by the processes we call evolution.

Now how can this choreography of device, effect, and proper function help us naturalize *intentionality*? The answer is that we should look upon our ordinary intentional acts of believing or desiring or hoping or intending in the same way as we look upon the activity of sticklebacks, organs, and limbs. We should look upon them as the activity of biological devices whose proper or intended effects define their proper functions. Believing is the activity of a device which is designed by evolution to have the effect of producing true beliefs in the believer. A true belief is one which is an accurate 'map' or in some sense is an accurate account of how the

---

[3] Millikan writes of this 'outcome' side of biologically proper function as the 'consumer side' of the 'system' (1989a: 285–6).

world is, which in turn will enable the believer to find his or her way in the world. That is, for belief-producing systems to function properly, they must deliver *true* beliefs at least some of the time, for true beliefs are the effects which belief-producing systems were selected to have by natural selection.

Any device, whether it be a belief or something else, is said to produce or give rise to a content in so far as the effect of its proper functioning can be said to be about something beyond itself. In regard to beliefs and other intentional acts, content is revealed not by the effects of their everyday function but only by the effects of their *proper function* in their evolutionarily *proper or normal conditions.*[4] That is, the content of a belief is the effect the belief system was designed to have when it was functioning properly in the proper conditions. For the effect a belief system is designed to have is the production of accurate or true maps, or beliefs about the world, which in turn will enable the possessor to find his or her way around the world. The contents of beliefs are about the world in somewhat the same way as accurate maps or true pictures are. Thus, in so far as beliefs are thoughts of ours, and the contents of such beliefs are dictated by their mapping function, and the success of that mapping function, then 'It turns out that we cannot know *a priori* either *that* we think or what we think *about*, just as we do not know *a priori* whether what we think is true' (Millikan 1984: 6). Of course, in a particular case or instance, the proper effect of a key or a belief system may not be revealed by the use to which it is put. The key might be used to pick someone's teeth, and the belief system may map the environment incorrectly and so produce a false belief. It could even happen that in the majority of cases some particular person's keys and belief system do not function normally or standardly. Maybe it could be the case that most keys and most belief systems, no matter to whom they belong, are nowadays improperly employed most of the time. So statistics or averages have nothing to do with it.

To recapitulate, the contents of our beliefs and thoughts and desires and hopes are set by the effects of the proper or standard biological function in the normal or proper circumstances of the systems whose effects they are. By way of further elucidation of this biological

---

[4] In Millikan (1984) she employs the term 'Normal' for this special sense of 'normal'.

account of content and intentionality, consider the waggle dance of the honey-bees. A scout bee returns to the hive and dances. This dance enables another group of sister bees, from the same hive, after close observation of the same dance, to fly to where there are flowers with nectar and pollen (bee food). The dance is *about* the whereabouts of nectar and pollen because that has been the biologically standard 'reading' of it by honey-bees for who knows how long.[5] Just as evolution has secured the success of the dance of the honey-bees, so evolution has secured the success of human beliefs when they function, biologically speaking, in a standard way.

While describing the honey-bee's waggle dance as intentional, in much the same way as a human belief is, Millikan reminds us of an important difference. In regard to a thought or belief, a human not merely functions, in respect of some bodily part (presumably, in this case, some brain state or brain network), in a biologically proper or standard fashion, and thereby gives his or her thought or belief content, he or she (generally speaking) realizes this. He or she realizes its significance. On the other hand, a bee does not. A human, again generally speaking, can be said to know what her belief or thought is about. For a human has the ability to test whether the content of his or her belief truly matches or 'maps' the world whereas a bee cannot do this. Indeed that is why beliefs and thoughts *represent* while, strictly speaking, waggle dances do not. (On this point, see especially Millikan 1989*a*.)

Biology, then, when seen against its full evolutionary background, is the firm foundation for human knowledge which we have been seeking. It is a foundation without Cartesian or empiricist foundationalism. By reference to biology, we have succeeded in naturalizing intentionality. We have biologized intentionality. This whole approach, Millikan points out, can be extended to meaning. We can produce a 'biosemantics'. Thus the meaning of an indicative sentence, for example, will be that part of the world which, in a biological sense, it standardly maps from the point of view of an interpreter (the proper 'biological co-operator' in this system) when the sentence (which is a type of conventional sign) is true. Indeed the biological function of uttering such sentences is to map the world accurately or truly.

---

[5] Nowadays there is a lively dispute as to whether in fact the waggle dance performed by the scout bee does operate as a ritualized and miniaturized version of the journey to be undertaken by the follower bees. See Wilson (1971, ch. 13).

A similar story is to be told about the meaning of our mental contents. Meaning is not attached to a content as a simple property of it in the way that shape is a simple property of this piece of driftwood. The meaning of a mental content, such as the content of a belief, is what it is 'about'. What a content is 'about' will only be revealed when we see the content as the effect of a biological system that has a proper function in a normal or standard environment. Just as the meaning of an uttered indicative sentence is what it standardly or properly maps from the point of view of a standard interpreter, so the meaning of a belief content is what it standardly or properly maps when it is viewed by the believer as the standard effect of a system functioning normally in its biologically normal environment. As Millikan herself puts it:

Thus the intentionality of a public-language sentence [what it is about, its meaning] is not derived from the *intentionality* of the inner representations [thoughts in the head, or other inner signs] that it Normally produces or expresses. Sentences are *basic* intentional items. (1984: 90)

The position is that intentionality is grounded in external natural relations, Normal and/or proper relations, between representations and representeds, the notions 'Normal' and 'proper' being defined in terms of evolutionary *history*—of either the species or the evolving individual or both. Hence nothing that is either merely in consciousness or merely 'in the head' displays intentionality *as such*.

On the other hand, this means that there is no way of looking just at a present-moment person, e.g., at his speech dispositions or at his neural network patterns, that will reveal even the intentional nature of his uttered sentences or inner representations, let alone reveal *what* these represent . . . Ideas, beliefs, and intentions are not such because of what they do or could do. They are such because of what they are, given the context of their history, *supposed* to do and of how they are supposed to do it. (1984: 93)

This account clearly allows for Brentano's point that mental content must be describable irrespective of how the world actually is here and now. My thought, or belief, or sentence may be about the house next to the river in the village of Sneem, but in fact (unknown to me) there is no longer any house there. It was swept away in the last flood. Nevertheless, my thought is still about this non-existent house, because what my thought latches on to is the world not as it is but as it is supposed to be (or would be) if my thought were true. The content of my thought is what it properly or normally, in the biological sense, produces in an appropriate 'consumer' in 'optimal conditions' (i.e. when it is accurate). The content of a thought (or belief, or utterance) is what it is *meant* or *supposed* to do. One can say, therefore, that Millikan has given an account of meaning in terms of 'meant-ness'.

In her more recent work, Millikan has explored the relation between folk psychology and professional psychology in the light of her own theory, which, to borrow a section title in one of her papers, views 'psychology as a branch of biology' (1986: 55). She argues that folk psychology is a good starting-point, perhaps *the* starting-point, for modern professional psychology, especially since the latter has adopted the programme of turning itself into cognitive science. This is so because the belief–desire-type descriptions of our folk psychology do pick out real natural kinds. Beliefs and desires are the bearers of intentionality and the containers of content in a literal because biological way:

If I can make it plausible that the entities that folk psychology postulates are indeed defined by their proper functions, and make plausible that the proper functions with which folk psychology endows these entities very likely *are* had by some special parts or states of the body, that would be enough to show that cognitive science can probably use folk psychology as a starting point. The job of cognitive science would then be, in part, to explain what the Normal constitution of these psychological entities is and *how* they Normally perform their defining proper functions. (1986: 57)

Thus the real relevance of folk psychology to psychology as cognitive science is not its role as an explanatory lawlike *theory*, on the basis of which one might predict future human behaviour (for if it is that, it is a feeble theory and so a feeble first step to a more rigorous lawlike theory). Rather its real relation to and relevance to psychology as a formal cognitive science is as a first-glance map of those inner biological *items*, and the relations between them, which really do guide our behaviour in a biological and intentional manner. Of course the details in regard to these inner biological items, and their proper functions, must be a matter of laborious discovery by neuropsychologists and physiologists and biologists and cognitive scientists.

This last part of Millikan's theory, about the relation of our folk psychology to our neurophysiology, is both reminiscent of and different from Fodor. Like Fodor, she believes that the belief–desire descriptions of our folk psychology do carve nature at its joints. But for Fodor, because psychology is a 'special science' and not a ground-level physical science, these 'joints' are unlikely to be physiological joints as recognized by a physiologist. On the other hand, for Millikan, beliefs and desires are real and recognizable physiological and biological items in the head. For they have evolved just as surely as our livers and hearts and lungs have. Where she differs very radically from Fodor, of course, is in her contention that the *contents* of these beliefs and desires are *not* in the head and so are immune to investigation by 'methodological solipsism'. For contents can only be individuated by reference to their proper (and in that sense 'normal') biological function, which in turn is only discoverable by reference to their evolutionary history. Our brain states or processes, which are beliefs, are like screws or bee dances. They are essentially incomplete activities or processes when viewed in themselves. For we do not and cannot really know what they are about (their contents), till we see them functioning, and see the effects of their functioning, and then work out their normal function and proper effects in a biological and evolutionary sense. Fodor, on the other hand, holds that beliefs are brain states or processes, though they are brain states or processes picked out at a 'higher' or 'special science' level which cross-cuts the brain states or processes described by neurophysiology. For the brain states or processes in question are of a linguistic or quasi-linguistic kind, and defined in terms of the Representational Theory of Mind and the language of thought hypothesis. They are states or processes with an informational content which is expressed, or perhaps encoded, in a language of the brain. Beliefs and desires and other propositional attitudes, according to Fodor, could be individuated in principle by translating or decoding a brain's use of its own linguistic or quasi-linguistic representations. One need not refer to anything else. This methodological solipsism is all that is required.

MORE FROM MCGINN

In his book *Mental Content* Colin McGinn extends and defends the teleological-cum-biological account of intentionality expounded by Millikan, though he mentions also other sources of inspiration.[6] He

---

[6] In McGinn (1989*b*: 143 n. 40), McGinn refers to Stampe (1979), Dretske (1986), Fodor (1984), and Papineau (1987) as additional sources of inspiration.

suggests that, in the first place, a teleological account of beliefs or desires might be expressed as a variety of a more general viewpoint about mental states, which might be called 'Externalism'. In other words one could begin by explaining that the teleological account of intentionality could be expressed as the view that the identity conditions for individuating a particular propositional attitude, such as a belief or desire, must make reference to something external to the subject of the belief or desire.[7]

As a way of illustrating and arguing for this basic part of the teleological account, McGinn makes considerable use of Putnam's Twin Earth thought experiment.[8] In somewhat simplified form, this thought experiment can be explained as follows: Imagine two people, biologically identical (a person and his *doppelgänger* if you like), who live on two planets which are identical in all respects except one—call them Earth (our planet) and Twin Earth (its almost identical twin). The respect in which they are not identical is that what is water on Earth (H_2O) is not water on Twin Earth (it is XYZ). On the other hand, water on Twin Earth tastes the same as water on Earth. It has the same colour, taste, feel and, indeed, all the other experiential and so phenomenal qualities that water on Earth has. Thus, to someone drinking or swimming in Twin Earth water, it would appear to be the same as ordinary (Earth) water. While it would *seem* to us to be the same as ordinary water, *in fact* it would be physico-chemically different. Strictly speaking, Twin Earth water is a different 'stuff'. This being so, if Fred on Earth (let us call him Fred$_E$) has a belief about ordinary water and his *doppelgänger*, Fred on Twin Earth (let us call him Fred$_{TE}$), has a belief about Twin Earth water, then their beliefs are different. This will be so even if they themselves have the same experiences, when drinking or swimming in, or doing anything else with, the water on their own planet. This will be so, also, even if they are both ignorant of the physico-chemical difference between ordinary water and water on Twin Earth. The point is that the content of a belief is what the belief is about, not how what it is about might 'strike' (i.e. be phenomenally experienced by) the believer.

---

[7] In fact McGinn distinguishes two versions of externalism. In a weak version of the thesis, the identity conditions of a mental state merely make reference to 'some item belonging to the nonmental world'. In its strong version, the conditions will involve reference to some item belonging to the non-mental world 'in the environment of the subject'.   [8] The classical source is Putnam (1975*a*).

It would follow from the externalist viewpoint that a believer is not necessarily the best judge of what his or her own belief is about; that is, a believer could be ignorant of the content of his own belief. For what a belief is about is what it 'maps' or 'hooks on to' in the world (at least when it is a belief about the world) and, of course, a believer could be ignorant of the real nature of this thing or event. It is a bit like a fisherman casting his line into the river, success-fully, and thinking he has hooked a trout when it is only a pike. If we take an externalist view about mental acts, such as beliefs, de-sires, hopes, intentions, and so on, then there is always the possibil-ity that what their contents are is a discovery waiting to be made.

Humans, and to a certain extent other animals, McGinn continues, have mental contents which must be given an externalist explana-tion for good evolutionary reasons. For it is in so far as humans and other animals are designed by evolution to cope with their environ-ments that they have a cognitive life whose individual bits and pieces are intimately connected up to the environment. Beliefs and desires, in humans at any rate, are inner states (probably brain states or processes) whose content is a relation between an inner state and things external to it (McGinn 1989*b*, pt. 2, esp. 79 ff.). It is at this point that McGinn's account meshes closely with Millikan's. For he goes on to explain that this relation should be explained in terms of 'relational proper function' (1989*b*: 144 ff.).

Where McGinn noticeably extends Millikan's account is in con-nection with his contention that 'the relational proper function of representational mental states [such as beliefs and desires] coincides with their extrinsically individuated content'. Function fixes, and is fixed by, content (1989*b*: 147). If I interpret his account correctly at this point, it is because the content of my belief is fixed by reference to its proper function, evolutionarily speaking, that it takes the form it does in my brain. Beliefs, for example, have the incarnated shape or structure they in fact exhibit because the shape must subserve the relational 'purpose' it was designed by evolution to carry out. That is, it must have a shape apt for hooking on to the world and 'meshing' with other mental states, such as (especially) desires. For desires connect humans up to their behaviour in the world. The shape in question is a 'logical' one (1989*b*: 152), at least in the first instance, though this in turn will dictate its physiological shape (1989*b*: 169). On the other hand, we would be in error if we looked to language, or anything logico-linguistic, for further clarification of this concept of 'logical shape'. Mental states are not little inner conversations, nor do they involve inner computations. 'Logical shape' is best explained in terms of the brain's power to 'model'. The logic in question, then, is the logic built into the brain's employment of models. As McGinn himself puts it: 'The basis of content is more like an engineer's workshop in which no one speaks. There are no volleys of verbal activity occurring in the recesses of your brain, only the production of vastly many practical models. You are not a secret speaker of some hitherto undeciphered language; you are more like the maker of a very sophisticated atlas that covers much more than ordinary geography' (1989*b*: 208).[9] I take it that the phrase 'much more than ordinary geography' implies that, while some of the models might be perceptual ones (and so somewhat like internal products of cartography), others will be more like rationales (and so somewhat like internal rational explanations or justifications or predictions, that is, more like a map of the logical space in which objects and events are placed).

At any rate, McGinn is emphasizing that, in so far as they are partly in the head, then propositional attitudes are more like models of definite shape or contour than sentences expressing propositions written out in the language of the brain. The models have been designed by our brains, when prompted by external or internal stimuli, and, in turn, our brains have been designed by evolution. They have been designed to register the world, and mesh with desires and other appetitive states, and so to prompt and shape appropriate action or reaction. To open up someone's head and to look at a particular brain state or process is a bit like finding a key in a street. Merely by looking at it, you cannot know whose it is or what it will open or close. The same is true of the brain states which are the internal part of our mental states. It is only when brain states are placed in a relational context that they become mental states. It is only when a brain state is placed in its relation to the world via the sensory systems, in its relations to other brain states via cortical connections, and in its relations to behaviour via the central nervous system, *and*, especially, viewed in terms of its relational proper function (its evolutionary role), that we will see it as a mental state with content.

---

[9] In connection with the concept of mental (brain) models, McGinn refers especially to Craik (1943) and Johnson-Laird (1983).

UNDER FIRE FROM FODOR

In his Donnellan Lectures, delivered at Trinity College Dublin in 1989,[10] Jerry Fodor posed a series of objections against the teleological theory of intentionality which amounted to the most sustained attack yet made on this account. Fodor describes his first objection as the failure of the teleological account to solve the 'disjunction problem'. The disjunction problem, or some close relation to it, Fodor maintains, is a problem that besets any externalist theory of content. In a slightly adapted form,[11] the disjunction problem might be described as the problem any externalist theorist has in distinguishing between the external causal conditions which generate a true belief (i.e. acceptable or normal conditions) and those which generate a false belief (i.e. unacceptable and abnormal conditions). However, let us take an example and so put this point more clearly in the context of the teleological theory. Let us say that on Monday the presence of a platypus causes me to have a belief that there is a platypus over there, but on Tuesday, owing to some causal mix-up, the presence of a goldfish causes me to have a belief that there is a platypus over there. Now, unless a teleological theorist can specify which of these states of affairs constitutes a 'mix-up' and which a successful 'hook-up', the teleological theory is useless as a way of individuating the content of my present belief by reference to the external conditions which gave rise to my present belief. But how, Fodor asks, can a teleological theorist do this in terms of a vague reference to evolution and biologically proper function?

The teleological theorist's likely response[12] to this challenge is to explain that a belief that there is a platypus over there is the correct description of the content of my belief because the state of affairs whereby the presence of a goldfish causes me to believe that there is a platypus over there is functionally aberrant. The belief in question is one that is, in an important respect, based on a perception

[10] The lectures were entitled 'Problems of Content in the Philosophy of Mind', and the queries or objections referred to occur in his second lecture, which was entitled 'On there not being an Evolutionary Theory of Content; or, 'Why, if you've been waiting for Darwin to pull Brentano's chestnuts out of the fire, my advice to you is: Forget it'.

[11] Adapting it to the context of specifying the content of mental states rather than to the problem of specifying the meaning of terms.

[12] I base the teleological theorist's responses to Fodor partly on Millikan (1991). (Ruth Millikan kindly allowed me to see this in MS form.)

of the immediate environment. Only some flaw in my visual system, or in the connections between it and my belief-forming system (to keep it artificially simple), can generate such a belief. Flaws in biological systems are not part of proper biological functioning and so not what is selected by evolution as survival-enhancing. Beliefs about the world that are accurate help humans negotiate their way in the world but beliefs about platypuses when goldfish are present do not.

Fodor's retort to this is to say that the appeal to evolution in this context is no more than an act of faith. For a start, not each and everything that humans possess is survival-enhancing or even useful in any way, and our belief-generating mechanisms may be one of the non-survival-enhancing, more or less useless things with which humans are endowed.[13]

A teleological theorist would probably respond in the following way: 'Yes, of course, it need not have been the case that belief-generating mechanisms are survival-enhancing or even useful, but as a contingent matter of fact they are. Try surviving for a week without counting on the bulk of your beliefs being true. Try *not* believing that the food in the supermarket is not poisoned, that your house is still where it was when you left twenty minutes ago, that there is a stream of traffic between you and the phone booth on the other sidewalk, and so on.'

Certainly, as Fodor is quick to point out, that beliefs turn out to be useful does not show that they were designed by evolution to have such uses. It may turn out that everyone nowadays uses screwdrivers only to open paint tins, but that is not the purpose for which they were designed. The teleologist would probably have no difficulty accepting the general point but suggest that it can hardly apply in the case of belief or desire. As the teleologist might put it, 'Sure, even if beliefs have a use, it is possible that humans discovered this use for their beliefs by trial and error, rather than it being the case that beliefs were designed by evolution to have this use. It is possible but hardly probable. Given the general acceptance of the

---

[13] In his review of Millikan (1984), Peter Godfrey-Smith writes, 'Her model explanations are biological, yet it is well known that within biology there has lately been a reaction against the "Panglossian" or "optimising" view of natural selection. Stephen Jay Gould and Richard Lewontin spearhead the reaction, claiming that the products of evolution are not collections of independently selected, perfectly functioning parts, but a tangle of engineering compromises, including many features with no function' (Godfrey-Smith 1988: 559).

Darwinian thesis, that natural selection is the architect of the central action-guiding features in any organism, and since beliefs and desires are the central action-guiding features in humans, then it is very reasonable to assume that our belief-generating mechanisms were designed by evolution to have the uses they in fact have, and that, generally speaking, having beliefs that can be employed in these ways is survival-enhancing.' A teleologist could go on to point out that it does not follow from this that every belief works properly and so fulfils its survival-enhancing purpose. All that is needed is that humans have a mechanism that can generate survival-enhancing decisions on the basis of survival-enhancing beliefs when those rare occasions arise. Feet are for walking with the dog as well as for running out of the way of a runaway bus, but none of us may ever be called upon to use our legs for the latter life-preserving purpose. A teleologist does not have to tell a survival-enhancing story about each and every belief, just as he or she does not have to tell a survival-enhancing story about each and every step his or her legs take.

On the other hand, Fodor does seem to hit the mark when he suggests that a teleological view of intentionality seems to end up making everything that has an evolutionarily proper function the possessor of content in exactly the same way as mental acts possess content. A teleological theory of intentionality seems to make states of our hearts and livers and lungs to be kinds of mental state. In more detail, according to a teleologist about intentionality, I should be described as having a belief *about* there being a ferocious dog just outside the door, because a particular brain state (or, more likely, a particular network of brain processes) in me has been selected by evolution to produce responses appropriate to what, in our folk psychology, would be described as having just such a belief in just such a context. Therefore, according to such a teleologist, it ought also to be the case that I should be described as having a belief *about* needing oxygen or needing to speed up my respiration rate, because the present state of my lungs has been selected by evolution to produce responses appropriate to what, in an extended folk psychology, would be described as having just such a belief in just such a context. Or, to put this another way, what is so special about brains? Why, when handing out intentional awards, should we discriminate in favour of brains but against hearts, livers, and lungs?

McGinn seems to have some sort of answer to this objection,

which may not be open to Millikan. He can reply that a mechanism is to be described as having a content not merely if it has a normal function shaped by evolution but also if its normal function achieves its purpose by generating internal models. Millikan may or may not want to venture along the same path, though she does distinguish between a human belief and the nearest equivalent state of, say, a stickleback or a honey-bee by saying that beliefs involve representations or maps identified by the believer while the nearest equivalent states of the stickleback and honey-bee do not. So, if we take it that Millikan's response is along the same lines as that of McGinn, then Fodor could reply that such a response involves a major retreat from an externalist position. For now the major role in specifying content seems to have been taken over by an internal item, a model or representation or map in the head. Indeed Fodor might suggest that such a response is not a thousand miles away from his own position on intentionality as explained in his Representational Theory of Mind.

A different sort of reply, which is, I suspect, the one Millikan might prefer to give, is to say, 'Yes. A heart and a lung do have a sort of content. Anything that is biological does. There is no clear cut-off point between content (or "the aboutness of biological proper function") in some psychological sense and content (or "the aboutness of biological proper function") in a non-psychological sense. After all, part of my contention is that a mature and successful psychology will be seen as just a part of biology. On the other hand, to say this is not to deny that there will be important differences in the way content is *realized* in the case of a non-psychological item such as a heart or lung and in the case of a psychological item such as a belief. But the differences should not be described as the difference between content and lack of it. Or if they are, all that is happening in terms of such a distinction is that, in a more or less arbitrary fashion, someone is deciding that one sort of inner something-or-other which has a proper function and proper effect should not be said to have a content because its function is not a mapping, nor anything cognate.' In short, Millikan can reply that it is a strength, not a weakness, of her theory that it blurs the distinction between states of our lungs and beliefs. If this goes against our intuitions, then so much the worse for them. Because they are probably Cartesian or Brentanian intuitions, or at least rationalist ones of some hue, then they are better interred anyway.

PROBLEMS WITH INDIVIDUATING PARTICULAR BELIEFS AND DESIRES

Fodor is also at least close to the mark when he suggests that if, as seems to be the case, an evolutionary teleological account can only specify the normal function of belief mechanisms and desire mechanisms *in general*, then it is of little use in specifying the function of *particular* beliefs or desires and so for individuating the contents of particular beliefs or desires. How, for example, could reference to evolution and proper function ever help us work out that my present desire is to be rich, and that I have a belief that a liking for pea soup reveals a strong defect of character? There is nothing survival-enhancing about these particular beliefs and desires, and this is probably true of most of our quotidian intentional states. So an appeal to evolution is of no help in individuating the content of most of our ordinary beliefs and desires. Nor is it of any use to say that the proper function of my desire to be rich is to lead to behaviour that would bring it about that I be rich because this is the proper function of desire mechanisms in general (i.e. the proper function of desires is to lead to behaviour that would satisfy those desires). This response, Fodor would reply, only endorses my point. All that can be said by a teleologist, when asked to individuate the content of this belief here or that desire over there, is to talk in a general way about the proper function of belief mechanisms being to provide accurate beliefs about the world and the proper function of desire mechanisms being to lead to behaviour which would satisfy the desires which are generated.

Millikan and McGinn can reply that a teleologist *can* employ evolutionally proper function to individuate the particular content of a particular desire or belief. One just notes the behaviour which emanates from the person in question, then, against the background assumption that the person's belief and desire mechanisms co-ordinate to produce behaviour which is appropriate to the way the world is and appropriate to the satisfaction of some particular desire, one then works back to what the belief or desire in question must be. For example, I can work out that you have a desire to be rich by observing that you keep saying to people 'I want to be a millionaire before I'm 40' and that you are always engaging in risky business deals with a particularly rich pay-off. You may never become rich but it may be obvious that you want to be.

Fodor would probably respond by saying that, in the above example, we are given a credible account of how an observer might decide that someone probably has a desire to be rich. However, any reference to teleology or evolutionally proper function is now marginal. Content is individuated by reference to ordinary behaviour combined with the general assumption that people act rationally most of the time. This is how most of us, who have never heard of, much less employed, the concept of biologically or evolutionarily proper function, individuate another person's beliefs and desires. We just study output (behaviour) in the light of input (the person's likely understanding of the context) and guess, with varying degrees of accuracy, what someone's beliefs and desires are. Moreover, the further we get away from simple cases of behaviour satisfying my desire *in toto* to complex cases where the behaviour stemming from the desire is a long way from being the optimal or proper satisfaction of my desire, then the more marginal seems any reference to biologically proper function as a way to individuate the content of my desire. For example, let us say that my desire is to drink a really good chateau-bottled Bordeaux rouge of 1985 vintage, as it is my birthday and I would like to give myself a treat. I have been thinking of this all day. However, when I enter the wine-merchant's, I realize that I cannot afford a chateau-bottled Bordeaux of any colour or vintage. I cannot even afford a decent Australian or Californian cabernet sauvignon. So I end up with a bottle of Bulgarian red of uncertain provenance. It is the best I can do. My behaviour stems from my desire, but in no sense does it satisfy it. A great amount of our behaviour must be of this kind, and it is unclear how an appeal to biologically proper function could lead to the correct answer in these cases, unless it becomes modified to something like an appeal to 'the, pragmatically speaking, best possible satisfaction of the desire in question in these circumstances'. But such a modification seems to amount to an admission that an appeal to biologically proper function is useless in such cases.

It could be said that the core of Fodor's attack on the teleological approach to intentionality is his contention that to appeal to evolution as a way of individuating mental content is to employ a very crude instrument. Evolution is the 'selection' of *types* of organism by the environment on the basis of behaviour. So, at most, what can be said to have survival value is types of behaviour, not particular refined or precise instances of mental content. Evolution is indifferent to whether you *desire* a pork sausage or a vegetarian nut cutlet, if *eating* either fulfils the function of assuaging your hunger. As Fodor himself puts it: 'Darwin has nothing to say to Brentano; the whole point of Darwin's enterprise was to get biology out of Brentano's line of work' (1989, lecture 2, 18). The teleologist would want to say that Brentano's line of work is obsolete. To seek to do it is like advertising as a witch-doctor in the age of modern medicine. If at present there are difficulties in describing how one individuates particular intentional states in a biologically useful way, then this is no more than the difficulty that a biologist might encounter in describing how one can individuate particular functions in certain types of insect. How *exactly* does the waiting honey-bee, for example, 'read' the waggle dance of the scout bee? Is it by sight, or hearing, or through felt vibrations, or scent, or what? Biology is full of discoveries waiting to be made, so why should we think that it would be otherwise in the realm of biological psychology?

To say this, however, Fodor might wearily respond, is to lead us into the commerce of IOUs handed out by that notoriously unreliable borrower Future Science. For how is one to square these hopes about the future of biology or biological psychology with the common conviction, rationalist or not, that we can and do individuate one another's beliefs and desires and other propositional attitudes, and with our conviction that we do this by making reference, not to supposed biologically proper functions, but just to ordinary people's actions and reactions in a known context?

FURTHER CRITIQUE

Fodor is not the only critic of this teleological approach to intentionality. P. F. Snowdon, for example, in a review of David Papineau's book *Reality and Representation*, which, among other theses, defends a teleological-cum-biological approach to psychology, puts the following shrewd point:

Due to a random mutation, a creature is produced with a new sense organ and connected neural system which provides it with information about aspects of its environment. The system performs a highly advantageous function and persists and spreads. It therefore gets selected to perform that function. However, how do we characterize in cognitive, representational terms the very first creature to possess it? In it, the system had not been *selected* for anything, because the processes of selection had not had [a] chance to operate. (1988: 630)

In other words, Snowdon is suggesting that, according to the teleological-cum-biological view, the first inner product from this new sense organ could not be considered to be about anything (to be a content), because no evolutionally proper function for the sense organ has yet been established. The environment has yet to test this randomly produced sensory system for survival value or fitness. On the other hand all our intuitions tell us that here we have a new sensory system because, in much the same way as our other sensory systems, it reacts to stimuli from the environment. Furthermore, the story about how this system or process was produced by random mutation (or recombination, perhaps) will not be science fiction. It will be merely an account of the usual biological birth of any new system or process in an organism. For every new biological system or process must, in the beginning, be untested by evolution. Selection for fitness can only begin *after* a biological system or process has emerged. As Snowdon observes, such a consideration should incline us to the view 'that "biologising" content underestimates (even if other approaches overestimate) the degree to which psychology is individualistic' (ibid.).

It is not clear to me what reply the teleological-cum-biological view should or could make here. One response might be to say that the first content produced by such a randomly produced sensory system could only be, at most, a rough and random proto-content. The organism whose system it is would not yet have integrated the system into its behaviour, so a content that leads to no behaviour, and *a fortiori* to no biologically proper behaviour, cannot yet be a content in the biological sense. It is only half-way to being a content, for it is not yet about anything, for 'aboutness' is secured by behaviour and its consequences; just as what a key is 'about' is revealed when it opens a particular lock. According to the biological view, it is only about something definite when it has a proper function which is established or embedded by the evolutionary test of fitness or adaptation to the environment.

The critic's reaction would be to say that this sort of response from the teleologist would still rule out, as being contentless behaviour (and so non-cognitive behaviour), the first time that the organism *did* indeed *act* in response to the sensory stimulations. For now the organism has responded as a result of (as a causal consequence of) the incoming sensory stimuli from its brand new sensory system, but, according to the teleologists, the behaviour has not been anointed by the evolutionary process of selection. What has not been selected by evolution has no proper (or Normal) function, and what has no proper function is not 'about' anything and so lacks intentionality. For evolution, being a long-term process, cannot operate in terms of a single first piece of behaviour produced via a new sensory system.

The critic might add that, in general, the teleological view seems to be too long-term in its view of content. It is like judging a painting, not on its contents, but according to its provenance. If it has been in the possession of Bernard Berenson, then it must be good. Running together content and its biological role, as seen through evolutionary binoculars, will indeed transform beliefs and desires into biological categories, and there is nothing against one taking a long biological view of anything. But why should we accept that this is the *only* view of psychological states and processes? Why is the short what-is-going-on-here-and-now view to be dismissed? It seems not merely legitimate, but historically accurate, to say that psychology is interested in the short view, and has the task of discovering the workings of the mind-cum-brain, not the biological usefulness of those workings. To take a specific example, the psychology of emotion seeks to describe the relation between the outer 'bits and pieces' of emotion, the behaviour and expression we ordinarily label 'fearful' or 'angry' or 'jealous', and the inner 'items', such as beliefs and desires and wants and needs. It is a further, and distinct, question whether fear and anger and jealousy have a survival-enhancing function. In somewhat the same way, cognitive psychology seeks to describe the nature and workings of human beliefs and desires and so on, and leaves to others any question about their survival value or biological usefulness.

Finally, it occurs to me that the teleologists join the queue for a lot of trouble when they so readily accept our folk psychological categories of belief and desire as biological ones (or, at least, ones that can be connected up to biologically proper functions). For such categories do not seem to be biological ones, and any search for their biologically proper functions seems bound to produce bizarre results. For nowadays more and more philosophers and psychologists, and I am one of them, are suggesting that our vocabulary of propositional attitudes—our vocabulary of beliefs, desires, hopes, wants, intentions, wishes, and so on—does not carve nature at its biological or physiological joints. It is a cultural artefact. It is generated from a viewpoint which is much more panoramic than that of physiology and much less historical than that of evolutionary biology. It is part of a folk psychology, which is a useful, and probably indispensable, way of making sense of ourselves and others from the outside looking *on* but not *in*. But it is not the vocabulary of either biology or physiological psychology and, if we try to do biology or physiological psychology on the basis of it, we will end up doing rather odd things. We will end up having to do a sort of old-fashioned linguistic analysis as a first step. For we will be forced, as an initial clearing and cleaning-up exercise, to trace out the speech acts, and concepts, and distinctions, and 'logical geography', and 'language games', of our folk psychological discourse about our own and others' minds. Then, in the next phase, we will try to pin down the items that have been sifted out by this clearing and cleaning in purely biological or physiological terms.

Would not a thoroughgoing doctrine of psychology as biology deny *any* role to our belief–desire-type vocabulary, on the grounds that it is hopelessly infected with Brentanian (if not Cartesian and Platonic) assumptions about the nature of mind? The obvious platform from which to deliver such a doctrine would seem to be biology itself. The platform should be that there are only those mental items or types of item (in a teleologist's ontology) which are sanctioned by a mature biology. We seek to discover the biologically proper functions of biologically proper organs and devices. What could be simpler? This would certainly overturn rationalism, as well as our intuitions. Perhaps it is the price, the cost, that gives a teleologist pause.

The price, presumably, is the one of which Quine has so frequently reminded us;[14] namely that, if you reduce psychology to biology or neurophysiology or, ultimately, physics, then *ipso facto* you will be involved in a purely extensional vocabulary, and your thesis will be a physicalist one. In such an enterprise all talk of propositional content and propositional-attitude intentionality must be left behind. To try to *reduce* talk of propositional content and propositional-attitude intentionality to something which can only be described with an extensional vocabulary is to miss the point. Such

[14] For references, and some quotations, see Ch. I.

reduction is impossible. You cannot reduce what is not about objects and events and causal relations to what is.

The dilemma for the teleologists is that, if they take this path, they will have achieved (or given us a programme for achieving) a reduction of psychology to biology, and shown us that we should not consider humans as special cases in the history of evolution. Psychology will disappear. If they do not take this path, then they have preserved psychological items, such as beliefs and desires, in their ontology, but are landed with the unappetizing task of making non-biological categories into biological ones without bizarre results.

The teleologists' reply to me, I presume, is that I am unnecessarily pessimistic. You can lie in bed and be up at work at the same time. The trick is to see that our psychological intentional vocabulary *was* really a biological one all along. It is just that we failed to see this. Evolution led us to employ our belief–desire vocabulary, just as it produced in us hearts and lungs, and since evolution only deals in biological currency, beliefs and desires will be discovered among our biological coins in our purse of proper functions. We must not be faint-hearted.

What is certain is that a 'top–down' strategy has continued to dominate the scene; that is, the strategy of taking our vocabulary of the propositional attitudes as the starting-point in a philosophical psychology of intentionality and then seeing what 'lower-level' realities this vocabulary, when properly understood and construed, picks out. As we shall see in the next two chapters, the energy and ingenuity employed by these, arguably the most sophisticated of all the top–down strategists, has been simply prodigious.

4

The Information-Processing Approach

INFORMATION-PROCESSING SYSTEMS

I have placed this information-processing account of intentionality after that of Ruth Garrett Millikan's and Colin McGinn's teleological or 'biologically proper functions' account though, chronologically, it comes earlier. I have placed it after because it could be argued that it combines the best of the two immediately preceding accounts, namely of both the Fodorian representational account and the 'biologically proper functions' account. For Fred Dretske, on whose information-processing account I will be concentrating, has produced what seems to me to be a very sophisticated and plausible account of the representational aspect of mental content and combined this with a teleological (behaviour-guiding) interpretation of its cognitive aspect. But to say these things at this stage can only serve to confuse the reader, and any such confusion would be an insult to Dretske, who is one of the most skilled expositors in the current *dramatis personae* of contemporary philosophy of mind. So I need to go back and begin where Dretske himself begins.

The core of Dretske's account of intentionality lies in his account of the human brain and its perceptual organs as an information-processing system, which in turn is based on 'information theory' as espoused by communications and computing people. The flour and butter that go into this information-processing account of our mental life are purely physical ingredients. So Dretske's account of the intentionality of mental functions is materialistic. It is yet another project aimed at naturalizing intentionality.

The first part of Dretske's cake was baked in his book *Knowledge and the Flow of Information*, the first draft of which was produced in 1975–6. The final published version appeared in 1981. In the preface Dretske outlined his recipe. Out of the lower-order, purely physical, raw material which is information, and via information-processing mechanisms, it is possible to produce the 'higher level accomplishments associated with intelligent life'. For these higher-level accomplishments amount to no more than more efficient ways of processing information.

Dretske's first major work was *Seeing and Knowing*, published in 1969. In a sense the title of that book sums up his long-term projects in epistemology and philosophy of mind. For these projects are an attempt to show how, by beginning with an account of those information-processing input mechanisms we call the senses, and by treating the brain as an information processor, we can build up an account of those paradigm sophisticated intentional states knowledge and belief.

In *Knowledge and the Flow of Information* Dretske explains that communication theory ignores (rightly ignores) the question 'What is information?' in order to concentrate on the question 'How does one quantify the amount of information that is carried from a source to a receiver?' The second question is usually answered in terms of a 'narrowing of the possibilities' (which, in fact, may only amount to a more favourable 'distribution of the probabilities') in regard to any situation. If I were, say, to play a game of 'Twenty Questions' in order to discover what object it is in this room that you are thinking about, I could begin with the question 'Is it in the left-hand side of the room or the right-hand side?' Your answer to my question will immediately halve the possibilities. Then if I ask the question 'Given that you have said that it is in the left-hand side of the room, is it in the northern half of that half or not?' Your answer will again halve the possibilities. And so on. Each answer to my questions increases my information, and this increase can be quantified as a ratio between the possibilities existing before any answer is given (or the 'amount of information at the source') and the possibilities existing after the last answer is given (or the 'amount of information at the receiving end of the communication chain').

Let us see this point in simple mathematical terms. If we lined up eight different hats on a hat stand and agreed that, as the method of choosing which hat to wear today, I engage in a series of flips of a heads-and-tails coin. We agree beforehand that heads are to denote the left-hand side and tails the right-hand side. Each flip of the coin will present me with a binary (or 'two possibilities only') decision. Do I select a hat from the left-hand side or do I select one from the right-hand side? It will take me three binary decisions to choose my hat for the day. The first decision will be whether to take my hat from among the four hats on the left-hand side or from among the four hats on the right-hand side. Let us say that the coin lands with a head facing upwards. I choose the left-hand side. The second binary decision is to choose, from among these four hats on the left-hand side, whether to take a left-hand side hat or a right-hand side one. The flipped coin makes its decision for me. I take the right-hand side. The final binary decision is to choose from these last two hats which one it is I am actually to put on my head. The flipped coin tells me to choose the hat on the right-hand side, the white peaked cap with 'New York Giants' emblazoned on it.

It has taken three binary decisions to choose my hat, so that, in information-theoretic terms, the amount of information I have gained (if expressed in *b*inary dig*its*) is three *bits*.

There are some important points to note here. First, any situation 'that has possibilities' is a possible source of (further) information. For, in theory, any spectrum of possibilities can be cut down to fewer possibilities by a suitable information-processing system. Second, the information-processing system is a causal system, though we must not confuse any knowledge of the causes involved with knowledge of the information involved. For, put bluntly, a receiver may receive information from a source without knowing anything at all about the causal processes by which it received the information. Third, no amount of knowledge about the causal processes at work, or the amount of information produced by those processes, will tell us either what the information is (its content) or what in general information is (what is its nature).

INFORMATION AS SEMANTIC CONTENT

The semantic aspects of information, how it embodies content, are of no interest to communication theorists, and rightly so. Yet it is these aspects that are essential to Dretske's project of naturalizing intentionality in information-theoretic terms. So in effect Dretske wants to extend information theory so as to produce an account of how information *informs* the receiver so that it (or he or she) generates beliefs or knowledge. In doing so, Dretske wants to make a number of important distinctions—namely to distinguish information carried by a signal from its meaning, perceptual information from conceptual information, and conceptual information from cognitive information.

For Dretske the beginning of everything—everything cognitive and intentional and so mental—lies in the notion of information: 'Information is what is capable of yielding knowledge, and since knowledge requires truth, information requires it also' (1981: 45).[1] That is, information is, as Gilbert Ryle would have put it, a 'success notion'. You only have information if what you learn from some information-gathering and -processing system is true. If I tell you a load of old lies, though each of my uttered sentences may be perfectly grammatical and convey all their conventional meaning, so that you understand them perfectly, you receive no information. To put it in a way that the philosopher of language J. L. Austin might have put it, my sentences could be said to comprise properly completed speech acts; nevertheless, you receive no information by means of them. For information is a commodity that must be able to produce, in a recipient that is properly attuned to the conveyer or vehicle of that information, *knowledge*. In fact the recipient may fail to gain the information because he or she or it is not properly attuned to receiving the signal or perhaps, having received it, is unable to interpret it. However, the signal must be at least capable of inducing knowledge in optimal circumstances.

If the information in question is a message, then information becomes an all-or-nothing concept as well. For you only receive a message if you receive all of it. With regard to sending messages, the name of the game is to send all that is at the source, without loss, to the receiver. If the message is 'You left the light on in the bathroom', it is of no use your receiving the information 'You left the light on'. For you may know already that there is always a light on in the entrance hall at that time because it is on a timer-switch. It comes on automatically at five o'clock. So just to receive the information 'You left the light on' is no message at all.

It is also important to note that there is a distinction to be made between information *as carried* and information *as received*. Information as carried by an information-processing system, right up to the

---

[1] In fact the 'truth element' in Dretske's account of information is quite complex. For, put baldly, Dretske's position is that a signal only carries information about its source given that the probability that the source is as the information represents it to be is more or less 100%. Dretske himself has expressed his position in the following way: '*Informational content*: A signal r [at the receiving end] carries the information that s [an indexical or demonstrative element referring to some item at the source] is F = The conditional probability of s's being F, given r (and k [the previous knowledge possessed by the receiver]), is 1 (but, given k alone, less than 1)' (1981: 65).

point where it is received by a recipient, is usually much more diffuse than the same information after being received by the recipient. For most often a recipient has some prior knowledge, background knowledge, which acts as a sieve on the incoming information. To vary our previous example, I might know, but you (the conveyer of the information) do not, that only the bathroom light could have been left on. For only the bathroom is part of a completed ring circuit in the house wiring (for I am rewiring the house). Given my background knowledge about the house wiring, the information 'The light is on' tells me, but not you, that the *bathroom* light is the one that has been left on.

All forms of belief and knowledge go beyond the mere reception of information in just such a sieving or 'cutting down of the possibilities' way. For information, when it is still in the human perceptual systems and central processing systems, is quite diffuse and more or less unusable, until *it has been selectively sifted*. This diffuseness is not just a matter of the sheer amount of information coming into our brains through our perceptual systems, it is also a matter of the way any incoming information is automatically nested in other information. The information that a stone was thrown into the air by a boy implies that the stone will have to land back on earth somewhere, perhaps on someone's head. For throwing heavier-than-air objects into the air, by reference to the law of gravity, implies that it will come rushing back to earth soon enough. In informational terms 'that a stone was thrown into the air' is *nested* in the information 'that heavier-than-air objects, when thrown into the air, must fall back down to earth'. Now the term 'nesting' here does not imply that any person, or even impersonal processor, is actually making an inference; it merely implies that the information in question, by reason of its meaning (conventional or natural), has an implication in respect of other information. Perhaps someone could make explicit what is so nested, but the term 'nesting' has no such implication. The important point is that information entering any system is almost always diffuse and, so to speak, able 'to gallop off in any direction', because it is nested in other information.

ANALOGUE VERSUS DIGITAL CODING

Dretske suggests that while our human perceptual systems are rather catholic and diffuse in the way they take in information, the more this information becomes transformed into real cognitive states (that is, information with content that can guide the possessor of such information's behaviour), then the more narrow and focused and pertinent and usable the original perceptual information must have become. To put this in information-processing terms, Dretske makes use of a central information-processing distinction, namely that between digital and analogue encoding.

A digital device is a binary device, that is one with only two discrete informationally relevant states. Thus a simple 'light on–light off' system encodes, digitally, the information that current is flowing through some electrical system such as a radio, or that it is not. There are no informationally relevant intermediate states. On the other hand a light bulb 'that has many positions', that is one that can gradually brighten up from a position of emitting no light at all to one of emitting a light of such-and-such candle power, would be an analogue system. Thus a light bulb that can gradually brighten from darkness to regular room illumination, and back again, could be used to measure the amount of current flowing through the circuit to which it is attached. The more the current, the brighter the light emitted by the light bulb. The light varies directly with the amount of current flowing. The light bulb's brightness is an encoding in analogue fashion of the amount of current.

The information from our 'variable-brightness' light bulb system is comparatively indeterminate compared to the 'on–off' light bulb system. The on–off light bulb system will tell you quite definitely all that is to be told in regard to the information it carries. That is, either that the current is flowing or that it is not. On the other hand the variable-brightness light bulb system will carry a lot more information but less definite information. It may tell you that the current is stronger now than it was five minutes ago, but only if you were around five minutes ago to note how brightly the bulb was then shining. It may also tell you the amount of current in the circuit in relation to many other possible amounts of current flowing through the system, though it will not in isolation present you with any such comparison. Much less will it quantify any flow of current it registers in its analogue fashion. All this analogue system does, so to speak, is just continuously register according to its own loose and diffuse system of calibration (the brightness of the light bulb) the differences in the currents in the system. It is up to you, an observer, to make something definite and usable out of it.

Dretske puts forward the view that our human perceptual systems are analogue systems whose information becomes transformed into cognitive content precisely in so far as the information becomes digitally encoded. Humans (and presumably some 'higher' animals) are hybrid digital–analogue information processors. To extend our previous example, the same light bulb that registers the amount of current flowing through it in analogue fashion might be adjusted so that it also has a digital role. It might, for example, be hooked up to an additional system such that, when the brightness of the light bulb reaches a certain candle power, via a photoelectric cell, it switches on a buzzer. By clever employment of a voltmeter we could discover that the buzzer is triggered (is turned on) by any current that is x volts or more. Given that the light bulb is emitting light, the buzzer has now come to signal, in its digital role, either that the current is less than x volts or that it is x volts or more. The photoelectric-cell-with-buzzer system has transformed the analogue information into digital information or, more accurately, extracted digital information from analogue information. As in all such transformations or extractions, a quantity of information is lost along the way. In return there is a greater determinacy in the information that remains. If our desire was to monitor when the circuit's current reached or went beyond x volts (for this, say, constituted some danger), then we can be said to have discarded some information for the sake of some particular important relevant piece of it. This has been achieved, so to speak, by applying a sieve or grid to the flow of information. Precise information has been sieved out of the flow of available information.

Dretske suggests that the interplay of our human perceptual and cognitive systems is based on this transformation of information from analogue to digital form. Indeed it is 'the successful conversion of information into (appropriate) digital form that constitutes the essence of cognitive activity' (1981: 142). The perceptual system of which my nose forms a prominent part might register in an analogue way the presence of some smell in the kitchen that could be Gorgonzola cheese or else a dead dog or else football gear my son had previously left in his locker at school for over a month but has now dumped in the kitchen. But I will not *know* what is in the kitchen, not even this disjunctive list of possibilities, until some information is extracted and encoded in digital form, that is until some of the incoming sensory information has been extracted and made precise.

CONTENTS, BELIEF STATES, AND INTENTIONALITY

Another way of putting this is to say that the transformation from sensory information to real knowledge involves the generation of specific *contents*, which utilize *concepts*, and so produce *beliefs*. As Dretske himself puts it in *Knowledge and the Flow of Information*: 'To occupy a belief state a system must somehow discriminate among the various pieces of information embodied in a physical structure and select *one* of these pieces for special treatment—as *the content* of that higher-order intentional state that is to be identified as the belief' (1981: 174). So now it is time to see the details of Dretske's explanation of how physical structures which carry information in analogue form can be transformed into physical structures that carry information in digital form, so that this digitalized information becomes a true semantic content and so able to be the content of some mental act such as a belief.

Dretske tells us that the meaning of a structure is derived from its informational origins. It is here that his account connects up with evolution, genetic inheritance, species adaptation, and individual maturation. A human acquires the concept of red by being exposed to red objects—by having his visual perception (his sight) stimulated by red objects. Internally some structure will be selected as the analogue registering structure for 'red stimulation of the visual system' if the person concerned is also exposed to a good number of things which are not red. However, such a structure becomes one which has semantic content, and so one which is presenting a utilizable concept of red to the person whose brain houses that structure, only when this structure has been made precise and determinate.

Though I found Dretske's account uncharacteristically elusive at this point,[2] I take it that what is important from his point of view is that it is the perceptual input system plus central neurological states *alone* which sharpen up and make determinate and so digitalize this otherwise diffuse analogue information about red objects. The process by which the analogue information about red objects becomes focused on the redness of red objects is the process of neurological selection by which certain neuronal structures adapt so as to react selectively only to red objects or objects that can fool the system

---

[2] Brian McLaughlin also seems to find Dretske elusive if not unconvincing on this point (see 1991*b*, esp. 643 ff.).

into reacting internally as it would to red objects.[3] Dretske may feel that to go beyond saying this is to enter the field of neurophysiology without a licence.[4]

From Dretske's point of view an important corollary of this account is that semantic content has nothing to do with the behavioural output of the system, at least as regards its genesis as semantic content. Of course, when this semantic content is utilized so as to guide behaviour, it is employed as a map (or something which functions as a map) by which the person whose head houses this semantic structure finds his way about the world. Semantic contents become *beliefs* in so far as they are used as maps or representations to guide output, verbal or gestural or behavioural.

For Dretske it is *information* that manufactures meaning, not behaviour. So those philosophers are wrong who look for the explanation and individuation of content by reference to behaviour. Of course, we may learn or guess that Mrs Bloggs over the road believes that I am a parasite on the community by watching how she behaves in my presence and by hearing what she says or pointedly leaves unsaid. But if Mrs Bloggs does have that belief, then it was formed in her by input, by information about me (or what she thought was information about me). She says and does what she says and does *because* of what she believes, not vice versa. To think otherwise is to confuse the epistemological problem of trying to work out another's beliefs with the philosophical and psychological problem of explaining how the contents of beliefs arise. As Dretske himself explains:

This account of belief, though still skeletal, has an etiological cast. That is to say, a certain type of structure acquires its content, the sort of content we associate with belief, by its informational origins. An internal structure develops (during learning) as a system's way of completely digitalizing information about, say, the *F*-ness of things. This way of encoding information (as the semantic content of an output-determining structure) makes the information so encoded relevant to explaining the system's behavior. It is

[3] Though it is not our concern here, Dretske does have an elaborate and sophisticated account of innate concepts (1981: 231 ff.). In the case of innate concepts it is not the individual's environment that has been the driving force in selecting a particular structure and so in individuating a content but the *species'* past evolutionary history.

[4] I expect that at this point Dretske would find considerable comfort in the 'neural Darwinism' of neurophysiologists such as Gerald Edelman. See e.g. Edelman (1985).

this origin that defines the content or meaning of the internal structures. It defines *what* a system believes when one of these structures is later instantiated with respect to some perceptual object. *That* a system believes something depends, partially, on the *effects* (on system output) of these internal states, since to qualify for cognitive content an internal structure must have executive responsibilities. But the content is determined solely by the structure's origin—by its information heritage. (1981: 201–2)

Content, and so intentionality in general, looks backwards to its informational origins not forwards to its behavioural effects, if any. On the other hand, it is probably true to say, from an evolutionary point of view at least, that it is difficult to see how a system could or would develop an ability to digitalize or extract precise content from diffuse analogue information *unless* this was utilized in some way so as to aid its adaptation to the environment. To put this another way, unless internal semantic content had some related output in terms of action or reaction, it is not clear how an organism's ability to generate such contents could have been 'selected' or been 'found to fit in with' the environment in which it lives. To be selected the internal semantic world has to have some interface with the external environment.

In very general terms then, intentionality is a feature of digitalized information, that is structures which react in a precise and selective manner to some feature of the environment. The structure must not, however, be confused with the information it carries any more than a symbol should be confused with what it symbolizes. Information is the beginning of intentionality, and so constitutes original intentionality, in so far as the structure realizing the input information has the potentiality to cause someone to learn something *about* the environment from whence it came (or about whatever else it is about). The same structure, in a different person, or in a different organism, having a different etiology, may carry quite different information.

Strictly speaking a structure with precise or semantic content does not constitute a *concept* till it has become part of a belief, that is until the content has gained a functional role wherein it controls output of some sort. As Dretske puts it, 'In this respect a concept is a two-faced structure: one face looks backwards to informational origins; the other face looks ahead to effects and consequences' (1981: 214–15).

Thus semantic content becomes a cognitive content when it gains a functional role rather than a purely representational one.

REPRESENTATIONAL SYSTEMS

In his book *Explaining Behavior* (1988), Dretske sets out to demonstrate how human behaviour—at least when correctly individuated as a process that is partly inside the agent and partly external—is to be explained in terms of reasons. For reasons for actions are a hybrid of relevant antecedent beliefs and desires (or other cognate cognitive and conative states). These in turn are internal physical structures which are both representational and functional. They are functional in terms of the behaviour-guiding powers of the information represented by these structures.

So it is to Dretske's account, in *Explaining Behavior*, of how exactly beliefs and desires are to be identified with internal information-carrying representations in the brain, which cause bodily movements (or a deliberate refraining from them) in virtue of the information represented, that I now wish to turn. For this later account adds a considerable amount to the earlier one. In particular it explains these internal information-bearing structures and their functional role by means of an extended and very sophisticated account of representational systems and reason-guided movements.

In chapter 3 of *Explaining Behavior*, entitled 'Representational Systems', Dretske first defines any representational system as one whose function it is to indicate something about some object or event or condition or state of affairs outside itself. Dretske then goes on to distinguish three kinds of representational system. First there are *conventional symbols* (Representation Systems, Type I), such as ⊗, which means 'No parking here' in some countries. This is a purely conventional representation. Its representational function is wholly conferred on it by humans. The symbol has no natural connection with what it has come to symbolize. It has no intrinsic powers of representation. The indicator (or 'aboutness') function of such symbols is wholly assigned by humans. We could have said, 'Let ⊗ indicate the presence of a Tourist Information Office' or 'Let ⊗ indicate the male sex'.

Then there are *natural signs* (Representation Systems, Type II), such as footprints or cloud formations. Such natural objects or structures or events become signs in so far as humans, recognizing their natural causal connections to other objects or structures or events, use them as indicators of those other objects, structures, or events. Thus we humans consider footprints as a sign that humans (human feet) have recently passed this way. Or, through experience, we come to recognize that grey clouds which have a dark underside are a sign of impending rain. So we call them 'rain clouds'. What is natural and so intrinsic to such signs is that they form part of some natural causal interconnection. Feet cause footprints. Rain very often follows the appearance of that sort of dark cloud, and contrariwise rain does not seem to have any causal connection with other sorts of clouds. What is not natural but conventional is that we humans, having worked out the causal connections (at least roughly), adopt the cause (or part cause) as a sign of the effect, or vice versa. Rain clouds are the sign of rain in so far as they are observed to precede rain and believed to have some crucial role in causing rain to fall. Footprints are a sign of the presence of humans in so far as they are one of the more obvious effects of humans passing by, at least in certain conditions.

Finally there are *wholly intrinsic natural indicators* (Representation Systems, Type III): 'Natural systems of representation, systems of Type III, are ones which have *their own* intrinsic indicator functions, functions that derive from the way the indicators are developed and used *by the system of which they are part*. In contrast with systems of Type I and II, these functions are not assigned. They do not depend on the way *others* may use or regard the indicator elements' (1988: 62). Every animal depends upon such indicators, for every animal, or type of animal, must live in some sort of harmony with its surroundings if it is to survive. So it is no wonder that every animal, including the human animal, has sensory systems which help to construct internal structures which carry information about the environment and function as guidance devices for the animal's behaviour in that environment. These internal structures are partly constructed by the selectional pressures of the environment in the history of the species of which that individual animal is a member, and partly constructed by the influence of the environment during the local history of the maturation of that individual. The visual system of a certain sort of frog has developed an internal structure that is activated only when a certain sort of fly is in sight, because that sort of fly is the right sort of nourishment for that sort of frog in that sort of climate and terrain. What is more, this same internal structure will be part of the explanation of the tropic behaviour by which, at least when he is hungry, the frog tries to leap up and swallow that sort of fly whenever its visual system indicates the presence of a fly of just that sort, or of something that looks very like it.

Such an internal structure (presumably in the frog's brain), since it carries information about the presence of something outside the frog's visual system (indeed outside the frog as well), is a true representation. For it is an indicator of something beyond itself. It is a wholly natural and non-conventional representation because no human or animal, including the frog in whose brain it is housed, has had any hand in setting up its indicatory powers. Like natural signs, such internal information-bearing structures are wholly constructed by the causal powers of nature. But in the case of these internal information systems indicators, the employment or deployment of these structures as action-guiding devices is also more or less internal to the system. For no outside *cognitive* agency has had a hand in it. These structures guide behaviour in the way they do because, again, the selectional powers of evolution and of individual maturation have ordained that they do so. Thus these representational structures can be said to have 'pure' intentionality or 'original' intentionality or 'intrinsic' intentionality. Besides, it is in so far as these sorts of representations are at the heart of the cognitive powers of humans that humans can generate non-intrinsic indicators (that is, invent conventional symbols or employ natural signs). For it needs cognitive skills to invent or employ something as the sign of something else.

These internal systems structures, whether they be in the brain of a frog or of a human, are nevertheless true representations, for they have a true content. Or to put this another way, these internal structures have a *reference* and a *sense*. Their reference is what they are about, what it is in the environment (to keep it uncomplicated) that they pick out. Their sense is the particular expression or form taken by the structure that does this indicating. Such internal systems indicators clearly do refer because they enable the animals in whose heads they are to act upon that referential information, to 'hit the target' with their actions. Thus such internal structures may act as maps or behaviour-guiding structures (expressions) for that animal.

BELIEFS AND DESIRES AS ACTION-GUIDING INTRINSIC REPRESENTATIONAL STRUCTURES

In humans we call such action-guiding structures with contents *beliefs* and *desires*. 'For beliefs, normally a prominent part of one's reasons for acting (desire being another prominent part), are special kinds of representations. Beliefs are those representations whose causal role in the production of output is determined by their meaning or content—by *the way* they represent what they represent' (Dretske 1988: 52). Beliefs (and their relations) are internal cognitive representations and desires (and their relatives) are internal conative representations. However, to put it in that way is to separate beliefs and desires artificially. For the very same structure, with the same informational content, can act both cognitively and conatively, can be both a belief and a desire. For these roles are *functional ones*. It is the *use* to which these internal representational structures are put that makes them into either beliefs or desires or both. More accurately, it is the use to which the *contents* or *indicatory powers* of these internal structures are put that makes them into beliefs and desires. In jargon terms, it is in so far as the causal connections they have are also semantic connections or information-based connections, and that the former depend upon the latter, that these internal structures become beliefs or desires.

We will see that there are *some* processes—those in which genuine cognitive structures are developed—in which an element's causal role in the overall operation of the system of which it is a part is determined by its indicator properties, by the fact that it carries information. The element does *this* because it indicates *that*. This connection between a structure's meaning and its causal role, though not direct, is, I shall argue, the connection that underlies the explanatory role of belief. Beliefs are representational structures that acquire their meaning, their maplike quality, by actually *using* the information it is their function to carry in steering the system of which they are a part. (Dretske 1988: 80–1)

Why we accord the titles 'belief' and 'desire' only to the internal representational structures of humans, and not to those of frogs or computers, is partly a matter of convention. But that is not the whole story. In part it is also related to the fact that, in humans, these internal structures have a holistic character. They are intertwined and interconnected with other such structures on the basis of their semantic character. This latter point can be described in another way, by saying that, in humans, these internal structures also have the status of concepts.

There is yet another reason why we accord the titles 'belief' and 'desire' to the internal representational structures of humans but not of frogs or computers. In humans, perhaps in dogs, but certainly not in frogs, these internal information-bearing structures are modifiable by learning. They are plastic. Another way of putting this is to say that frogs have only *implicit* beliefs while humans have *explicit* beliefs. An implicit belief is just an internal representational structure that disposes the possessor to act in a certain determinate way. It disposes, say, the frog to leap up and try to swallow flies or flylike objects moving in the air. An explicit belief, on the other hand, is an internal structure which is a multi-track disposition. It is more sophisticated as regards its function. For it disposes the person in whose head it resides to do actions of a certain type rather than merely a token determinate piece of behaviour. Moreover, the type is defined in a conceptual way, namely as actions aimed at achieving a certain goal or aim. A human's more sophisticated behaviour is directed *towards* achieving some purpose or goal rather than *by* a goal. How this goal is to be achieved is left fluid and behaviourally underdetermined, which in turn allows an agent guided by such structures to be versatile.

In saying that goal-directed human behaviour is not fixed once and for all but is modifiable by learning, intentionality is not being slipped in by the back door. For Dretske makes it clear that, by 'learning', he means no more than the processes of 'habituation' or 'reinforcement' or 'classical conditioning' or, in short, the sort of account of learning that a classical psychological behaviourist would give.

Strictly speaking the term 'behaviour' is one that should be reserved for bodily movements which are part of certain processes. These processes are ones which begin internally with those structures that have assumed the functions of beliefs and desires, which cause our muscles to engage, and which in turn cause those bodily movements (or deliberate refrainings from bodily movements) which are aimed at reaching the goals *indicated* by those beliefs and desires. Thus it is only in connection with behaviour thus defined that it makes sense to explain a human's behaviour in terms of *reasons*. For reasons are nothing over and above those antecedent beliefs and desires which are the beginning of those processes we truly call 'behaviour'.

Accounts in terms of reasons (beliefs and desires, and their close relatives) are not, then, in competition with neurophysiological accounts. Neurophysiological accounts explain *how* an action came about, while explanations in terms of reasons explain *why* an action occurred and *why* it took the shape it did. Ultimately such accounts in terms of reasons only make sense, as we have seen, when explained in terms of intrinsic natural representation systems. In turn such intrinsic natural representation systems only make sense when explained in terms of information-bearing structures which have causal powers in virtue of the information they carry.

So we have come full circle. Dretske has set out for us a long and intricate argument to the effect that we humans, even as regards our most sophisticated purposive behaviour, are purely physical information-processing systems. He has naturalized intentionality.

SOME PUZZLES ABOUT BELIEF

Dretske's account of how to naturalize intentionality in information-processing terms is indubitably a dazzling *tour de force* spread over two major books (and a number of papers). If he has pulled it off, then he has produced what every such 'naturalizer' of intentionality dreams of, namely an internal representation which is self-understanding or self-interpreting. This, an unsympathetic critic of this enterprise might say, is like claiming to have made frozen lasagne that cook and eat themselves. However, Dretske deserves more than such flippancy. So let me bring forward some puzzles or problems that some might have in regard to the information-processing approach.

The first puzzle that occurs to me arises in connection with Dretske's account of beliefs as internal action-guiding maps. Following Ramsey (1960a: 238) and Armstrong (1973: 3 ff.), Dretske describes beliefs as 'maps by means of which we steer' (1988: 79, italics removed), where the maps are 'representational structures that acquire their meaning, their maplike quality, by actually *using* the information it is their function to carry in steering the system of which they are part' (1988: 81). Or, again, 'beliefs are precisely those internal structures that have acquired control over output' (1988: 84).

Put rather bluntly, my worry here is that, if we accept Dretske's view of the nature of belief, then it follows that, in normal circumstances, no one is ever aware of his beliefs. For Dretskean beliefs are neural structures (or processes in neural networks or some such), and humans, unless they are neurophysiologists, have no knowledge of their neural structures.

Seen from another angle, Dretske's view might be described as follows: The best we humans can do in regard to attributing beliefs to one another is to work backwards from a combination of input and output, though mainly output or behaviour, to in-the-head states. We get hints and clues about beliefs but are never directly acquainted with them. For example, I might work out that you believe that the New York Giants will not even make it to the Superbowl this year, much less win it, by taking notice of various input–output clues. I may notice that you no longer scan the sports pages avidly and that you pass over articles about the New York Giants without giving them a second glance. It may suddenly occur to me that this is the first time in many years that you have ceased going regularly to the Giants' home games. In addition, it may not escape my notice that your conversation now seems studiously to avoid the topic of football altogether. You may not at any time have uttered the words 'I do not think the Giants will make it to the Superbowl this year' or 'I do not believe that the New York Giants will win the Superbowl', but I have a firm basis for attributing to you a belief that the Giants will not win the Superbowl or even get to it. On the other hand, no one, no one at all except some future neurophysiologist, has direct access to the structural neural state which is the belief. The belief as such is inaccessible.

Connected with this worry about the internal private nature of Dretskean beliefs as such is another one about their internal nature. This worry, in blunt form, is about whether it even makes sense, neurophysiologically, to align beliefs with some particular internal or central neural structure or structures. For the sake of setting up the discussion, let us assume that the above story about a supporter of the New York Giants is a fairly uncontroversial account of how we might attribute a belief to someone; that is, such attributions are made 'outside-in' so to speak, not 'inside-out'. Let us also assume for the moment, along with Dretske, that beliefs are internal or central states of some sort. If this is so, why should we ever imagine that our attributions of a particular belief to someone, even when the attribution is well grounded, picks out a *particular single* (even if highly complex) neural structure? Indeed it seems much more likely that the truth of the matter would have to be very different, namely that our ordinary common-sense attributions of beliefs to someone could not possibly be the basis for 'homing in on' or picking out a particular single neural state or structure.

The point might be explained in the following way. Let us, for the sake of discussion, allow that any particular external action or reaction could be correlated with a particular internal neural structure or state. If so, then it would seem to follow that one internal neural structure or state will be the neural basis which caused you to refrain from reading the sports pages. Another quite different one will be the one which caused you to refrain from going to the Giants' home games. Yet another one will be that which caused you to avoid football as a conversational topic; and so on. For the neural areas that control reading are quite different from those that control motor activity, and so on. Which one of these neural structures, then, is the one to which we should give the description 'belief that the Giants will not make it to the Superbowl this year'? Or should we say that the neural state or structure which should bear that belief description must be a large conjunct, namely neural structure a plus neural structure b plus neural structure c plus neural structure d, and so on? We would have to take into account that these listed neural structures would not necessarily occur in the believer's head at one and the same time. For at some stage he might change some part of his overall action or reaction pattern, without changing his overall belief. However, for the sake of argument, let us pass over these difficulties.

Unfortunately this 'conjunction view' will not do either. For we might be prepared to attribute the belief on the basis of just one or two such behavioural clues. So the belief description would apply when only a selection from the foregoing conjunction of neural structures was instantiated in the head. But this must mean that the answer then becomes a disjunct. For I now attribute the belief to you on the basis of observing a selection from the possible behavioural episodes which I (or an 'average common-sense observer') would allow as manifestations of or clues to just that belief. If this is the case, then the neural structure which is to be counted as the belief in question will be neural structure a and neural structure d *or* neural structure b and neural structure d *or* neural structure d and neural structure z, and so on. The possibilities are endless, and the complications endless. Indeed the accumulation of such complications in this account of beliefs as internal action-guiding neural structures seems to amount to something like a *reductio ad absurdum* of the account; that is, it seems that it could not really be like that.

Let me put this latter point in more general terms. While we, in our adult, linguistic, conceptual, conscious life, may make these 'from the outside' attributions of propositional attitudes to one another—attribute beliefs and desires to one another—there is no reason to think that such attributions will carve the brain at its neurophysiological joints. Indeed, as I have endeavoured to make clear, there is every reason to think that they would not. If so, then it looks as if it is a mistake to look for beliefs (and desires, and other such cognitive and conative states) at the level of brain functioning. At this point at least, I am not wanting to deny that there may be maplike, representational features instantiated in our brains. I am merely arguing that, even if there were, these are not the sorts of things which should merit the labels 'belief' or 'desire' or 'hope' or 'intention'. To think otherwise seems to be to confuse an important neural segment or factor in the brain's genesis of the external actions and reactions, in terms of which we gain clues for the attribution of beliefs and desires to one another, with the far more complex and panoramic and macro reality which is the referent of our terms 'belief' and 'desire'. It is a bit like saying that a beach is a bit of sand. Leaving aside that pebbly variety of beach found on the east coasts of Scotland and Ireland, of course you need a heap of sand in order to have a beach. But that is not enough. You also need a coastline and sea, and all this to be spread out and arranged in a certain way. The attribution 'This is a beach' is a macro or 'large view of things' attribution.

IS THE BRAIN AN EPISTEMIC ENGINE?

The point I want to make in this section is related to the previous point. In the previous section I put on paper my doubts about attributing such states as beliefs and desires to neural structures. In this section I want to question whether it makes any sense at all to hold that the brain operates at an epistemic level.[5]

Most people, I think, would be prepared to agree that a system which comprises internal structures which cause things to happen in virtue of those structures is certainly a syntactic system. It also seems reasonable to claim that, since such internal structures are also information-bearing structures, then such a system is a semantic

---

[5] For what I think is a similar point—though put in terms of a claim that Dretske's position will fall foul of a form of scepticism—see Alston (1983: 454).

engine. For if information is a semantic concept, as it seems reasonable to maintain, then an information processor is *ipso facto* a semantic processor. However, I believe that genuine doubts can arise about the level of intentionality of such information-processing systems. For it is arguable that the information-shaped neural structures (or configurations of neural networks) are *never known as information in or by the brain itself.* Indeed it is arguable that these internal information-bearing neural structures are *never interpreted*, by the brain or anything else. That is, it is arguable that the brain is not an epistemic engine.

According to Dretske's account—and I suspect it is about right—the brain causally employs information-bearing structures, and does so in so far as the structures express the information they bear. But the brain as such does no more than that, and that, I suggest, is not sufficient ground for maintaining that the brain *interprets* its own information-bearing states.

After all a rat trap causally employs analogue-plus-digital information as information (though it does not manufacture information-bearing structures in the process). For when a rat places its paw on the flat platform-like part of the lever that releases the spring which closes the jaws of the trap, the system called 'a rat trap' is acting in accordance with the information it receives. Moreover, this information is analogue information with a threshold factor built in to it; that is, it is analogue information which is transformed into digital information (at least in Dretske's sense of the terms 'analogue' and 'digital'). For the lever part of the system is a simple analogue system, while the spring-and-trap part of the system is a binary device. The lever reacts initially in an analogue way, such that the greater the weight on it the greater is the amount by which the lever is depressed. When it is depressed, roughly speaking, to the degree that even a smallish rat would depress it, then the lever system becomes a switching device for activating the spring-and-trap system. When the weight of someone or something pressing on the lever is x or greater than x, then the jaws of the trap close. If the weight is less than x, they do not. A rat will release the spring, a fly or beetle will not.

No interpretation of an epistemic sort goes on in the brain because no such interpretation can go on. No such interpretation can go on because the brain is a purely causal analogue-cum-digital processor. This means that such a processor cannot stand outside one of its own causal processes, in terms of which it receives information from the environment (or from anywhere else), and note the significance of any resulting information-bearing structures. The brain does not make associations between its own states and something outside those states, in the environment. How could it? How could it step outside itself so as to be in a position to make or note a relation or association between something in itself and something in the environment? *A fortiori* how could the brain be in a position to note that the relation between that-something-in-itself and that-something-in-the-environment is one of the former being an analogue (or digitalized) impress of the latter?

No interpretation of an epistemic sort goes on because no such interpretation need go on. The brain is a superb information processor but as dumb as can be as regards interpretation or knowing that one of its own states is *about* something else. It is better that things are like this. The brain no more needs to know that the pinprick on the arm to which it is connected by nerves is *about* a pin that has been left in the shirt by the manufacturer than the rat trap needs to know that the weight on its lever is *about* a rat putting its paw on the lever. Both pieces of knowledge are superfluous to the tasks in hand.

The point I am making might be made clearer in terms of a *carry–use–interpret* distinction. Take the following example. I might *carry* the number 1729 on a plastic card in my right-hand trouser pocket. I am the bearer of some numerical information. So is the plastic card in my pocket.

Then I might *use* the number on the card in my pocket to gain entry to the top-security bioengineering building where I work. For the security system might comprise a mechanism, at the right-hand side of the heavy bullet-proof door, that can read numbers which have been set out in a specially embossed 'readable' way on a certain size and weight and type of plastic card. If the number is one of those which have been apportioned to legitimate employees, then the mechanism will release the catch on the door and sound a buzzer at the same time. So this sophisticated security system, just as much as I, can be said to use the number to allow me to enter the building.

Finally, someone in the pub, seeing my card lying face-up on the table, might *interpret* or explain the significance of the number on it. She might say to me, 'I see that you work in the bioengineering building at the university. All numbers from 1000 to 1999 signify that the person to whom the card has been issued works in the bioengineering building.'

My point is that, in regard to its own internal representational structures, the brain can carry these structures, and use them, but it cannot interpret them. Its 'interpretation' must stay at the level of causally employing or using those information-shaped structures to shape and guide and direct some effect. This may involve extremely sophisticated neural structures and connections, and extremely sophisticated electrochemical processes, but nevertheless the processes are cognitively blind.

In one sense, then, I believe that Dretske is absolutely correct when he describes the human brain as a Representation System Type III. I think the brain is an information processor, which probably works in something like the information-processing way that Dretske describes. But I think that it is not brains but a much larger parcel of the human organism that does the understanding and knowing and believing or, in general, has an epistemological life. Important factors in human understanding and knowing and believing are some of the brain's *products*, in particular I mean the employment of language and consciousness, and the production of purposeful behaviour. But products like consciousness and the employment of language are no more *in the brain* than are other products such as the movement of one's limbs or the growth of one's beard.

Put in even more broad terms, I cannot help thinking that any attempt to explain our mental life more or less in terms of the workings of the brain alone is doomed to failure. I think that this is so whether it be a case of an explanation in terms of some elimination of mental talk in favour of descriptions of brain activity or whether it be an identifying of the core of mental activity with certain structural-cum-functional aspects of the brain. For the brain is just the engine of our life, and you cannot reduce a ship or a car or an aeroplane, or the life of a human, just to its engine, no matter how important and central the latter is. So it would be, to me at any rate, simply astonishing if the mental life of a human (or for that matter his or her sporting life or sexual life or digestive life) was more or less reducible to brain structures and their functions.

BRAIN-LEVEL FUNCTIONAL ACCOUNTS
AND CONSCIOUSNESS

Let me air a final doubt. I can imagine someone saying that an information-processing account of our mental life will always end up being unable to cope with consciousness *if* it limits itself to just brain processing. But perhaps this point can be made clearer by referring to the distinction between 'I moved my arm for good reason' and 'I was aware that I moved my arm for good reason'.

Let us allow, for the sake of concentrating on the present point, that the information-theoretic account of what is happening in my brain, when I can be said to have moved my arm for good reason, is adequate. This means, in brief, that an adequate explanation of this action of mine can be given in terms of information being taken in to the brain by my sensory systems, which leads to the selectional formation in my brain, through a process of analogue-plus-digital encoding, of certain information-expressing representational structures. These structures in turn, via interconnection with other cognitive and conative structures already in place in the brain, lead to an output which is shaped and directed by, and so appropriate to, these information-expressing representational structures. So the question becomes, now, 'Can the same sort of brain-level information-theoretic account of intentionality make sense of the similar yet importantly different case, namely when *I was aware that* I moved my arm for good reason?'

I suspect not. For consciousness is a *product* of brain functioning, not a segment of it. It is a product or result of a certain level and type of activity in certain areas and networks of the brain. Not untypical extracts from neuroscience textbooks, with no philosophical sermons to preach, are the following:

Consciousness is the *result* of interplay between three neuronal systems . . . (Pansky *et al.* 1988: 220, italics mine)

Problems of knowledge, experience, consciousness and the mind—all of them a *consequence* of the activities of the brain . . . (Zeki 1993: 7, italics mine)

. . . the reticular formation is necessary for the *maintenance* of normal wakeful consciousness. (Brodal 1992: 296–7, italics mine)

I suspect that sometimes we are tempted to think of consciousness as a part or segment of brain activity, and so to be subsumed under any description of its functioning, because we are tempted, perhaps with good reason, to situate consciousness 'in the head'; that is, we are tempted to situate it more or less in the same place as the brain. Not the least reason for our being tempted in this way, I suspect, is our knowledge of the direct causal connections between brain functioning and its product consciousness, in both directions. Not merely does neuronal activity cause consciousness but conscious episodes can directly cause neuronal activity, without going via any of our sensory input systems. Consciousness seems to have more immediate and more intimate connections to neuronal activity than do any of the other products of neuronal activity, such as running and jumping and talking and laughing.

Consciousness may well *have a function* without this function being a brain function. In addition, it may well function *physically* without this physical activity being of the same physical type as that possessed by neurones and their activities. Since consciousness is a product of the evolution of animal species, it would be surprising if consciousness was not physical in some way. If I was urged to guess at its function (given that it has a function), then I would suggest that consciousness seems to have an integrative function. It seems to allow us to put different sorts of information together and then to make something coherent out of the *mélange*. To put this another way, its function may be not so much to process in parallel as to process in unity. Or, more accurately, its function may be to produce a unified point of view from the brain's parallel processing. Hence it is not surprising that consciousness seems to be the source of our sense of a self or of ourselves as single persons who do certain things and are on the receiving end of other things, no matter in what part of our organism the activity is taking place. It may also be advantageous (in the evolutionary sense, as well as in a more personal sense) to have this awareness of ourselves as single agents rather than simply to be a non-conscious but very clever, even single-minded, aggregation of systems.

Another way of making my point might be in terms of *perceptual experiences*.[6] Well known to neurophysiologists, psychologists, and more recently philosophers of mind is the curious case of *blind sight*. Blind sight occurs when, through some damage to the visual

---

[6] I borrow my examples from Heil (1991: 1 ff.). Heil uses the examples to make a different, if related, point.

cortex, a person can take in visual *information* from the environment, and to a limited extent act on that information, and so demonstrate that he is able to form action-guiding 'maps' or beliefs. On the other hand, he is not aware of seeing any objects or events in that blind-sight region of the environment. That is, the person would say he was blind in regard to those objects or events. The person *sees* with the blind-sighted part of his eye, and so takes in perceptual information, and can form beliefs on the basis of the information, but has no *visual experience*. The latter, the visual experience, must then be something other than information and its processing.

A similar point might be made by means of a thought experiment. Let us imagine that a visitor from another planet arrives on Planet Earth. Such an alien visitor passes all our visual tests. It sees what we see. However, when the creature dies, and we open up its head, we find that its brain physiology matches our own excepting that it has no neural basis for awareness or experience (perhaps there is a part of the reticular formation that is missing). Our natural conclusion would be to conjecture that such a creature is like a human with total blind sight.

Now Dretske is alive to such an objection, and does include the term 'perceptual experience' in his information-theoretic vocabulary. For in *Knowledge and the Flow of Information*, he writes 'For the moment I merely wish to develop the idea that the difference between our perceptual experience, the experience that constitutes our seeing and hearing things, and the knowledge (or belief) that is normally consequent upon that experience is, fundamentally, a coding difference' (Dretske 1981: 143). In short, Dretske believes that the sting can be taken out of all such references to *experience* and *awareness* and *consciousness*, whether in regard to perception or anything else, in terms of the information-theoretic approach. In the case of perception, for example, a perceptual experience is just that stage, in the processing of information coming in through the visual system, which stays short of being cognitive. It is part of the analogue encoding phase. For once things are encoded digitally, then they have contents and so are either cognitive or precognitive. So while experiences are not epistemic or cognitive states they are information states and so would be an item on any completed information-theoretic flow chart of our perceptual and cognitive life. So there is no need to attempt to make something out of the 'so-called phenomenal character of . . . experience' (Dretske 1981: 91).

If I have correctly described how Dretske would account for perceptual experiences, it might be said that the same basic query remains. It is just that now it must be put differently, namely as 'If you give the label "perceptual experience" to that early analogue, pre-content, non-cognitive, phase of information processing, how do you distinguish between that early phase when it involves blind sight and when it does not?' For one can imagine a newborn infant who sees with an unimpaired visual system some item in the left-hand side of the environment, and another newborn infant with blind sight in regard to the same item. Both, presumably, are at the same stage of preconceptual, contentless, non-cognitive, analogue encoding. So, in Dretske's terminology, they can both be said to have visual experiences. Yet the two cases are clearly different. Must we say, then, that there is a distinction to be made between *visual experience type 1* and *visual experience type 2*? If so, why cannot we make the distinction in the traditional way, by saying that the first infant was *conscious* of the item in the environment while the second was not?

Fred Dretske's information-processing approach to intentionality still seems to me to be a brilliant, meticulous, and convincing account of the brain's analogue and digital processing and of its level of intentionality. On the other hand, I have attempted to air my feeling that it does not give an altogether convincing account of certain aspects of human intentionality, namely of the epistemic and conscious life of humans. Perhaps I should have said that it does not *yet* give a convincing account. For maybe it can be extended to show that in fact it can take care of the puzzles I have brought forward. I myself, however, will leave the discussion at this point in order to give space to another project of naturalizing intentionality, which could be said to be 'in the same line of business'.

5

The Purest Functionalism

This is the last chapter dealing with specific contemporary approaches to intentionality. Strictly speaking, the approach discussed in this chapter pre-dates almost all of the other approaches. On the other hand in general this approach, and in particular the main text for discussion in this chapter, have both been much slower than other accounts in surfacing and in making their impact, at least in philosophy of mind. Even the reviews of the central text have been slow to surface. They have leaked out over six or seven years rather than appeared soon after publication. The reason for this may be, at least in part, the complexity of this approach, and the density and difficulty of the text in question, Brian Loar's *Mind and Meaning* (1981).

Perhaps the most notable early texts in regard to the functional role approach to intentionality have been those texts in philosophy of language of the 1970s which discussed functional role semantics. For it was from these that a functional role view of intentionality has been mined. As regards functional role semantics, I have in mind, especially, the work of Gilbert Harman, and most notably his book *Thought* (1973) and his papers 'Meaning and Semantics' (1974) and 'Language, Thought and Communication' (1975). In 'Meaning and Semantics' Harman gives a summary of this functional role semantics view of meaning:

Let me elaborate. I say that meaning depends on role in conceptual scheme rather than on truth conditions. That is, meaning has to do with evidence, inference, and reasoning, including the impact sensory experience has on what one believes, the way in which inference and reasoning modify one's beliefs and plans, and the way beliefs and plans are reflected in action. For me, the meaning of the relevant sort of sentence is determined by the thought it would normally express. The nature of that thought is not in the first instance determined by its truth conditions; it is, rather, a matter of psychology. For a thought, as I am using this term [to refer to a belief, a hope, a supposition, etc.], is a psychological state, defined by its role in a system of states that are modified by sensory input, inference, and reasoning, and that have an influence on action. To specify a thought is to specify its role in such a conceptual scheme. To specify the meaning of a sentence of the relevant sort is to specify a thought, so to specify its meaning is to specify a role in a conceptual scheme. (1974: 11)

In that same paper Harman himself traces his own conceptual role account, which in turn he describes as a functionalist theory, back to the behaviouristic philosophy of language of Quine's *Word and Object* (1960) and even further back to verification theories of meaning. In his paper '(Nonsolipsistic) Conceptual Role Semantics' (1987), Harman also mentions as a precursor Wilfrid Sellars's paper 'Some Reflections on Language Games' (1954).

It is now time to discuss this functional role account in the context of philosophy of mind and in detail. As I have already indicated, I shall do this in the context of a discussion of Brian Loar's *Mind and Meaning*. The opening words of Loar's ambitious, wide-ranging, and very clever book are the following: 'The attention that philosophers have lavished on propositional attitudes in the last hundred years has been thoroughly appropriate; there are few concepts whose explication would yield greater philosophical dividends than those of belief, desire and their content' (1981: 1). True to his word Loar develops his accounts of intentionality, action, truth, and meaning in terms, at least ultimately, of the propositional attitudes. Indeed he could be said to have put forward a propositional-attitude theory of mind, for he would consider whatever the realities are that underlie our propositional-attitude ascriptions as the core of mind. To echo his own words above, while his book is very closely written and of great complexity, and demanding of considerable powers of attentiveness and stamina, the result is rich in philosophical dividends.

While, at the appropriate places, I will sketch in its connections with his theories of truth and meaning, in this chapter I will concentrate almost entirely on trying to isolate and make perspicuous his underlying theory of intentionality. This theory, for reasons of its origins and for reasons which will eventually emerge, might best be called 'the functional role theory of intentionality'. While it is a functionalist theory, and indeed more centrally and purely functionalist than any other functionalist theory, it differs from the majority of functionalist theories. It differs from such theories in eschewing both any sort of teleological explanation and any explanations in terms of a language of thought or, indeed, of representations of any kind. However, in certain places, he does draw upon the notions of isomorphism, sentence, and syntax. What, on the other hand, he does share with all other contemporary theorists in this area, functionalist or otherwise, is a belief that one can and should *naturalize* intentionality, in this case by seeking a physicalist account of what propositional attitudes really are. So it is also a reductionist theory and entails a *type–type* reduction of the propositional attitudes to brain states, but it does not entail a reduction to states which are in any way structurally isomorphic with the linguistic structure of our propositional-attitude vocabulary. In a sense the precise physical structure (though not the causal powers) of the brain states with which the propositional attitudes are identified is irrelevant. In a real sense the propositions of propositional attitudes are also irrelevant. For while they (or their 'semantically active aspects') act as indicators or 'indices' of the various roles played by propositional attitudes; they are not to be taken literally at the 'business end' of the explanation of those attitudes. Strictly speaking, even the 'indexing' role of propositions could be taken over by some (say, more formal and artificial) indexing system.

For Loar, then, beliefs and desires are real physical states with real causal powers as well as real functional roles; hence his thesis is a strongly realist one. Beliefs and desires are real intentional states because they are expressible or 'indicated' in a precise way by linguistic expressions with (propositional) content. This latter position seems to imply that, while he is strongly realist about the reduction of the propositional attitudes to physical states, he is in fact far less realist about the intentionality of those states.

However, these rather sweeping descriptions of the functional role theory of intentionality may only serve to confuse. So, in what follows, I will try to fill in at least some of the details of Loar's functional role theory of the propositional attitudes, and then attempt, critically, to prod and probe it a little.

THE ASCRIPTION–INTERPRETATION DISTINCTION

Loar's starting-point is to stress that the correct way to approach an account of beliefs and desires and the other propositional attitudes, philosophically speaking, is via a distinction between *epistemological* considerations and *metaphysical* ones. Epistemological considerations involve singling out the conditions for correctly *ascribing* or attributing propositional attitudes to persons. Thus the epistemological considerations ensure that the beliefs and desires we are referring to in our functional system are 'interpersonally ascribable' and so genuinely part of our community's psychology. Metaphysical considerations involve the grounds for claiming that propositional attitudes are of such-and-such a nature or, to put the point in another way, the grounds for *interpreting* the propositional attitudes in one ontological way rather than another. It is in the latter that Loar is ultimately interested, for it is the metaphysical considerations that further Loar's complex project of reducing the intentionality of the expressions of the propositional attitudes to non-intentional physical states.

But first the *epistemological* considerations or the conditions for correctly attributing or *ascribing* the propositional attitudes to other persons or to oneself. In practice, Loar explains, we guide and circumscribe our attributions or ascriptions in a number of ways. This is best seen in regard to beliefs, for belief might be accorded the status of core or chief propositional attitude. For when we attribute to some person, say, a belief that it is about to rain, we do so by taking into account the nature of persons (that they are intentional beings of the sort that have goals and plans, and so intermediary beliefs and desires), the social background of the person or persons in question (their social context, including what sorts and depths of knowledge they are likely to have), the immediate environment that such a person is likely to be aware of (or the perceptual context), the normal response by any rational person to that sort of environment, including the presumed ability to engage in some basic sorts of induction and deduction (or the principles of logical rationalization), the likelihood that such a person is 'socially co-operative' (likely to tell the truth, be relevant, be serious, etc.), and finally the person in question's observable actions and reactions, especially their utterances (or, in general, behavioural considerations). Thus the basis for our ascription to some person, say, Mary, of a belief that it is about to rain, might be that, first, we saw Mary go out the back door and into her back garden, and then look up at the sky. At the same time we might have noted that the sky was full of dark clouds of the kind normally associated with rain. Second, we might have presumed that Mary had the knowledge and ability to recognize the clouds as rain clouds and to respond to that knowledge in a sensible way. Finally, we might have waited around till Mary went out of the house a quarter of an hour later, and then noted that she wore a raincoat and carried an umbrella. Given our knowledge of Mary's background, culture, immediate environment, and current behaviour, and our knowledge of people in general, we attribute to her a belief that it is about to rain.

However, what Loar is really interested in is the *metaphysical* status of our propositional attitudes. To put this another way, we should give to our propositional-attitude terms—believing, desiring, intending, willing, and so on—a functionalist *interpretation* for important ontological reasons. The reasons that circumscribe us here are those which exercise control over our desire to say, metaphysically speaking, exactly what beliefs and desires and the other propositional attitudes really are. The motivation which produces, for Loar at least, a functional role account of the propositional attitudes is a desire to find a theory which will give a *naturalized* (that is, one that is not at odds with the explanations of natural science) and *realist* (that is, one that is embedded in objects, properties, or events about which there are grounds for saying that they really exist) explanation of the propositional attitudes. We are driven to accepting that our beliefs and desires and intentions and willings are *real* states because, quite simply, it seems impossible to deny that such states are real causes of human behaviour. We are driven to considering our beliefs, desires, and other propositional attitudes as *functional* states for the (not so simple) reason that, motivated by the desire to find a realist and naturalized interpretation of our intentional attitudes, we find that a functional role interpretation works better than any other. In short, as a psychological theory about how certain in-the-head cognitive and appetitive states of humans are organized causally or sequentially, functionalism has no peer. Such a theory may not produce detailed descriptions of the internal structure or composition of those internal brain states, but that is not important from a philosophical point of view. Such details should be left to the neurophysiologist. Furthermore, such a functionalist interpretation of human psychology is a generalized or 'type' explanation. It is designed to produce generalizations about human cognitive functioning, not for spelling out what *exactly* Mary or Fred is *now* believing or desiring or likely to do. That is, in terms of certain perceptual, rationality, output, and truth conditions we set out to define *a functional theory* in terms of which we are able to delineate *the functional system* which individuates the various *functional states* of believing, desiring, willing, and so on.

Loar stresses that a certain sort of 'relativity' is to be taken into account in regard to the realization of the functional system. As Loar himself explains: 'While belief in general involves a certain kind of functional system, different functional systems may apply throughout the range of societies and species that have beliefs. Interpersonal ascribability requires sharing some such functional system, and, in particular, input conditions, for example among those who conventionally are deemed capable of the same beliefs as *us*' (1981: 67). Loar also seems to imply that a certain amount of 'plasticity' should be taken into account. By this he seems to mean that, in applying the functional theory, we should realize that the same *belief that p* will be embedded in slightly different ways in different people and in the same individual at different times.

What this whole, very complex package entails will be made a little clearer, I hope, in what follows.

FUNCTIONAL ROLE, TRUTH-FUNCTIONAL ROLE, AND PHYSICAL STATE

It should be made clear at this point that the brain states which are picked out by the functional role theory do not have merely functional properties according to the theory. For if they did, that would produce some sort of sleight-of-hand regress from functional role to functional role. The 'states' are real states with *real structure* (though the theory cannot tell us the details about this) and *real causal powers* which are *picked out by their role or function*. Thus, if we call their functional role a *second-order* property, then whatever properties these brain states have, which are independent of their functional role, will be their *first-order* properties.

Nevertheless, while a functional explanation as such may not tell us about the actual structure or composition of the internal states which have the designated functional roles, such an explanation can still have considerable explanatory, if no real predictive,[1] power.

---

[1] As Brian Loar pointed out to me, in correspondence, his 'functional system, as picked out by his functional theory, is not very predictive. This because of two factors, the negative nature of the rationality constraints (Loar: 1981, e.g. 72), and

Because a functional role theory of the propositional attitudes is put in place as a theory of human cognitive and appetitive powers and subsequent activities, then, in so far as it is a good theory, it will enable us to give an explanation, a *true* explanation, of the internal cognitive economy of ordinary humans.

It follows from this functional role account of the propositional attitudes that *type–type* psychophysical correlations are possible.[2] For the functional role theory first correlates types of propositional attitude as described by our common-sense psychology (such as beliefs or desires or intentions or willings) with types of state individuated by functional role according to a more theoretical and 'professional' psychology (such as state with functional role x or state with functional role y). The functional role theory then points out that there are type–type correlations between types of state individuated by functional role and types of brain state. However, even putting it this way is somewhat misleading. For most likely the reduction would have to be more *holistic*.[3] It would have to be in terms of a network of states exhibiting a certain pattern of logical and rational interrelations (which at a higher level we call a 'network of beliefs, desires, etc.') being found to mirror the pattern of 'counterfactual relations' (that is, hypothetical or dispositional interrelations) in a network of non-functional states with first-order structural and causal properties.

What is relevant, and of the utmost importance, is that the network of lower-level first-order states, because it mirrors the higher-level network of second-order states demarcated in terms of functional

the fact that the belief–desire–willing condition contains an override clause (1981: 89–90). Prediction is more the job of "our standard scheme for attitude ascriptions" (1981: 127 ff.). The principles that make up this scheme are in large part contingent —i.e. not constitutive of the relevant functional system, but contingent generalizations about the functional states thereby constituted.'

[2] A type–type correlation is to be distinguished from a token–token correlation. A *type* is a kind or class of thing. A *token* is an instantiation or actual member of a class. Thus 'coin' indicates a kind or type of thing. The actual embossed metal disc which is picked out or referred to by the description 'the one and only coin now in my left pocket' is a token of the type coin. A *type–type correlation* is a correlation between two types of thing. A *token–token correlation* is a correlation between two tokens. To say that a Rolls Royce is a car is to make a type–type correlation. To say this coin in my pocket is the only piece of metal in my pocket is to make a token–token correlation.

[3] See Loar (1981: 17 ff.), where there is a discussion of the difficulties with such broad or holistic psychophysical correlations and reductions.

role, becomes thereby also a network *organized in a rational way*. For, in a logical and rational way, that is how, both in common-sense psychology and more theoretically, we individuate particular beliefs and desires, and interpret the interrelations of a belief–desire network. In turn, this would mean that the lower-level network of non-functional states, with which the higher-level network is correlated, operates counterfactually in a rational way. For the lower-level brain networks have been demarcated precisely in so far as their causal powers or dispositional properties (their counterfactual relations) are isomorphic with a rationally and logically organized higher-level network. Strictly speaking, perhaps one should say that this lower-level network is not so much rational as *isomorphic with* the rational. To say otherwise would be to fall into something like a category confusion. It would be to confuse levels of explanation. Physical states in the brain are not rational, but their higher-level *doppelgängers*, beliefs and desires, are. Nevertheless, as Loar himself points out, 'there is no incoherence in the idea that certain physical states *meet the demands of rationality*' (1981: 25, italics mine) or that the rational interplay of our propositional attitudes does indeed find an echo in (some sort of) physical theory.

Our ordinary expressions of the propositional attitudes—'He believes that it will rain today', 'She hopes that the train will not be late', 'Mary desires to have better relations with her colleagues'— are relational. For these ordinary expressions display our cognitive and appetitive attitudes in terms of a subject or person attitudinizing over a content expressed in propositional form (i.e. as a that-clause or to-clause). They relate an attitude to a content (or proposition).

For Loar, this relation of the attitudes to propositions should not be taken at face value when we come to spell out, in terms of the functional role theory, what is really going on at the level of the brain when we believe so-and-so, and desire such-and-such. We should not search inside our heads for propositions, or sentences which assert or express propositions. And, *a fortiori*, we should not go in search of a language of thought or language of the brain from which these sentences might be fashioned. On the other hand, what should be taken at face value are the pointers we are being given by our use of these ordinary, common-sense propositional-attitude expressions. For these expressions make it clear to us, or should make it clear to us, that our propositional attitudes operate in two distinct ways. They are *functionally relational* in so far as they form part of a network of propositional attitudes, and they are *truth-functionally relational* in so far as they have a connection with a content which is 'about' something. In so far as they are functionally relational, they have connections with perceptual input, behavioural output, and, especially, with other propositional attitudes. That is, in so far as they are functionally relational, they have a *functional* role. On the other hand, in so far as they are truth-functionally relational, they have a connection with a content which involves relations (especially that of correspondence) with extra-mental things, such as states of affairs in the world. So this truth-functional relation often involves a relation to the world, for its propositional content can be true or false in regard to how the (external) world is. That is, in so far as they have relations to the world (or to something else they are about), and so are expressed as having contents, propositional attitudes have *truth conditions*.

It might be easier, as does Loar himself from time to time, to call the former functional relations a propositional attitude's *horizontal* relations, and the latter truth-functional relations a propositional attitude's *vertical* relations. Horizontal relations amount to a propositional attitude's functional role, that is, its functional relations that mirror the logical relations between the propositional attitudes, while vertical relations (at least under one aspect) are its truth conditions. For a propositional attitude's rational and logical links to other propositional attitudes, and to perceptual input and behavioural output, are what defines or demarcates its functional role, and a propositional attitude's content's connection, or would-be connection, to states of affairs (taken very broadly) is what defines its truth conditions. So the horizontal relations could also be called the *logical* relations, and the vertical relations the *truth-conditional* relations.

CONSTRAINTS ON NATURALIZING INTENTIONALITY

But what figures do these horizontal and vertical dimensions really carve? What work do they do at the level where we use the functional role theory to pick out real states with first-order structural and causal properties? How, more bluntly, does talk of these two dimensions really help us to naturalize intentionality?

The answer is, according to Loar, that it is above all else the horizontal or functional role (or functional role aspect) of propositional attitudes which allows us to demarcate real states (and real content) at the lower level. For, first, we work out the functional role of a particular person's belief—say Mary's belief that it is about to rain—in terms of its higher-level logical and rational connections to perceptual input (such as Mary's going into her back garden and observing dark lowering clouds), to other cognitive and appetitive states, that is to other propositional attitudes (such as Mary's belief that dark lowering clouds presage rain in the immediate future in this climate at this time of year, and her knowledge that she has to leave the house in five minutes' time, her desire to keep her appointment, and her desire not to get wet) and to behavioural output (Mary's putting on a raincoat and arming herself with an umbrella just before she leaves the house). Then we *look for an isomorphism* between relations at the higher level of propositional-attitude explanations (though in their tidied-up, more theoretical form, as we shall see) and relations at the lower level of description of real physical states with structural and causal properties. We look for a network of such lower-level states whose *dispositional and causal* (i.e. counterfactual) interrelations mirror the *logical and rational* interrelations at the higher (though theoretically refined) level (Loar 1981: 59 ff.).

In its simplest formulation, it is a propositional attitude's role in the explanatory system, which we call our ordinary, common-sense psychological explanations (in terms of beliefs and desires and the other attitudes), that becomes *the indicator* that, at least eventually, helps us to pick out lower-level 'naturalized' states.

It is not quite as simple as that, however; it never is. For to be successful in this process of homing in on or picking out lower-level naturalized (that is, brain) states, we need to elaborate and systematize our ordinary employment of our concepts of belief and desire. We need to tighten it up philosophically into a functional role theory. In order to do this we would need, first, to exercise great care in our attributions of propositional attitudes to persons. However, Loar spends considerable time explaining that to attribute even apparently uncomplicated perceptual beliefs to someone is not the simple, straightforward affair it might appear to be (1981: 65 ff.). For example, it is not really a sufficient basis for attributing to Mary a belief that there are dark lowering clouds in the sky to know that in fact there are such clouds in the sky and to see Mary looking up at the sky. To be sure that Mary has come to believe that there are such clouds in the sky, you would need to be certain that Mary can see well enough to observe them and that she was attentive to them and that in raising her eyes towards the sky she was not just exercising her neck muscles. Now to go further and to attribute to Mary a belief that it is about to rain, you would need a lot more information. You would need to know whether Mary is capable of making a connection between dark lowering clouds and the onset of rain, whether in fact she knows about the connection, and whether or not she is sceptical about the usefulness of this alleged connection in this climate at this time of year, and so on. The matter is not simple and straightforward at all.

In practice, in our ordinary everyday attribution to others, and to ourselves, of beliefs, desires, intentions, and the other propositional attitudes, we just do the best we can. But, Loar warns, this is not good enough if we are to use this higher-level, common-sense, folk psychological theory about the rational interplay of our beliefs and desires as a way of demarcating and indicating naturalized lower-level states. Somewhat paradoxically the major way to correct the deficiencies in using the higher-level folk psychological theory to pick out lower-level states is to put it to work. If the attempt to pick out a lower-level state is misguided, then this will soon be apparent. It will be apparent through a failure to find isomorphism. For example, it might be apparent through a failure to find an isomorphism *between* the discovered logical and rational interplay between my belief that it is about to rain with my other beliefs, my desires, and my intentions, and with my actions and reactions, *and* the interplay of counterfactual relations (dispositional and causal relations) between the best candidates inside my head for being the naturalized physical correlatives of these beliefs, desires, intentions, actions, and reactions of mine. In other words, the constraint that, more than any other, turns our ordinary, everyday, minimal constraints into (something more like) a set of (not quite sufficient but) more formal constraints is embedded above all in the asking of the question 'Have we found, at this lower level, a dispositional and causal (or counterfactual) interplay that mirrors the logical and rational interplay at the higher level?' or, to put it simply, 'Has an isomorphism of relations, between the two levels, been discovered?' Perhaps this constraint might be dubbed *the isomorphism constraint* or *the correlation constraint*.

It should be clear that, to test for isomorphism, we would need a well-worked-out higher-level formal theory even to begin to individuate states at this lower physical level (that is, the real natur-alized brain states described in terms of their non-functional first-order causal properties). Quite clearly such a well-worked-out higher-level theory will depend a lot upon progress in theoretical psychology and, when this lower level comes to be identified with brain states, the individuation and reductive process will depend on progress in neurophysiology as well.

Perhaps Loar's clearest and most emphatic account of the con-straints with which we must operate when we seek to naturalize intentionality are in his article 'Social Content and Psychological Content' (Loar 1988).[4] In that article Loar suggests that our common-sense psychology's individuation of the propositional attitudes gives us the clue that, in our efforts to naturalize intentionality, we must individuate the propositional attitudes in two important ways. Our ordinary, common-sense psychology first of all makes clear to us that we capture, and express in that-clauses, what we believe (that is, the content of our beliefs) through 'deference to the usage of his [the speaker's] linguistic community' (Loar 1988: 110). What I believe is *what I am understood to believe by the speaker's 'linguis-tic community'*. If I say that I believe that I have arthritis in my leg, then what I believe is whatever is usually understood by those around about me to be the content of the that-clause 'that I have arthritis in my leg'. So one way to naturalize intentionality, and so individuate the propositional attitudes at the lower level of brain states, is by working backwards from the socially ordained semantic content of our propositional attitudes to brain content. Though I am not clear how this is to be done in detail, I take it that Loar means that, first of all, we are to use our linguistic community's beliefs to help us pick out what it is in the world (or whatever 'state of affairs' is in question) that is referred to by the contents of our propositional-attitude expression. Then, as a second step, we are to work back, via causal links, to what it is in our brain that is linked to that object

---

[4] This article discusses Tyler Burge's influential paper 'Individualism and the Mental' (Burge 1979). I should make it clear that Loar (1988) also represents a slight change of view. For in this paper, as different from *Mind and Meaning* (1981), the social or content role alone now attaches to the propositional core of an intentional attitude. For the psychological or functional role is now attached to the propositional attitude as a psychological whole.

or event in the world (or other state of affairs). This should give us some indication of which brain state is the instantiation of the belief or at least the belief-type in question.

On the other hand, our common-sense psychology also makes it clear that a propositional attitude has a conceptual role. This conceptual role is its relations to other propositional attitudes. So *what I conceive about things* is, to a great extent, elucidated and individuated by my belief's conceptual role in my psychology (that is, how my belief that I have arthritis in my leg fits in with other beliefs, desires, intentions, and so on, of mine). For I might, quite mistakenly, conceive of arthritis as inflammation not merely of the joints but of muscles as well. So another constraint on naturalizing intentionality must involve matching up, at the lower level, the relations between a brain state (presumably the one we have already homed in on via its social role or 'role in the linguistic community') and its neurophysiological neighbours with, at the higher level, the relations of an expressed belief of mine with other relevant expressed (or at least discoverable) beliefs and desires of mine.

This former sort of content might be called *social content* (or *broad* content) and the latter sort *psychological content* (or *narrow* content). The constraint related to the role of a content of a belief of mine in the linguistic community might also be called the *semantic constraint*, and the constraint related to the role of that same belief in the network of my beliefs, desires, and other propositional attitudes might also be called the *network constraint*. But it is the latter constraint, the network, or functional role, constraint, that is still the most important because it is the most constraining.

FUNCTIONAL ROLE SEMANTICS

While it is, strictly speaking, not our concern here, it may help to shed some further light on Loar's account of intentionality if we see, however briefly, how it connects up with his theories of meaning and truth. In briefest form, Loar gives not only a functional role account of how intentionality can be naturalized but also a functional role account of how meaning can be naturalized, for the latter depends upon the former, not vice versa.

Loar's arresting account of meaning is derived most immediately from Ramsey (1960*b*) and Russell (1967, first published in 1912), but then overlaid with his own account of the propositional attitudes. On the other hand, while it is seen as an alternative to Grice's and Schiffer's theories of meaning in terms of communicative intentions,[5] it has been heavily influenced by that account as well. The trick, Loar might have said, is to reverse the usual perspective on meaning. In regard to the meaning of our utterances, do not look outwards from uttered sentence to the world or convention or custom or anything else, but look inwards (even further 'inwards' than the Gricean and Schifferian accounts would have you do) to the connection between the speaker and his acceptance or adoption of the sentence. Not merely does our talk about beliefs and desires depend for its accuracy and usefulness upon the fact that it mirrors the internal functional and truth-functional economy of our real in-the-head beliefs and desires, the very meaning of the words we utter depends upon the reality of the same internal functional and truth-functional economy. Put more crisply, it is a speaker's real in-the-head beliefs, thoughts, and, especially, intentions that drive the chariot called 'meaning of a sentence', and it is above all what I have labelled Loar's 'network constraint' that does the work of telling us what are a speaker's beliefs, thoughts, and intentions.

So Loar's theory of meaning is, in a real sense, a physicalist theory of meaning as well as a physicalist theory of the propositional attitudes, because it is the internal, real, physical realization of propositional attitudes in the head that, via their causal links with 'accepted' sentences, give meaning to our utterances. It is a theory of meaning that employs wholly non-intentional items—brain states plus sentences described purely syntactically—as its bricks and mortar.

It is also a propositional-attitude theory of meaning in a deep sense. We do not believe sentences, which independently have meaning, say in some conventional or 'external' way. We give meaning to sentences by adopting or accepting them, though, presumably, they must already have some acceptance by the linguistic community as well, otherwise their use as an expression would not communicate anything. In accepting sentences, what we do is to link them in a literal way with what we already believe or hope or want or intend. Perhaps we could put it this way. We *endorse* that particular concatenation of words, that particular sentence, *as what we already believe and so mean*. Meaning begins in the head and works its way outwards, not vice versa.

---

[5] The central references would be Grice (1952, 1968) and Schiffer (1972).

In more detail, Loar explains, the meaning of a natural language sentence is given 'by specifying what [some person] z would be *believing* by accepting [some sentence] s' (1981: 212). For when a speaker utters s, he or she intends (at least when backed up by various implicit expectations) the hearer to understand (believe) something on hearing s. If Mary says to me 'Get your umbrella', then Mary *intends and believes* that in uttering those sounds she will get me to believe that she, Mary, wants me to get an umbrella. She also believes, or at least has the implicit expectation, presumably, that I know what an umbrella is, that I know where one is to be found, and so on. What is clear is that, on this account, it is essential to see language as aimed at communication, and in turn communication as having the purpose of getting something from the speaker to the hearer. The speaker must first 'have meaning' in order to adopt or accept a sentence as the vehicle for carrying meaning to someone else.[6] But this having meaning is, ultimately, no more than having in one's head physical states with certain non-intentional roles.

Thus this means that 'ascriptions of public language meaning are derivative from ascriptions of content to intentions and beliefs' (Loar 1981: 238). In less formal terms, if you want to work out the meaning of some word, then see it in the context of an utterance. If you want to work out the meaning of this utterance, then first work out the speaker's intention, which in turn means that you must work out what it is that he or she believes and, via that, what he or she is trying to get the hearer to believe. Thus, at this point, Loar's 'reverse version of the more usual accounts of sentence meaning' is grafted on to the functional role theory of belief and intention so as to produce a version of a functional role semantics for natural language. For example, the truth conditions of a simple indicative sentence which contains no indexicals,[7] one such as 'Snow is white', are the truth conditions of 'the belief that snow is white' and an integral part of the satisfaction conditions of the intention 'to get the hearer to believe that snow is white'. The belief is correct, and the

---

[6] Though it is even further from our concerns here, Loar (1981, sect. 9.5 ff.) develops a propositional-attitude-based theory of language learning as well.

[7] Indexicals are terms which index someone or something or some event or some time or place only in so far as you, who hear or read the indexical term, know by whom and when the utterance (or text) containing the indexical was made (or produced). Thus 'I' is an indexical which picks out the current speaker, and 'you' an indexical which picks out the current hearer. 'Yesterday' is an indexical which picks out the day before the utterer used the word 'yesterday'.

sentence is true, if and only if, in fact, snow is white, and the communication is successful if and only if the hearer has come to adopt the belief 'that snow is white', which the speaker intended. If you want to know the meaning of the sentence 'Snow is white', then you have to work out what it is that an utterer of the sentence 'Snow is white' believes he is, in the context, trying to get a hearer to believe. This, in turn, means that you have to work out the content of the speaker's propositional attitude of believing or intending, for this contains, embedded in it, the content of the belief he or she intends the hearer to adopt.

THE RESULTING NATURALIZATION OF INTENTIONALITY

It should be clear that Loar takes our ordinary everyday explanations of the actions and reactions of ourselves and others, in terms of the interplay of our propositional attitudes, as the foundation of everything to do with naturalizing intentionality. His programme for naturalizing intentionality is, in short, a 'top-down' strategy. For his strategy is, first, to take our ordinary propositional-attitude explanations, and then produce a tidied-up and stiffened-up version of them. That is, a version with clear constraints—a formal version of the social and, especially, psychological, constraints—applied to the individuation of the propositional attitudes. In particular this process of tidying up involves discovering the logical and rational (or hypothetico-deductive, 'practical syllogism') connections between beliefs, desires, and the other propositional attitudes, that is, their psychological content. In turn these logical and rational connections between our propositional attitudes could be said to be possible only in so far as our attitudes have propositional content which is truth-functionally constrained, that is by their social constraints. That is, the intentional attitudes have a practical propositional logic because they (or at least our ascriptions of them) are fabricated out of propositions. Then, using what we have found out about the nature of our propositional attitudes as reduction-directing *indices*, we should be in a position to see the mirror image of the logical and rational functioning of this dynamic network of propositional attitudes in the network of counterfactual relations (or dispositional and causal properties) of the physical states at the lower level of the brain.

However, it should be clear by now that we should give primacy of place to the logical and rational (that is, the functional) relations between our propositional or intentional attitudes as the prime precision instrument for carving out the lower-level, physical *doppelgängers* of those intentional attitudes. This should enable us to avoid a lot of dead ends. It should enable us to avoid, for example, setting out to search, at the lower, physical level, for things that resemble the comparatively irrelevant linguistic or syntactic features of our explanations in terms of the propositional attitudes. We will avoid postulating a language of thought or language of the brain which could incarnate or express the propositions which are at the heart of our propositional-attitude expressions. Loar's belief is that we can cut through all that linguistic business by realizing that what is salient—at least for the task of *individuating* our propositional attitudes—is the logical and rational interplay of our propositional attitudes when we employ them in a schema of explanation. That is, to naturalize the propositional attitudes, concentrate not on isolated propositional attitudes but on their *functional role*. Strictly speaking, you could not concentrate on them in isolation without concentrating on their logical and rational interconnections, for they are individuated in terms of those connections; just as, if you are seeking the meaning of some linguistic expression, you should not concentrate on the syntactical features of the expression itself but on its *role* in communication. If we do concentrate on the functional role of the propositional attitudes, that is on their logical and rational economy, then we will not be mesmerized and misled by their comparatively superficial linguistic features.

At any rate, it is this starting-point that has given Loar a highly original method for naturalizing intentionality. He naturalizes intentionality by seeking, primarily, an isomorphism between this salient functional 'horizontal' feature as it operates at the higher, tidied-up level of propositional-attitude explanations and as it operates at a lower, physical level. That is, he seeks the mirror image, in terms of the dispositional and causal interactions of states at the lower, physical level, of the logical and rational interactions of the intentional states of our higher-level propositional-attitude explanations.

The second strand of his strategy for naturalizing intentionality is to give further precision to it by bringing in the social or truth-functional dimension of the propositional attitudes. I take it that the reason for this is as follows. If the strategy only relied upon the functional role or second-order properties of the propositional attitudes, then it is possible that two or more sets or networks of lower-level states could instantiate or realize the same pattern of functional roles. This problem will be overcome by adding the additional constraints associated with the truth-functional role or 'broad' content of the otherwise 'narrow' or psychological contents of the propositional attitudes. For, in effect, this gives us a second set of interconnections or interrelations by means of which we might more accurately plot states at the lower level. For at the lower level of physical naturalized states the truth conditions of a particular content will, when they are 'about' the world, be realized as counterfactual relations (dispositional-cum-causal connections), via sensory systems, to objects or events in the world.

At this lower level the 'truth' of a content will be realized as a particularly 'reliable', because reliably action-guiding, counterfactual relation or set of relations. So 'truth' has come to be interpreted, at the lower level, as a brain state's 'reliable causal connection' to the world (or some other state of affairs); because it is only in so far as the causal connections are reliable that, at the upper level of our common-sense psychology, we can say 'Her belief that so-and-so is true'.

So the strategy of naturalizing intentionality might be summed up, as Loar himself explains, in the following way:

The picture of the role of propositions has so far been this. First, their logical relations *mirror* counterfactual relations among first-order state-types, and the truth conditions of observational and basic action propositions are correlated with causal relations between perceptual circumstances and certain states (observational beliefs) and other states (willings) and certain actions. This mirroring of counterfactual relations enables each proposition (conjoined with some marker of belief or desire) to encode a second-order functional state. Secondly, propositions encapsulate a correlation between functional states and possible states of the world (their truth conditions), this correlation being of interest in part because of the reliability of beliefs as indicators of those states. The interaction between the role of the concept of truth, and the counterfactual relations that constitute the functional theory, determines, among the many possible assignments of propositions to functional states, a certain special one. (1981: 122)

We could see this from the bottom up rather than from the top down. If, to be fanciful, the bottom level of states, which are describable in terms of first-order, non-functional properties, could speak, the most extrovert and talkative of those states might say, 'I am a physical state, a brain state, with a real physical structure. I have a content or an "aboutness" partly in so far as I have been formed and put in place through the causal influence of stimulation to the perceptual apparatus of the person in whose head I reside, partly through my dispositional and causal connections to other internal physical states, and partly through the dispositional and causal effects of myself, and other states, on the actions and reactions of the whole organism in whose head I am situated. I am also an intentional state because I am the physical *doppelgänger* of what, in your common-sense psychology, you call "a belief that it is not now raining".' In more objective mode, since Loar seems confident that the lower-level physical states will turn out to be neurophysiologically sanctioned brain states, then the 'naturalization' story, in regard to a particular state, might go like this: Brain state B_{123} is an intentional state because the functional role theory (or theoretical psychology, backed up, presumably, by neurophysiology) picks it out as the realization of a particular belief which might be expressed in our ordinary, common-sense psychology as 'Bill's belief that it is not now raining'.

A HIGH-RISK STRATEGY

As we have seen, Loar's basic strategy is to naturalize intentionality in a top-down manner. It is the strategy of using our ordinary, common-sense propositional-attitude expressions, such as 'belief that so-and-so' and 'desire for such-and-such', when tidied up and stiffened up into a tight-knit functional role theory, as indices of physical states which are their realization. That is, the formally regimented propositional-attitude expressions (as least for particular persons at a particular time and in a particular context) index real physical states in much the same way that scientifically authorized expressions, such as '70°F' and '85°F', index real physical states. The central process in the task of putting these indices to work in regard to our propositional attitudes is the process whereby it is discovered which counterfactual causal relations among brain states mirror the logical and rational and truth-functional relations of our theory-delineated propositional-attitude indices. Such a strategy clearly amounts to a very clever way of avoiding the problems usually associated with functional theories, such as those associated with positing innate representational or quasi-linguistic systems in the brain. It is a clever way of avoiding having to find an answer to such questions as how these representations come to function as symbols or representations, and, given that they do, how they can be understood or interpreted by the brain or some part of it, and so on.

However, in regard to this strategy, a very basic, one might almost say innocent, question comes to mind. What if it turns out, after empirical investigation in the future, that *there is no echo at all at any physical level* of the logico-rational network of propositional attitudes as defined by the abstract functional role theory? We cannot presume a priori that there must be. So there is a reasonably high risk that an empirical investigation may show such a network-to-network reduction to be factually false. Scientists, or whoever are the proper investigators, might fail to find any way of dividing up the lower-level, physical, inside-the-head world so that, in its functional mode, it mirrors the functional interrelations of the upper level.

Let me come at this point from a slightly different and more radical angle. Why should we even presume that our ordinary propositional-attitude expressions—our ordinary talk of belief, desire, hope, intention, want, and so on—are *literally in our head*? After all, I might say, 'I have a good chance of doing so-and-so' or 'I am happy'. It does not follow from such locutions that we should postulate or look for real items labelled 'a chance' or 'a state of happiness' inside human heads or even inside humans. Chances can be genuine and happiness real in other ways. Similarly, it might turn out that beliefs and desires are real but not real items inside real human heads.

To suggest that beliefs and desires can be real and naturalized without being real items inside heads is *not* to reduce the propositional attitudes to, say, 'just a useful way of talking' or 'just a useful way of explaining'. For I am not suggesting a purely pragmatic or purely instrumentalist role for our talk, at any level, about beliefs and desires. There is plenty of room between that rather dismissive way of naturalizing intentionality and the Loar method of naturalizing intentionality as real physical states in real heads. For example, as I myself will attempt in more detail later on in this book, the propositional attitudes might be naturalized, not by *shrinking them downwards* into little inner somethings, but, so to speak, by *expanding them upwards* into big holistic somethings. Such somethings might be states (still with Loarian counterfactual interrelations) *of whole persons in a context.* Our propositional attitudes might be best construed as real states of the whole human-in-a-context envelope rather than particular enclosures inside that envelope. Inner brain states may be part of the story, but just one part among many. For it may be through some 'trick of our ordinary mental discourse' that we are led into looking for beliefs and desires inside heads or inside brains, in the way that it is a 'trick of the light' that might make a child look for a bent stick in a pool of water.

We might have an almost incorrigible inclination to locate beliefs inside our heads, but this might be because, first, we place such importance on our heads and brains. They are what make us intelligent. That is where, in ordinary discourse, our higher cognitive and appetitive life is located. 'She's got a lot of brains', 'I need to get my head right', 'If you only used your brains a little more', 'He's got nothing between his ears.' In addition, we locate consciousness in our heads and, if reductively inclined, in our brains. Thus *the conscious expression* of beliefs and desires and hopes and wants will *ipso facto* be located by us in our heads. But, even allowing this location for consciousness, expressions in consciousness are still just *expressions*, they are not the real thing.

Loar has certainly thought of this objection and he may feel that his modification of his type–type reduction thesis by talk of its 'relativity' and 'plasticity' will mollify the critic who brings forward such an objection. I am not so sure. For modifying a type–type reduction in that way is a way of saying, in effect, that 'It might turn out that the brain state, which is the realization of "a belief that I am too old to play rugby", is realized as brain state B_{127} in Fred but brain state B_{902} in Bill, or as brain state B_{127} in Fred on Monday but B_{787} in Fred on Wednesday'. That is, the modifications merely soften type–type reduction in the direction of token–token reduction. But the more you move in that direction the more you weaken the correlation between the upper level of our propositional-attitude talk and the lower level of brain states as described by neurophysiologists. The correlation becomes something which is not formal or tight any more, but highly contingent and *ad hoc*.

However, even a softening of type–type reduction in the direction of token–token reduction—whether or not one travels all the way along that road—does not touch the deeper worry underlying this critical point. For this deeper worry is that perhaps it is straining credulity to expect that our ordinary, common-sense talk of beliefs and desires, and their interplay, should be any basis at all for discovering neurophysiological natural kinds. Why should beliefs and desires, which are ascribed or attributed 'from the outside looking on', tell us anything much about our very inner innards? After all, the cleverest MENSA member from the Woop Woop tribe could watch a sausage machine produce sausages day after day but thereby gain no knowledge whatsoever about the inner workings of the sausage machine. Why should she? Why should she expect the form or 'syntactical properties' of a sausage to reveal the intricacies of the 'machine states' of the sausage machine? And why should our ancestors, who invented our common sense, or folk psychology, of the propositional attitudes, have been in any better position as they studied their fellow humans 'from the outside'?

TIDYING UP AND TIDYING AWAY

One important thrust, perhaps the central impetus, of Loar's functional role theory is to supply himself with a set of precision tools for carving out naturalized states which are the realities behind our ordinary, common-sense employment of the propositional attitudes. The task of supplying himself with such a set of precision tools involves various tidying-up enterprises. The *horizontal* dimension of our propositional attitudes (their functional role) is tidied up by imposing on any ascription of the attitudes certain constraints derived from the relations of the attitude in question to other attitudes. First, and centrally, there are the constraints of logic and reason. The interplay of beliefs and desires and the other propositional attitudes must obey the general laws of rationality. But there are other constraints on the horizontal dimension which I barely mentioned previously. In particular there is the constraint which might be called the 'belief–desire–intention' constraint. This constraint is that which is put in place by specifying the right relationship between a propositional attitude and its output in action and purposeful reaction. That is, any attribution of a propositional attitude must not merely fit in (in a logical and rational way) with other beliefs, desires, and attitudes with which the subject in question has been provisionally credited, but must also fit in with his or her past and present behaviour. The ascription to me, say, of a belief that I will get rich by investing in pedigree turkeys is not really sustainable if

I *never ever* talk about turkeys except to express extreme distaste in regard to them, appear to know nothing about them when questioned about their habits and needs, and also demonstrate little or no interest in doing anything just for the sake of gaining more money.

The *vertical* dimension of our propositional attitudes (the truth conditions attaching to their contents) is tidied up by introducing a quite formal and regimented Tarskian language with its attached formal theory of truth. In such a Tarskian schema, truth is a formal relation between expressions or sentences in that formal language and the things these expressions denote. Thus Loar favours the replacement of propositions in his formal functional theory of propositional attitudes by Tarskian sentences. Thus *beliefs that p* have the same formal truth conditions as *Tarskian sentences expressing that p*. Such Tarskian truth conditions are a variant of a correspondence theory of truth (or, in Tarski's phrase, must satisfy 'the material adequacy condition').[8]

So, in effect, Loar has produced a precision set of tools for naturalizing intentionality. He has produced a Tarski-tidied and functionally fenced-in theory of the interrelation of the propositional attitudes, and of the attitudes and the world, and a recipe for how to employ the theory for the project of naturalizing those attitudes. Now, let us assume that, by employing such a formal sanitized theory of propositional attitudes, we do indeed find correlations between them and physical states. We do, in short, naturalize sanitized propositional attitudes by finding the mirror image of their logical relations and truth conditions in the counterfactual causal relations of some lower-level physical states. Now, why should we accept that this process really has naturalized beliefs, desires, hopes, wants, intentions, and so on, *as we know them*; that is, as we know them in their ordinary, common-sense, or folk psychological, garb?

Let me put this point in terms of an analogy. Let us suppose that I am an exorcist in medieval Europe and I regularly attribute, to those troubled souls who come to me, such things as 'good demons' and 'evil demons'. In making the latter class of ascriptions I employ the species terms 'obsessing evil demons' and 'possessing evil demons'. Among the latter I regularly make use of such particular

---

[8] The Polish logician Alfred Tarski's most famous paper on truth is probably 'Der Wahrheitsbegriff in den formalisierten Sprachen' (1935), trans. and repr. as 'The Concept of Truth in Formalised Languages' (1983). The reader might also consult Tarski (1944).

denoting labels as 'Satan', 'Asmodeus', and 'Beelzebul'. However, let us say that I am a rather honest exorcist and readily own up to having great difficulty in knowing when and where I should say that someone is possessed by Satan rather than, say, Beelzebul or Asmodeus. Along comes a medieval philosopher of mind who offers help to me. He says, 'I'll tidy up for you this whole business of attributing demons to possessed persons.' He then proceeds to set out a series of functional conditions and behavioural conditions for the ascription to humans of various particular possessing evil demons. For example, he tells me that a person should be considered as possessed by Satan if and only if (*a*) he is of sufficient social or religious status to merit possession by the Prince of Darkness himself (that is, the person must be either of the status of a secular prince or above, or of a cardinal or pope), and (*b*) such a person must be heard to utter phrases that have been attributed to Satan in some standard orthodox version of the Bible. The philosopher then goes on to outline for me the different antecedent conditions which are to be counted as grounds for attributing to someone possession by Asmodeus or Beelzebul.

The question here is, why should we accept this tidied-up version as *the* account of possession by demons? Of course, my friend the medieval philosopher, being a very clever student at the University of Paris, may carry through his programme *with success*. That is, success as displayed by my now being in possession of clear and useful guide-lines, of a no-nonsense, tangible, naturalized kind, for attributing possession by demons to people. Indeed I could use these guide-lines to go on and produce, with his help, a formal guide for exorcists. But why accept *this* tidied-up version rather than another one which may be equally clear and useful?

The problem is not that the tidied-up account will be indeterminate, that is that it will not give clear guidance as to what demon is at hand, or whether any demon is at hand. The problem is why should I accept *this* tidying up rather than some other one which does the task of tidying up equally well? To translate this back into the context of Loar's tidying up and fencing in of our propositional-attitude ascriptions, why accept his tidying up rather than another one which may turn out to be equally useful?

Loar's answer seems to be that another schema will *not* be equally useful. It will not be equally useful because it will not be equally reliable as a guide. That is, it will not be as reliable in the tasks of interpreting actions, predicting actions, and guiding actions. In a sense, Loar might put it, his functional and truth conditions amount to reliability conditions. For when applied, such conditions pick out common-sense propositional-attitude ascriptions which have a long history of reliability. In short, we should accept his tidying up because it is tied so very closely to our common-sense schema of propositional attitudes which has worked so reliably for so very long a time.

But how could Loar, or anyone else, demonstrate a priori that no other tidying up—say, one which is not so functionalist and uses some version of a coherence theory of truth rather than a correspondence one—might not work equally well?

Allied to the problem above is this one. While we might indeed acknowledge the usefulness, perhaps the indispensability, of our common-sense employment of the propositional attitudes, it could be argued, without too much difficulty, that Loar's tidying up has distanced *his formal* functionalist schema of propositional attitudes from *our ordinary*, common-sense schema. Indeed the distance may be so great that his schema cannot bask in the reliability of the common-sense one. After all, Loar himself admits that he is substituting a quite 'narrow' psychological content for the rather 'broad' and basically social content of our common-sense propositional attitudes. But to have done so may have distorted the whole 'language game' involved in our ordinary attribution to others and to ourselves of the propositional attitudes. It seems, for example, to be central to our attributions of the propositional attitudes to ourselves that we do not have any privileged role in regard to such attributions. Others may sometimes, perhaps often, be in a better position to say what we really fear or hope or believe or desire than we are. This may be so because they will be less prone to deception, less likely to be subjected to prejudice, and have a wider area from which to draw evidence. Others may see more of our behaviour than we do and interpret it more neutrally and objectively. Obviously others see more of our facial gestures and body language than we do, to take just one example. Thus my friends may know, before I do, that I am in love with the barmaid at the Crown and Anchor and not, as I believe, interested in her recent travels in the Balkans. Or you might realize that my avowals that I am a rather liberal character are not in accordance with my real beliefs which subtly reveal themselves in my unguarded, illiberal actions and reactions. In general, then, our common-sense attributions of the propositional attitudes bestow upon those attitudes quite broad or as-interpreted-by-the-community content. This is so because, generally speaking, it is the 'common-sense community' which is the ultimate arbiter of what is correct and incorrect, acceptable or unacceptable, in regard to such attributions, though not necessarily in each individual case. On the other hand, Loar's account of the propositional attitudes is that, essentially, they have narrow content. His is an account of beliefs and desires as having individual or personalized content. That being so, it would seem to follow that the individual (or perhaps the 'individual introspector') ought to have a privileged position in the matter of deciding what are the contents of his (or her) propositional attitudes, because he has a privileged position in saying what is the functional role of any particular propositional attitude (in terms of the logical and rational interplay of the whole network of his own beliefs and desires).

Another significant way in which Loar's view of the propositional attitudes differs from our common-sense one is in the emphasis he gives to the interrelations among those attitudes. For Loar it is a necessary condition for a claimant to be accorded the title 'belief that so-and-so' or 'desire for such-and-such' that it be systematically related in a logico-rational way to *other* (presumably already canonized) propositional attitudes. *A belief that p* is partly defined by its role or function in a network. It is a holistic view of the propositional attitudes. That being so, such a formal theory of the propositional attitudes seems to run counter to our common-sense one, once again. For in accordance with our common-sense schema, it would seem to make sense to hold that a newborn infant or a primitive animal, or maybe even an adult with severe cognitive disabilities, could be the possessor of just one single belief or desire. A candidate for being such an isolated but genuine propositional attitude might be some very basic and primitive desire, such as a (non-conceptual) wanting that one's present (painful) state cease. But I shall take up this point again in the next section.

In general, however, all I need in order to make my point here is to make out a case that, in tidying up and fencing in our attributions of the propositional attitudes, Loar has changed their character, so that the reliability that attaches to our ordinary, common-sense schema cannot readily be transferred to a specialized, formalized, transformed abstraction from our common-sense schema. Just as I can no longer share in the glory attaching to the East Heathland

Cricket Club's victory in the annual village cricket champion-
ship when I am no longer a member of the Club, so a formal theory
of the propositional attitudes can no longer share in the glory attaching to the reliability of our common-sense, or folk, psychology when
the former involves a rather radical abstraction from the latter.

TOO FUNCTIONALIST FOR ITS OWN GOOD?

In his legitimate desire to naturalize intentionality, Loar puts more
weight on the functional role of propositional attitudes than does
any other functionalist theorist of the propositional attitudes. Thus
a belief is individuated more or less entirely by its functional role
in a network of propositional attitudes. Now, my problem with this
is that, ultimately, either it seems to introduce a certain kind of
utopianism into the theory or else it ceases to be a functionalist
theory in reality.

Let me take the utopianism horn of the dilemma first. Loar's very
pure functionalism—if it is to be used to individuate propositional
attitudes so as to help us naturalize them—seems to demand an
inordinate amount of knowledge about *the networks* of propositional
attitudes. By contrast, in our ordinary, common-sense attribution of
those attitudes, we rely on little or no knowledge of any networks
of attitudes. Indeed I suggest that we rely very little on such 'network knowledge' because, quite simply, it is not readily (or perhaps
even at all) available to us. For example, my attribution to Mary of
a belief that it is about to rain could have been made in a fairly
direct observational way and with little or no knowledge about Mary's
other beliefs and desires, hopes and yearnings, intentions and aims.
I might merely observe Mary from my seventh-floor apartment,
which overlooks her inner-city bungalow, and then attribute to her
the belief that it is about to rain. In more detail, I might make this
attribution to Mary more or less entirely on the basis of having
observed her going out into the back garden, looking up at the sky,
and then walking out of the front door with a raincoat and umbrella.
Certainly I may have placed those observations in a framework of
my knowledge of *human psychology*, but not of *Mary's networks*.
Attributions of propositional attitudes to a particular person are very
often no more than specific applications of generalizations about

humans. It could not be otherwise for the most part. For, even if we were able to gain an intimate knowledge of the cognitive and appetitive life of particular humans, we would become overloaded with information. We would not even have sufficient storage space, and we would be overwhelmed by the computational task of working out the logical and rational interrelations of the states of these myriad networks of attitudes.

Some people we do know fairly intimately, but they are few and familiar. With such people we may be able to predict even what they are going to say on the odd occasion. But even in such a case it is on the basis of something rather like behaviourist grounds, namely that this person had said just that sort of thing on just that sort of occasion in the past. It does not seem to be on the basis of inferences from network knowledge. Another way of putting this point would be to say that we attribute a belief to Mary in a way that is not vastly different from the way in which we attribute a belief to Mary's dog. I might attribute to Mary's dog a belief that his bone is buried in the left-hand corner of the garden, because I see the dog sniffing around in that corner and then, a few moments later, scratching around with his paws and growling. Part of my grounds for making that belief attribution to Mary's dog is that, last week, I had seen the dog doing much the same thing, in much the same place, and also observed him dig up a bone and start gnawing on it. I bring to this attribution, as 'background knowledge', little more than some generalized knowledge about dogs burying bones and then digging them up again, plus some more particular knowledge about this particular dog's habits. I do not need to try and work out anything about this dog's networks of attitudes or quasi-attitudes.

More generally, it seems fair to say that our *individuation* of the propositional attitudes, in respect of a particular person at a particular time, must be kept close to our *grounds for attributing* them to just such a person in just such circumstances. This must be so for the simple reason that we have little or no *additional knowledge* of people's attitudes other than that which we employ when making attributions of attitudes to them.

The other horn of the dilemma is the problem of how Loar might give a plausible account of how one 'grasps' (epistemologically speaking) a network and how at the same time he might preserve his strong, pure version of functionalism. Part of this problem is the problem about how, according to Loar, we could gain knowledge of the formal interrelations of a particular network. Presumably we begin by homing in on a particular belief, and then using it as the 'anchor', so to speak. Then we 'fan out from it', epistemologically speaking, via a knowledge of its logical and rational relations with other beliefs, desires, intentions, and so on. *But how do we establish the first 'anchor' belief?* We cannot call upon any network to individuate it, because, *ex hypothesi*, so far we have no knowledge of any such network. If we say that there must be some foundational beliefs and desires which are not defined or individuated in terms of a network, then we have a sort of Cartesian foundationalist epistemology at work in regard to our knowledge of our (at least formally precise) propositional attitudes. The real work is now being done, not by functional role (in a network), but by something else. The purity of the functionalism is lost. At its core it is not really a functionalist theory at all.

An alternative response is that we accept the rough and ready networks of propositional attitudes as described in our ordinary, common-sense schema (acknowledging that our knowledge of these must also rest, ultimately, on some foundationalist approach). Then we tighten up the ordinary schema into a formal 'professional' theory by forming the rough and ready interrelations into formally defined ones. But this would mean that, ultimately, the formal schema is based on the ordinary schema, which in turn, as we have already seen, is *not* based on the individuation of propositional attitudes by reference to networks.

There is another problem, which is related to the foregoing, at least in the sense that it seems to arise from Loar's very strong emphasis on the functional role in a network aspect of propositional-attitude individuation. This problem is that it seems impossible, according to his account, to individuate a belief in cases where the person has just one belief. Yet, intuitively, it would seem that such cases could occur. For example, a newborn infant or a severely mentally handicapped adult or a day-old puppy might have just one, simple, observational, non-conceptual, and non-linguistically based belief. Let us now concentrate, say, on the case of the severely mentally handicapped person. Let us suppose that this person is more or less a complete paraplegic as well. So this person has just one simple belief, a simple observational belief, namely that there is something (we would say 'something fuzzy' or 'some undifferentiated object') in front of his eyes. This belief is never of any use for finding his way about the world as he is entirely helpless and never finds his way about the world. Besides, the belief is so minimal it is hard to see how it could be a useful guide for anything. *Ex hypothesi* such a belief does not connect up with other beliefs and does not guide action. It has no functional role. It does nothing. It is, ontologically speaking, just a lower-level physical state which is the passive internal impress caused by stimulation to the visual system. It satisfies the *vertical* or truth-functional dimension of the propositional attitudes, but not the *horizontal* one. It has an informational content which can be true or false of the world (there may or may not be anything in front of his eyes). And the subject is aware of the content, so it amounts to an attitude to a content. It should then qualify as a simple belief. Rather that is what we, or some of us, intuitively, might say. However, on the functional role theory of the propositional attitudes, it would appear that it could not count as a belief as it lacks the horizontal dimension which is the individuating or defining one.

Loar, of course, could say a number of things here. One is that such an alleged belief just is not to be counted as a belief in terms of a more sophisticated, professional, formal theory of the propositional attitudes. The worry about this answer, this sort of answer, is that it is always rather *ad hoc*, indeed rather high-handed. It is a response that seems to amount to saying, 'If there are difficult or maverick cases, then just dismiss them out of hand as being just the product of our unsophisticated folk psychological stage of talk about the propositional attitudes'.

Another response is to allow that there are such simple beliefs with no apparent functional role. It is to allow that any functional role system must have some (or 'at least one') initial attitude which, because it is the *inaugurating attitude* of a person's future complex networks of attitudes, must lack a functional role. That is, Loar could say that any theory such as his must have *a foundationalist aspect* to it, otherwise how could it all begin. This is a reasonable response, but the cost in making it is that the theory thereby loses its purity. It cannot any longer be said to be a pure functional role theory, for the simple reason that the most important beliefs, the ones that start everything off, have no functional role. Besides, there is no reason to believe that such simple observational beliefs with no functional role occur only as the inaugurating step in the process of setting up cognitive and appetitive networks (or, in more personal terms, occur at the beginning of one's mental development). I suspect that over a lifetime I have had a lot of simple observational beliefs that have never had, and are never likely to find, a functional role in the networks of my propositional attitudes. For example, I might, while waiting in the dentist's waiting-room, have once observed a curiously shaped speck of dust. The simple observational belief that there was a curiously shaped speck of dust before my eyes just came and went and played no part in my cognitive and appetitive life thenceforwards. For the content of such a belief had no real interest for me. It did not connect up with anything I wanted or needed or even liked.

A reply which I do not think that Loar would want to make is that even a belief about there being a speck of dust before my eyes, or the mentally handicapped person's belief that there is something there, could be utilized, even if in fact they never are or will be. A map is a map even if no one ever consults it. It could guide someone to somewhere. One could think of a use for the simple beliefs about a speck of dust and about something being out there in front of one's eyes. So they have a functional role, even if unutilized by any network or system. The problem with this sort of response is that it would allow too much. If functional role is defined in terms of *possible* functional role or roles, then everything not merely has a functional role, it has a potentially infinite array of them. We just need to find another 'possible world' in order to find it yet another functional role. But this would seem to leave the task of individuation by functional role in tatters. It would be an infinite task.

I suppose that, deep down, as a gut feeling, I have great difficulty in believing that it makes much sense to try and find the physical equivalents inside our heads of individual items in our ordinary, common-sense employment of the propositional attitudes. All the queries I have voiced above have probably arisen, directly or indirectly, from that gut feeling. I take a broad, or social, view of our talk about beliefs and desires and intentions, and the rest of the attitudes, and I suspect that the way to naturalize them is not downwards. I feel that this is so, no matter how sophisticated the top-down strategy turns out to be, and none is more sophisticated than Loar's functional role theory of the propositional attitudes. On the other hand, I do think that there is real information and content and intentionality inside our heads, but that it is not of the propositional-attitude variety and that it is not linguistic or representational in any way either. My view is that the propositional-attitude variety of intentionality arises only at a very high, sophisticated, conceptual, whole-person-in-a-context level. But the filling out of these brief remarks of mine is the material of the final three chapters.

II
A Different Approach

6

A Brain's-Eye View of Intentionality

SOME LESSONS LEARNED

In Part II of this study I want to attempt the construction of at least the foundations of a new approach to intentionality. I want to base this approach both upon the undoubted gains which have been made over the recent history of theorizing on this topic and upon some facts about human psychology and neurophysiology which I believe have not been given the prominence they deserve.

At the beginning of this book I suggested that in modern times the problem of intentionality had become the problem of explaining how representations can understand themselves. Now, in retrospect, it seems to me that the message to be taken down and ruminated upon is that no representations in the mind or brain or anywhere else will ever be able to understand themselves. To think otherwise is to set oneself a project like that of producing a tennis ball that serves itself over the net. To make sense of intentionality, we have to start from a different point altogether, and not any sort of reductionist or instrumentalist one that simply dismisses the reality of the intentionality of the mind-cum-brain. We need to start from a standpoint which holds that the brain is really a processor that does house information-bearing structures, and so is a true semantic engine. On the other hand, it (the brain itself) is *not* an epistemic engine, for, in any strict sense of the word 'interpret', it does not interpret its own information-carrying contents. We have, then, no need to puzzle over intentionality in terms of the problem of how brain representations can understand themselves, or even how the brain as a system can interpret its own representations, because that kind of intentionality does not occur in the brain. Epistemic or truly interpretive intentionality occurs at a different point, or rather points, for it is arguable that epistemic or interpretive intentionality should not be confined to our adult employment of the propositional attitudes but appears earlier, at least in embryonic form.

We should not allow this sweeping away of the problem of how brain representations understand themselves to go to our heads. Sweeping away this problem will not sweep away the problems of epistemic or interpretive intentionality which, in its most basic form, is the problem of how humans come to recognize one thing as signifying another. What I am going to argue is that humans involve themselves in representations proper (as different from analogue records in the brain) at a relatively sophisticated age, when they learn to cope with language and other symbolic forms. On the other hand, even in infancy, humans move beyond the stage of playing host merely to analogue sensory experiences. For in infancy, via the medium of their sensory experiences, they learn that one thing can gain significance through another. When humans do get to the stage of involving themselves in representations proper, the important thing to remember is that humans invent such representations. They do not find their brains lumbered with them. Furthermore, it is in producing representations proper that humans understand them.

Briefly reflecting on Brentano's approach to intentionality should also be very instructive. He himself looked upon his task in philosophy of mind (though he himself would have rephrased that as 'in psychology') as, first of all, one of engaging in a direct, empirical, if irredeemably private, inner observation of the workings, especially the intellectual processes, of the mind (where mind was construed in a Cartesian or 'consciousness as a separate substance' way). The second task was to deliver a 'descriptive phenomenology' of his findings, where the phrase descriptive phenomenology should be understood as the careful description of the essential nature of the 'phenomena' or 'conscious appearances' observed by this method.

In one sense Brentano was right, in another sense perhaps not so. He was right to see consciousness as important for the understanding of intentionality, which in turn is the essence of mind; but wrong, I believe, in restricting intentionality to consciousness. For I see consciousness as a very important product of the brain but only one of the products which underwrite intentionality (another is language), and so only one of the products by which brains perform in such a way that they merit the evaluative (indeed honorific) title 'minds'. The point of consciousness, I believe, is not to gain access to an inner private world. Consciousness is one of the bridges, which evolution has produced, between brain and world. Being conscious of what is about us, or of certain actions and reactions, or of what might be the case in the future, is one of the things brains can do, for a person. Other things they can do are to enable us to speak to others, to move our arms and legs, to grasp things, to find our way about the environment, and to lie down and sleep. But Brentano was dead right in so far as he pointed to consciousness as the origin of *one type* of intentionality, even if in certain respects he did turn back to a medieval-cum-Aristotelian vocabulary and metaphysics in his description of this fact. For I am going to suggest that, developmentally speaking, the first forms of proto-interpretive intentionality are to be found in the conscious sensory experiences of an infant. In a sense that part of my account will be Brentano without the Aristotelian–Cartesian underpinning and with a dose of modern developmental psychology. A strange combination, I admit, but I believe it produces interesting results.

Clearly I do not think that we should accept the wholesome breeziness of the approach to intentionality which says 'Off with its head. There's no such thing as intentionality. Or, at most, it is just a feature of a certain sort of vocabulary.' There is no denying that this approach has its attractions. Among other things, at a stroke, it reduces cognitive psychology to the more manageable study of our mental vocabulary or, perhaps ultimately, does away with cognitive psychology altogether. However, this breeziness has hit upon something very important, namely that, in the strictest way of putting it, propositional content is only a feature of language or language-like systems. For the propositional attitudes, defined as they are in terms of propositions as contents, can only come into existence when language does. An infant can have no propositional attitudes because its attitudes cannot have propositional form. But where this line of thought is in danger of inducing severe agnosticism, if not outright atheism, about intentionality is in its tendency to make us blind to other non-linguistic forms of content. *A fortiori* it will inhibit any urge to investigate the link between non-linguistic and linguistic content, and the possibility that the former may turn out to be the foundation of and the prelinguistic precursor for later, more sophisticated linguistic content.

Finally the appeal to evolution and evolutionally proper function has also been both suggestive and misleading. While evolution tells us *why* an organism developed some capacity—why it developed a long tail or a short beak or a belief-producing system—it does not tell us *how* this capacity is to be explained, that is how it works. On the other hand, the biologizing of psychology must be partly correct. If intentionality is a real feature of humans, then almost certainly it must have been developed by the processes we call 'evolution'. I will argue that brains as such have a very primitive form of intentionality which makes use of uninterpreted contents. Nevertheless, this initial form of intentionality is absolutely essential, as it makes possible the initial contact between person and world upon which everything else is built. I will also argue that the first form of proto-interpretive intentionality, as found at the level of sensory experience, is not merely prior to language but must underlie it in the sense of making linguistic intentionality, and probably much other human output, possible.

The above comments are very general ones; just sweeping strokes of the pen. They must be understood both in terms of the detailed critique of Part I, and in terms of what comes next. For, in the rest of Part II, I will try to give some substance to those general comments above which suggest a different approach to intentionality. I shall begin on this task, then, by going back to the beginning. First, in this chapter, to the primitive yet foundational intentionality of the brain; then, in the next chapter, to the first flowering of proto-interpretive intentionality in the prelinguistic sensory life of human infancy. Finally, in the last chapter, I will investigate the nature of the intentionality of our propositional attitudes.

THE LAYERS OF INTENTIONALITY

At the heart of my own view of intentionality is something which I also believe lies hidden, if largely unnoticed, in the recent debates about the nature and whereabouts of intentionality. What I am referring to is my conviction that recent debates should teach us that it will be impossible to give an essentialist account of intentionality. The term 'intentionality' cannot refer to just one thing. Or, to put this another way, if the term 'intentionality' is used to refer to one thing which is common to all levels of intentionality, then that 'one thing' is going to be a rather minimal, empty, formal, shell-like 'thing'. At most it could mean something like the 'aboutness relation', that is the fact that all forms of intentionality will include an x of some sort which carries information about something, y, beyond itself. But to say that would be to say very little; certainly very little of real interest. My own view is that intentionality is a layered developmental concept: there are simple primitive forms and there are complex forms. The latter develop from and depend upon the former. They are all forms of intentionality in a developmental sense, in the way that the foundations, the supporting structure, and the completed house are all forms of a building, rather than in the way that an egg, a chicken, and a full-grown hen are all forms of domestic fowl.

In consequence, any question of the form 'Is intentionality in the brain or is it just a feature of language or is it here or is it there?' (one could call it the Scarlet Pimpernel Question) is liable to be misleading. For it follows from my view that intentionality is to be found in a number of places, though in a different form in each of those places. So that any question about the whereabouts of intentionality, put in strictly disjunctive form, must produce a partial and so misleading answer. To put this in a slightly combative way, I think that recent debates about intentionality have produced a misleading rivalry. In implicitly assuming that intentionality must be found in just one place, in the brain or in language or in consciousness or in some other place, much recent work on intentionality has been unwilling to make philosophical connections. I want to suggest that in our mental or intentional heaven there are many mansions. Some of these, certainly, may be mere mud huts or lean-to structures, but others are baroque *palazzi*.

So, now, let me set out my wares. Let me list the levels or layers of intentionality which form the structure around which Part II of this book is built:

1. *Brain-level intentionality.* A human (or a dog or cat, probably also a frog) receives sensory stimulation to its sensory systems (to its eyes, ears, etc.). This is laid down in the brain in a form which, I shall argue, should be called 'analogue records' rather than maps or representations. These analogue records, at least when they are formed into working brain networks, may, in turn, be subject to 'thresholds' or 'cut-off points', such that thereby they acquire some more determinate characteristics, but remain analogue in character.

At this level, intentionality is merely that of the primary or original analogue records. Such records record features of or about the environment via the medium of light-waves or sound-waves and so on. On the other hand there is no, and there need be no, interpretive or monitor component in the brain which can make the connection between the record and what it is about. At this stage only 'the system' or organism needs to make the connection *in behaviour*.

2. *Sensory experience intentionality*. Sensory experiences can guide our behaviour in the world. This is so even for a foetus in the womb. And this is so without fathering upon the foetus either nativist innate concepts or any empiricist 'hallmarking' of sensory experiences as 'from the outside'. Sensory experience, I will suggest, is the beginning of a new sort of intentionality, which in turn becomes the basis for a series of intentional layers associated specifically with conscious experience. Thus, after the development of memory, an infant (or a cat or dog, but probably not a frog) can learn to put two things together. After repetition or constant conjunction, or something like 'conditioning' if you are of a behaviourist bent, an infant may learn to associate a sensory experience with behaviour, or one occurrent sensory experience with another which can be recalled from memory into immediate consciousness. The infant can grasp the *aboutness* of a current conscious experience, but only in the sense that the current sensory experience more or less inevitably calls up the second. The infant cannot yet be said to *interpret* the prior experience in terms of the latter, for it has not learned the former as a symbol, or 'stand-in', for the latter. On the other hand, something, which is clearly on the same continuum with interpretation, goes on. Something which we might call *quasi-interpretation*.

To put this another way, this level of sensory experience intentionality might be seen as the primitive precursor of Proust's inescapable association of the madeleine with certain childhood experiences. It is Proust without the rich addition of language, concepts, and thought.

3. *Linguistic intentionality*. The infant begins to be a non-infant when it starts to use words, even if the few words it can employ would not give it the status of a language user. As soon as it can use even one word, an infant employs or is in possession of a new form of intentionality, namely that of conventional signs or symbols. Thus when a child starts to utter the sound 'Daddy' (or even 'Doddy' or 'Doody' would do), in a conventional and rule-governed way, and is prone thereby to conjuring up by means of its sensory memory the sight of a large, two-legged, hairy, noisy, shambling object, so at that point it can be said to be in possession of the *aboutness* of a conventional sign or symbol. It interprets, albeit in a primitive and non-conceptual way, the conventional sound 'Daddy' or its mangled

versions, 'Doddy' or 'Doody'. Soon these proto-words become words when they are used in a more creative yet less idiosyncratic way, and so the new world of language and speech is opened up.

4. *The intentionality of the propositional attitudes.* This final level of intentionality is a very sophisticated, culture-based, language-mediated form of intentionality. We attribute to one another, to whole persons, an *aboutness*. We say that he believes this and she desires that. We say what their actions, reactions, and inactions are about. We interpret them in a macro and from-the-outside-looking-on way, and in terms of highly sophisticated conceptual folk psychological schemas. Such attributions of the propositional attitudes to ourselves and others require language, which (as we have just seen) possesses its own form of intentionality. But we do not thereby reduce the propositional attitudes themselves to just features of language. They pick out real features of real humans *by means of* language.

In this chapter I am going to concentrate on the very first level of intentionality, brain-level intentionality. In the next chapter I am going to concentrate on prelinguistic or infant sensory experience intentionality. In the last chapter I am going to concentrate on the sophisticated intentionality of our attributions to ourselves and others of the propositional attitudes. I will treat of the intentionality of language use only in passing, only in so far as it enters into the discussion of the other three levels of intentionality. I neglect the intentionality of language as such, as it is the province of philosophy of language and has already received more than its fair share of attention.

In this chapter as a whole I want to argue that whatever it is that is formed or firmed up in the networks of the brain as a result of its sensory system's being repeatedly stimulated in a certain way, this product or residue, while it amounts to brain *content*, it is not a representation or symbol of any kind. I will explain it in terms of and refer to it as 'an analogue record'. Furthermore, I will suggest that, while it is true that all our sensory systems produce effects in our brains in a common currency, electrical impulses, this currency is not a language of any kind. I will argue that the brain does not encode or translate or interpret anything when its sensory and other systems are in operation, for it has no need to do so.

So it is time, now, to get down to business and so to begin the discussion of that intentionality which is to be found at the level of brain functioning.

LANGUAGES, CODES, AND ANALOGUE
TRANSMISSION DEVICES

In this section, my task is to outline a distinction between a *language*, a *code*, and an *analogue transmission device*.[1] For at the core of my position is the claim that the brain's transformation of light-waves, and sound-waves, and pressures on the skin, and so on, into electrical impulses is not a process of translation, nor one of encoding, nor any process of a linguistic or quasi-linguistic sort.

First, in very brief fashion, a *language* is a system comprising a set of different symbols and a grammar or set of rules for how these are to be combined in order to form words, and then sentences, and so about how they are to be employed in order to communicate information or engage in other meaningful expressions. A *code* is a series of different ciphers or non-significant marks[2] and is used, together with a set of transformation rules, for converting a language communication or text into covert form. An *analogue transmission device* is a vehicle for transforming, in a causally covariant analogue manner, certain properties of one physical embodiment into another physical embodiment. If it is a linguistic analogue transmission device, then in analogue fashion it transforms one embodiment of speech or text into another physical embodiment so as to aid the accomplishment of some task such as the transportation of the overt (or coded) speech or text from one place to another.

In a sense all three parts of the distinction—language, code, and analogue transmission device—could, in a particular context, represent species of linguistic vehicle. Language could be described as a vehicle for communicating a message or expressing what one wants to make manifest, though here admittedly the vehicle is symbiotic with the message: no language, no linguistic message. A code,

---

[1] As regards this distinction, I am indebted almost entirely to a splendidly astringent article by Roy Harris (1989).

[2] The marks employed as ciphers may be significant in another context. For example, I might use our ordinary arabic numerals to encode an English language text. I could equally have used newly invented marks as my ciphers, say a squiggle, followed by a plain vertical line, followed by a broken horizontal line . . . and so on.

however, is merely a vehicle for hiding a text or some other form of linguistic expression, for the encoder need not understand the original text. An analogue transmission device, finally, could be used as the means for the actual carriage of linguistic information, whether in overt or covert form, from one place to another by physical means. Thus codes and analogue transmission devices could be carriers of linguistic information, at (at least) one remove. In such a case what they would hide or transport is information (or an expression of something) which is already embodied in and so carried by the written or uttered sentences of some natural language.

Of the three parts of our distinction, strictly speaking only language has a grammar, for only it has a set of rules for generating any number of different well-formed sentences employing the words and punctuation marks of that language. A code has a set of rules, but these rules are not guide-lines for generating original expressions in the code but merely for converting an ordinary language (or similar) text into a code, or, for that matter, one coded message into yet another coded form, in order to ensure, say, even greater secrecy for the original message. An analogue transmission device, even when used to transmit linguistic information, such as does a telephone, does not operate by a set of rules and *a fortiori* according to a grammar. A telephone (or at least the ordinary old-fashioned, non-digital variety in the kitchen) merely transmits your spoken English or French or Spanish sentence along a telephone wire to a listener at the other end. Certainly a transformation has taken place, but a transformation is not a translation. When you utter your sentence, say, 'Would you like to come to lunch tomorrow?', into the handset of the telephone, the vibrations in the air of your voiced invitation set up resonant vibrations in a metal diaphragm in the mouthpiece of the handset. This vibration in the diaphragm, in turn, is transformed into electrical impulses which are conducted along the telephone wires to the ear-piece of the handset in the hands of the person receiving your invitation. The electrical impulses reaching the ear-piece are, via a process involving an electromagnet and another diaphragm, transformed back, reasonably accurately though strictly speaking imperfectly, into vibrations in the air like those you set up when you first voiced your invitation and which now resonate on the ear-drum of the listener.

It is also the case that the telephone has neither encoded nor translated your invitation to come to lunch. It has not encoded your invitation because it has neither understood nor, like the President's 'scrambler' phone, automatically followed a program or set of instructions for encoding what was a plain and open invitation to lunch.[3] It has not translated your invitation because it neither understands English or any other language, nor employs any device that tacitly does. To translate a text, a translator must understand at least two languages, so as to represent in a second language a text expressed in a first language. The telephone, as regards the task it has accomplished, has merely extended the range of your voiced invitation from twenty yards to twenty miles or 2,000 miles. A less sophisticated communication system, like the postal system, does much the same task as the telecommunication system. It carries information. The postman merely carries your message from A to B without, we hope, knowing what the message is. The telephone also carries the message from A to B without knowing what the message is.

Even if I tapped into your telephone conversation, I would not be translating the electrical impulses into English, nor would I be decoding them. I would merely be grafting on an extra, uninvited and unwanted, receiving device, like the one you and your telephone interlocutor possess, to the telephone line now employed by you and your interlocutor. A telephone tapping device is not translating the electrical impulses into English or some other natural language, because the device knows neither English nor any other language, and because the electrical impulses siphoned off by the device are not expressions in any language. These electrical impulses are not a system of different symbols with a grammar, nor do they result from a set of rules for how electrical impulses are to be combined in order to communicate or express something. Nor is the stream of electrical impulses a coded message, for no one or no thing has followed rules for transforming English into some series of marks not immediately recognizable as English. A simple encoding of your invitation 'Would you like to come to lunch tomorrow?' might involve the crude rule of putting in the place of each letter of the alphabet that letter in the same alphabet which occurs two places

[3] 'Scrambler' phones are programmed to follow automatically a set of instructions by which the sound frequencies bearing the message are altered in a regulated way, so that, while the message is thereby rendered unintelligible to a listener, the original frequencies, and so the original message, can be recovered by means of a decoding device.

later. Thus the rule would enjoin that for 'a' one should write 'c', for 'b' one should write 'd', and so on. In encoded form your invitation to lunch becomes 'Yqwnf aqw nkmg vq eqog vq nwpej vqoqttqy?' However, no one has programmed your telephone to do this or anything like it. Your telephone (unless, like the President's, it is a 'scrambler') cannot encode.

An exceedingly clever Martian who only had a device for recording the stream of electrical impulses along telephone lines (employed, let us say, by two persons conversing on the telephone in Mongolian) would never be able to decode the electrical impulses into a message in Martian or any other language. The reason for this is that the electrical impulses are not symbols, much less words, in a language. The impulses are not broken up into word-length, or sentence-length, or message-length bits, because the impulses do not represent words or sentences or messages. Unless one could first learn Mongolian, and then sit down for a long time with an electrical-impulse-registering-and-storing device, and then correlate Mongolian sentences, as spoken by a particular Mongolian, with their transformation into electrical impulses on telephone lines, one could never read off messages in Mongolian from electrical impulses. Even then the chances are exceedingly slim; about as slim as your chances of working out what messages the waves of electromagnetic radiation in the air just outside your house are carrying to the radio set in your kitchen if the radio were not switched on and receiving. Without the help of physical devices, such as a telephone or radio, which, zombie-like but quite accurately, transform electrical impulses or electromagnetic radiation into human speech, most probably you have no chance whatever of success.

THE BRAIN AS AN ANALOGUE INFORMATION TRANSMITTER AND PROCESSOR

In this section, then, by means of the preceding distinction, I want to try and put a bit more colour and detail into the claim that the brain is an analogue transmission device, though it does other tasks as well. The core of this claim is that the brain deals only in terms of analogue records, and that these analogue records, even when they form part of cell networks with 'threshold' or 'gate' effects, should be explained without reference to a language of the brain.[4]

But let me try and explain these notions of analogue transmission and analogue system by way of analogy. Think of the world heavy-weight boxing champion punching me on the nose. Let us imagine that, when he gives me a punch equivalent to two pounds in weight delivered to my nose at a speed of fifty miles per hour, my nose is flattened to a depth of two centimetres from its original perimeter but then bounces back to its original shape soon afterwards. Further, let us imagine that, when he gives me a punch equivalent to four pounds delivered at fifty miles per hour, my nose is squashed to a depth of four centimetres, and so on. Though my nose does not symbolize the punch, and there is no 'language of the nose' which represents or expresses the punch, the differential flattening of my nose mirrors the variation in the force of the boxer's punches. My nose alters covariably with variations in the weight of punch of my opponent. My nose resonates with its stimulation. If my nose did react in such a way to a boxer's punches, it would be an analogue system.

Something reasonably similar to this happens, inside a baby's head, in its brain, when it sees its mother's face. In such a case the basic physical account, briefly put, goes like this: The light striking the mother's face is reflected back into the baby's eyes. The different features on the mother's face (such as shape of face, disposition of the eyes and eyebrows, position of the nose and mouth, colour of hair and skin) are reflected in variations in the light entering the baby's eyes (such as in differences in wavelength, frequency, and strength, and in angle of entry of the light-waves). These variations in the light, in turn, are registered in an analogue way in the im-pulses generated in the brain's optic system, which stretches from retina to visual cortex and beyond. That is, the differences in stimu-lation to a sensory or input system are registered, in a purely causal way, as covariable differences in the brain's electrochemical impulses.

Put in more general terms, for some time now neuroscientists have been able to link stimulation of the retina of the eye of an

[4] The references to brain functioning make use especially of the work of John Dowling (1992), Gerald Edelman (1978, 1985, 1989, 1992), Patricia Churchland (1986), Peter Nathan (1987), Michael Gazzaniga (1989), and Edward Hundert (1989). I also profited greatly from correspondence with the neuropsychiatrist John Smythies and the neurophysiologist Roger Anwyl.

animal to the resulting electrical activity in the nerve cells of the visual cortex; that is, they can discover how the stimulation at the receptor end is recorded in terms of the activation of the relevant part or parts of the cortex. Generally speaking, though there are exceptions, the higher you reach on the evolutionary tree the more analogue cortical records (or 'maps', as the psychological literature very misleadingly tends to put it) there are in your visual system. Thus a cat has more visual analogue records than does a rat, and a rat has more than a frog. The human visual system is known to have analogue records that mirror the variation in stimulations to the system caused by the amount of available light as well as by the shape, surface, movement, orientation, and distance of objects.

The 'logic' of the brain's analogue system of information processing is a little bit like the 'logic' employed by a telephone system, for the latter is also an analogue system, not a symbolic or quasi-linguistic system. So it follows that your chances of reading off information in the human brain by trying to *decode* or *translate* the stream of the brain's electrochemical neuronal impulses, as measured by an electroencephalograph of some sort, say, are as slim as are your chances of reading off information from the electrical impulses flowing along telephone wires. For like the electrical impulses conducted by telephone wires, the electrical impulses conducted by the brain's neuronal networks form neither a language nor a code. For the brain does not contain any device that translates information or data from our eyes and ears and nose and mouth and skin into the symbols and phrases and sentences of a brain language or any other sort of language. That the brain reduces all of its analogue information into a *single currency* of electrochemical impulses does not mean that it has transformed such information into a *common language*, though on the surface this may appear to be so. In this context a currency is not a language or symbolic system of any sort. It is merely a single sort of flow or stream or medium of transmission of information.

Strictly speaking, your chances of reading off information from the human brain are much slimmer than your chances of reading off information from a telephone line because, unlike the telephone system, the brain is not a simple analogue transformation and transmission device. The point of the brain is not to transform what goes into one part of the head into something more easily transportable, then to carry it to another part, and finally to transform it back at some exit point into as exact a replica as possible of what originally entered into the head via one of the sensory systems (except, perhaps, for students at examination time). The brain is the command module of an action-producing system. At the very outset what goes into the brain is, at the point of initial transformation into electrical impulses, divided up into distinct aspects or parts. Then a selection for saliency in regard to action or reaction takes place. Much of this selection is automatic in the way a gravel filter automatically selects out larger pieces of gravel from smaller pieces. The mechanism has been 'designed' by evolution and 'firmed up' during individual development. Then what is left after this selection-cum-filtering process is registered in an analogue way.

Then these primal or basic analogue recordings are summated or brought together into more sophisticated records. Some forms of summation may involve a threshold or gate effect in networks. That is, when the intensity and frequency of the electrochemical impulses along certain neuronal pathways reaches a certain point or level or threshold, then the stream of impulses is allowed through the gate so as to exercise an excitatory or inhibitory effect in regard to activity in other pathways or other networks. A gate or switch, so to speak, has been opened up or turned on. But there is nothing magical happening at this point, when, as some might put it, the analogue processing is given a binary role. For there is no sudden conversion from uninterpreted brain content to interpreted brain content. The only information the brain has is the information it receives in analogue form, or combines with what might be called innate information (also in analogue form). What is let through the gate or beyond the threshold will still be in analogue form. If it were not so, and if the brain suddenly became a representational system, then the brain would not be able to cope. It would have to come up with an interpreter of the symbols or representations it had produced or else produce some of those magical representations that interpret themselves. But there is no evidence that the brain does either of these things. There are no grounds for believing that, midstream in the flow of information processing, the brain suddenly becomes an epistemic engine or a cognitive machine.

Any conscious experience probably occurs, like the behavioural actions or visceral reactions of the organism, at the end or product point of brain processing. In short, conscious experiences, even sensory ones, are highly sifted and selective and polished effects of brain processing, and not, as is sometimes imagined, raw experiences of what has just entered the brain's sensory systems. Nevertheless, as we shall see in the next chapter, sensory experiences themselves are analogue in character. So what should be clear is that anyone 'tapping into' our neural analogue system will get quite different results depending on the stage or point at which he or she taps into the system. Further, given that such a system employs a considerable amount of selection and association and summation, it would be more or less impossible to recoup any stimulus in its original form, as it appeared at its point of entry through one of the sensory systems.

The brain is a semantic engine but not an epistemic one. It is a semantic engine because it carries and processes and makes use of information. The brain can be said to have information because it has internal states or processes which have content. It can be said to have content because it has internal states or processes which contain in a causally covariant way the effects of stimuli from the environment upon its sensory systems, such that these effects are in turn employed to guide the organism whose brain it is in that environment. The brain's information is primitive, or raw, information because it is carried by and remains in the brain as uninterpretable analogue content.

Thus, in one sense, evolution, and individual upbringing, adopt the role of 'interpreter' in regard to the brain's analogue information. For it is evolution that has selected and shaped human brain structure and processing so that it does transform in an analogue way the stimulation from the environment such that the organism can then make use of it to survive in that environment. As adults, again ultimately by grace of evolution, we learn to interpret some analogue information in a new way, by giving sophisticated linguistic and conceptual interpretation to that version of analogue information that is expressed in our conscious sensory experiences.

Let me elaborate on the second part of this 'loop' from environment to brain to behaviour and so back to the environment. Just as it is evolution that has selected and shaped human brain structure and function so that it can reflect in an analogue way certain features of the environment, so it is evolution that furnishes the link to appropriate behaviour in that environment. The 'selectional pressure' of evolution is exerted through the interaction between the organism and the environment in which it must try, via its behaviour, to live and survive. So in selecting an organism, evolution must not merely select an organism whose brain can accurately gather information in an analogue way about the environment, but it must select an organism whose analogue records are also successfully relinked to the environment as causes, or part of a chain of causes, *of appropriate behaviour in that environment*. Thus, at the level of brain analogue records, the analogue information is *utilized by* the organism whose brain it is though *not known by* that organism. It is uninterpreted (except in a 'blind' causal way) but nevertheless very useful analogue information. Indeed part of the reason for calling it information is that it is action-guiding. It is informative in that *directive* sense.

MAPPINGS AND TRANSFORMATIONS

In the previous two sections I tried to shed light on the nature of brain functioning by discussing it in terms of a distinction between a *language*, a *code*, and an *analogue transmission device*. I did so in order to argue more precisely that the brain does not operate in the way a language user does. I suggested that, given the three parts of the distinction, the brain was an analogue transmission device, not an employer of a language or code, nor a translator or encoder. But this is only part of the story such that, if left like that, the account would be quite misleading. For also at the core of my account is a claim that the brain does not deal in maps (which are types of representation) of any sort. It deals solely in terms of analogue records (which do not represent). In order to shed some more light on this anti-representational claim, I want to introduce two additional distinctions, in this section between *mapping* and *transforming*, and in the next section between *maps* and *records*. The two distinctions are related, in that analogue records, so I will argue, result from entirely natural transformations, while maps result from the conventional (or partly conventional) generation of representations through mapping procedures. Furthermore, maps stand in need of interpretation if they are to have a function, while analogue records do not. Such records function in an unmediated causal way.

A *map* is defined by the *Concise Oxford Dictionary* as, in its primary sense, 'a representation (usually on a plane surface . . .) of (part of) earth's surface'. Let me extend this definition a little, so that *a mapping* may be defined as *a procedure designed to record something else, and the relations between features on that 'something else', in symbolic or representational form, for the use of some future interpreter*. Thus the end-product of a process of mapping is a map, and a map may be designed to reveal the actual features of some object or area or event, and to mirror the actual relations between these features, by being made up of a regulated graph or model or depiction or set of representations of those features and the relations between them. A map might be produced more or less directly by the cartographer according to some agreed rules of representation, or the map might be produced by the cartographer's exploitation of some natural physical transformation of what is to be mapped on to something he has introduced.

A *transformation*, on the other hand, is different from a process of mapping. A transformation might be defined as *a process whereby a purely causally covariant, analogue effect is produced by one form of matter or energy on another according to the laws of nature*. Thus a photochemical effect is a transformation. So is a photoelectric one. The causes in such transformations are not designed to produce their effects by means of the interpretation of inherent symbols, depictions, or representations. The effects or end-products of transformations are analogue records.

Let me illustrate the difference between mapping and transforming by means of a series of examples. In the first example, I will present a case of pure mapping; in the second example, a case of transforming being used as mapping; in the third example, a case of pure transforming, which nevertheless might be mistaken for a map or representation; in the fourth example, I present what I believe is a 'pure' transformation where there is no temptation to see it as involving any depiction, representation, or mapping procedure.

In our first example, a cartographer might produce a map by sailing a ship round the coast of an island and then, according to some basic rules—such as 'Let one centimetre of length on the map equal one mile of land or sea', 'Let the representation of land and sea be laid out in two dimensions', and 'Let these two dimensions be given a grid in terms of the conventional lines of longitude and latitude'—painstakingly depict with pen and paper the island's coastline. His depiction of the coastline may be guided by noting the ins and outs, the points and peninsulas and inlets and bays of the coastline, as prompted by the changes in direction of his ship as it hugs the coastline at a steady five-mile distance.

In our second example, the cartographer might simply fit a camera to the underside of an aeroplane and fly an aeroplane up and down the island in longitudinal runs at a steady height of 10,000 feet above the ground, making sure that each longitudinal run is as near as possible one plane-width to the right of each previous longitudinal run. By employing this procedure, the camera produces for the cartographer a series of photographic depictions, that is, conventional two-dimensional representations or depictions, which may be conjoined and then reduced in magnification and then finally converted into outlines. What is clear is that this modern cartographer has exploited the naturally occurring photochemical effect which underlies all photography. Early photographic plates (to keep the discussion clear and manageable) were coated with silver bromide, which is sensitive to light-waves. Developing consisted in producing a black deposit of fine particles of metallic silver on those portions of the silver bromide plate which had been exposed to light, thus generating the negative or first image. Producing the positive or finished picture from the negative is a similar photochemical process which 'reverses' the image by making the black portions into white and vice versa.

In our third example, we have no mapping, but there is a transformation. Someone drops a container of silver bromide. The top comes off. The contents spill out. Silver bromide will react to light even if it just happens to have been spilled on the floor. In such a case the reaction in the silver bromide on the floor is not a picture. It is a pure analogue transformation of light reflected from some object producing a chemical effect. Someone may recognize some object which has been 'photographed' by the silver bromide, but to do that would be to use it as a picture.

But we could take another example, a fourth one, in which, I believe, no one would run any risk of being misled into thinking that the transformation was a representation of any sort. In plants sunlight sets off the process of photosynthesis. Light energy causes chemical reactions in pigment (or chlorophyll) molecules which in turn bring about other reactions culminating in the formation of carbohydrates within the plants. At the first stage of this long series of processes the photochemical pigment cells are transformed by light in a highly regulated way. These initial changes, in turn, in a highly regulated proportional way, bring about other changes culminating in the formation of carbohydrates within the plant. The amount of carbohydrate produced in the plant, given some qualifications which acknowledge the role of other agents and of threshold requirements, is directly proportional to the amount of light falling on the plant. The carbohydrate does not map or represent or even measure the amount of light falling on the plant, it merely records it in an analogue way. Of course, a clever plant biologist might be able to produce a mapping or measuring device which *exploits* this natural transformation, but that is probably true of any natural transformation.

RECORDS AND MAPS

Before going on to relate these distinctions to brain functioning, in this section I want to say a little more about the end-products of *mapping* and *transforming*. For I suggested that the end-product of a procedure of mapping was a *map*, and that of the process of transforming an *analogue record*.

An analogue record is *something that is brought about when one thing is informed by or registers, in a causally covariant analogue way, the causal impact of something else upon itself, and so can be said to be transformed by that causal process.* Thus an analogue record is embedded with, and so carries, causally induced information. The analogue impress of the causal impact is the record. This analogue impress may be simple and more or less immediate, as when a foot makes a footprint on wet sand. On the other hand, the effect or impress may be very far from being simple and immediate. It may involve one or more physico-chemical transformations. Thus the production of carbohydrate in a plant's system is a record of the amount of sunlight received by the plant, but it is so via a number of very complex transformations. A footprint is an analogue record of a moving foot. An analogue record in some organism, involving as it does some natural transformation or transformations, does its work in a purely causal way. It does not require an interpreter.

A *map* on the other hand, is *a piece of information with representational or symbolic content deliberately produced so as to depict an array of objects or events and the relations between them. Representations* are artefacts made to resemble what they stand for according to some convention. *Symbols* are non-resembling and so non-depictive artefacts which are conventionally instituted as standing for something. Both representations and symbols stand in need of an interpreter who or which understands the conventions or at least can interpret them. Thus with maps the informational content can only have an effect via a process of interpretation or 'reading' of the symbolic system or depictive convention, though a machine can sometimes be programmed to fulfil such a task. On the other hand, my handwritten, rather badly drawn, and not completely correct map of where I live in Dublin could probably only be read by a human interpreter.[5]

Per accidens or contingently an analogue record may also be employed as the platform for some inferrer (such as a human or some humanly programmed inference machine) to infer. That is, it may be employed as a map. In such a case, the inferrer has come to use the naturally occurring analogue record as a sign of something beyond itself. He or she has come to interpret the various features of the analogue record. But, interestingly, in such a case the interpretation will be in terms of the causal chain of which the analogue record is part, not in terms of any conventions. The inferrer will use the analogue record as a sign of its cause or as a sign of its effect. Thus Robinson Crusoe inferred that he was not alone on his tropical island when he saw a footprint in the sand. He knew there was another human about because only human feet make footprints of that shape. If Robinson Crusoe was more experienced in regard to footprints, say he had been employed for many years as a tracker, he might have been able to infer the height and weight and gender of the owner of the foot that produced the footprint.

Though a footprint in the sand is the bearer of interpretable content, if in fact there is someone around to infer things from his scrutiny of the footprint, the footprint does not become thereby a map. It does not become a map because at no time does it involve the use of symbols or depictive conventions. A footprint is not produced *in order to* signify something beyond itself, though in certain special circumstances it could be. A footprint could become an internationally agreed sign, and so be given conventional meaning. It might mean 'This is a footpath', and some world-wide international committee for tourism could decree or suggest that rural footpaths and urban walkways be signified by inserting into the

---

[5] I am indebted to David Novitz, of the University of Canterbury, New Zealand, for valuable instruction about the nature of representations.

beginning of the footpath or walkway a concrete slab with the real impress of a real human foot. This committee might set up a world-wide competition to determine the world's most beautiful foot or else, in order to further the cause of world peace, the Chairman of the Chinese Communist Party might be invited to lend a foot.

THE MAPLESS, AND NON-REPRESENTATIONAL, BRAIN

What have these distinctions between mapping and transforming, and between analogue records and maps, to do with my account of the intentionality of the brain?

First my hope is that these distinctions will help make clear how the human brain can be an information processor without being a representation former or language user or map reader. For nothing I am claiming about transformation and analogue records denies that the brain is an information processor. It is an information processor, but there are other ways of carrying and processing information than by means of representations, or symbols, or maps. Since there are analogue records in the brain, which are *about* something beyond themselves, because they mirror in a causally covariant way, and often very precisely, certain features of the causes which transformed them thus, then it still makes sense to speak of *information* in the brain and of real brain content. A brain has the same sort of content as a footprint in sand or the carbohydrate produced by photosynthesis, namely as the analogue impress of a naturally occurring transformation.

Sometimes, of course, these analogue effects or records will last only a matter of milliseconds, at other times they will be further transformed into the real structural or neurophysiological basis for that same network to have a disposition to fire in just the way it did (or at least in much the same way that it did) when that same sensory stimulus (or one that is similar) next stimulates the sensory system in question.

But whether brain content, its analogue records, are transitory or have more permanency, the point is that they still do their work without being interpreted. They just go on their merry causal way.

It is important that we should not be misled into thinking that the brain is some sort of language processor or representational system by the fact that sometimes the stimulus that enters a sensory system is caused by an ordinary linguistic expression. For example, the human, whose brain is the receiver of stimulation, may be reading a book or listening to the radio. Nevertheless, what the eye receives is light-waves reflected from the page of the book, and what the ear receives is sound-waves produced by the mouth and tongue and larynx of the person or persons speaking. These light-waves and sound-waves are received by the human brain in the same machine-like way that an answerphone receives its language communications or messages. The message on the page or in the spoken words does not enter the ear or eye as understood message. It *becomes* an understood message if and when, *as output* from the brain, understanding (usually conscious but sometimes purely behavioural) takes place. But because all this happens so fast, our gifts of imagination may lead us into creating for ourselves a belief that information passes into the brain as understood information, rather than as dumb transformation. Later (though the 'later', at times, may only be a few milliseconds) this dumb transformation may produce understanding in the person in whose head this dumb transformation takes place. Even so, the understanding will not be *of* the record produced by this dumb transformation. The understanding will be *of some end-product* of the transformation process or *in some end-product* of the transformation process. The brain's *whole-person outputs* of action, reaction, emotion, understanding, thought, and speech are the results of brain activity, not some part of it.

Sometimes, of course, the brain generates analogue records from which the human person either cannot generate any whole-person-level output or cannot generate a particular sort of whole-person output. For example, the heard speech may come through the brain's transformation processes as garbled. At other times the brain's records might be ones which never emerge from the brain's transformation processes. No output might be forthcoming. The brain may not be able to integrate the incoming stimulation so as to produce a transformation into electrochemical activity that connects up with other electrochemical activity so as to prompt output. The brain, so to speak, may not be able to make anything of the incoming stimuli. At other times, also, the brain generates records which influence behaviour but never enter consciousness. We can act on peripheral hearing or vision without being aware of it.

What should be clear is that it is a mistake to look for intentionality which involves interpretable content at the level of the brain's

electrochemical activity. There is an intentionality involving interpretation that pre-dates language, but this intentionality, I will argue
in the next chapter, is to be found at the level of an infant's conscious
sensory experiences.[6]

Given this brief sketch of brain structure and function, we can see
how unimportant if not odd the task of the individuation of even a
basic brain record, in order to make out a case that it is a real
physical representational structure, becomes. For, from the brain's
point of view, it makes little sense to isolate this momentary part of
the activity of the whole system, rather than this part two milliseconds later, as *the* analogue record of something. In a real sense,
whole, fairly 'global' patterns of brain activity, and perhaps different patterns at different times, are the container of the record that,
for example, enables an infant to recall a visual experience of its
mother's face, or an adult to ride a bicycle. In short, we should not
be misled by my own use of the terms 'brain content' and 'analogue
record' into giving any structural-like solidity or permanency to
their referents, so that in turn we are seduced into thinking of them
once again as maplike or symbolic or representational.

AN ARGUMENT FROM AUTHORITY PLUS A SCHERZO

It is now time, I think, for an argument from authority. I have been
taking for granted a certain view of brain functioning, which I believe is supported by recent work in neurophysiology. This view I
have been attempting to put in a form which connects it up with
recent philosophical debates about intentionality. However, at this
point, I think it is time to quote from Gerald Edelman, who gained
the Nobel Prize for Physiology or Medicine in 1972. In the first
chapter of one of his more popular books, *Bright Air, Brilliant Fire*,
he has this to say:

In the last few decades, practitioners in the field of cognitive science have
made serious and extensive attempts to transcend the limitations of behaviourism. Cognitive science is an interdisciplinary effort drawing on psychology, computer science and artificial intelligence, aspects of neurobiology

---

[6] Or for that matter at the level of an adult's association of conscious experiences,
for an adult is not precluded from this sort of intentionality because an adult, generally speaking, is the possessor of language and so of sophisticated intentionality.

and linguistics, and philosophy. Emboldened by an apparent convergence of interests, some scientists in these fields have chosen not to reject mental functions out of hand as the behaviorists did. Instead, they have relied on the concept of mental representations and on a set of assumptions collectively called the functionalist position. From this viewpoint, people behave according to knowledge made up of symbolic mental representations. Cognition consists of the manipulation of these symbols. Psychological phenomena are described in terms of functional processes. The efficacy of such processes resides in the possibility of interpreting items as symbols in an abstract and well-defined way, according to a set of unequivocal rules. Such a set of rules constitutes what is known as a syntax. . . . Such well-defined functional processes, it is said, constitute semantic representations, by which it is meant that they unequivocally specify what their symbols represent in the world. In its strongest form, this view proposes that the substrate of all mental activity is in fact a language of thought—a language that has been called 'mentalese'. . . . I claim that the entire structure on which the cognitivist enterprise is based is incoherent and not borne out by the facts.[7] (Edelman 1992: 13–14)

Edelman's reasons for saying that the 'cognitivist enterprise is . . . not borne out by the facts' are centred on certain general claims he makes about brain functioning in his two recent, more popular accounts of his views, namely *The Remembered Present* and *Bright Air, Brilliant Fire*. These can be set out as follows:

1. '. . . the existence of extensive individual variation in cognitive systems . . . negates the fundamental postulate of functionalism' (Edelman 1992: 226). By this he seems to mean that, given there is such an enormous variation in individual brain anatomy, including the way individual brain networks are selected and firmed up for future use, largely during the maturation process, then there seems to be no possibility that there is anything like a common language of the brain or system of representations (see Edelman 1992: 223–6; 1989: 242–3).

2. The brain operates in a 'selectional' and not in an 'instructional' manner, so that even in regard to memory 'storage is not replicative and not mediated by codes' (Edelman 1992: 227; 1989: 244).

3. Even artificial neural network or connectionist systems are not adequate models of the human brain because these involve a

---

[7] I should mention that, to confuse matters, at least from my point of view, Edelman makes use of a concept of non-representational maps.

programmer or executive unit; such things do not exist in the brain (Edelman 1992: 227).[8]

4. '. . . the sensory signals available to nervous systems are truly analogue in nature' (Edelman 1992: 225).

Let me finish this chapter on a lighter note. A favoured theme in much recent science fiction is that of mind-cum-brain reading, where the Thought Police or Interstellar Guardians stick the hero's or heroine's head into a machine which reads off his or her thoughts. According to my account this could happen, but not in the way that science fiction writers would usually have it. The process of reading someone's mind-cum-brain would not and could not be a process of employing an Enigma Machine to decipher or decode the brain's texts. Nor could it involve any process of siphoning off the brain's electrical activity and treating it as a language which a clever archaeologist of the brain could eventually translate into one of our common natural languages.

The only way to build a machine that would be of use to the Thought Police would be to build the 'Brain Bridger'.* This would be like building a *corpus callosum* between brains rather than between the hemispheres of a single brain. Such a machine would be able to transfer artificially, through a thick cable of implanted electrodes, the electrical activity from the brain-to-be-read to the brain-of-the-mind-reader in the hope that it would be fed in at the right point and accurately enough preserved in the process; that is, in the hope that the transferred electrical activity would be usable by the receiving brain and used in the same way by the receiving brain. For the idea is that, by means of this borrowed or transferred electrical activity, the brain of the mind reader, after transforming it in the appropriate electrochemical way, would be able to produce the same output as the original subject's head produced or would have produced. This, clearly, would depend on individual brains being sufficiently alike, so that we could be confident that the same transformation processes occurring in response to x input in brain a also occurred in response to x input in brain b. For sameness of

[8] I myself am not convinced that connectionist networks do need any inbuilt executive system.

* Cf. Paul Churchland's account (Churchland 1981) of interpersonal communication via a transducer able to convert neural activity into microwaves radiated from an aerial in the forehead, and to perform the reverse.

output to be achieved, it would also have to be the case that the acquired brain networks of both brains (their 'central states') were sufficiently similar. In short, the 'Similarity Problem' would not be negligible in regard to the Brain Bridger. Genetically identical twins would be the best bet, but that would cut down severely on the usefulness of the Brain Bridger. Then again, if it were feasible, it may cut down upon the current regrettable and vulgar practice of interrogators of resorting to more crude means of obtaining information from their victims.

So the short account of the Brain Bridger above is definitely science *fiction*. I won't be calling in at the Patents Office on my way home.

7

An Infant's-Eye View of Intentionality

Strictly speaking, this chapter should be called 'The Intentionality of Sensory Experiences', for that title more truly reflects its aim. I entitled it 'An Infant's-Eye View of Intentionality' solely as a heuristic device. For I will use early infancy as the main source for my examples. I find it more helpful to use real examples, both because there is less risk of my inventing powers we do not have or situations that do not occur, and because it is easier on a reader if I say, 'Take the example of an infant who . . .' rather than 'Let us say that X at time t does y . . .' and so on . Of course we need such formal crispness from time to time, but, I suspect, not as frequently as we think we do.

I might also have called this chapter 'The Bogey of Consciousness', for the simple reason that recent debates on intentionality (as, to a certain extent, I have documented in Part I) have treated consciousness as if it were a bad philosophical smell. In so far as these recent debates have been prepared to bring consciousness into an account of intentionality, this has been the case only after consciousness has been deodorized; that is, after consciousness has been reduced to a describable function or task, or else reduced further to some brain or cell network process. Alternatively, it has been reduced upwards, so to speak, to being just a feature of a certain sort of vocabulary we call 'an intentional vocabulary', which may or may not have any real use or any discernible reference.

A phenomenal, or 'from-the-subject's-point-of-view', account of intentionality, or of anything else for that matter, being non-objective, is *ipso facto* assumed to be both a non-scientific account and an account which a scientific philosophy should shun. Moreover, if in fact some account of intentionality does bring in conscious states or sensory experiences, in the phenomenal sense, then it is believed that such an account is almost certainly morbid, because almost certainly infected with that dreaded virus of philosophy of mind Cartesianism.

There is yet another reason, at the back of the minds of many contemporary philosophers of mind, for having nothing to do with consciousness. This reluctance is associated with the almost universal desire to 'naturalize intentionality'. The goal of naturalizing intentionality is, of course, perfectly legitimate and a very sensible programme to adopt. However, what seems to go along with this programme is the assumption that consciousness cannot be part of any naturalized account of intentionality. For naturalizing intentionality is taken to mean making intentionality an ordinary, if elusive, part of nature, which in turn is taken to mean that, at least in the fullness of time, the proper account of intentionality should be given in terms of one of the natural sciences. Since intentionality is thought to be a feature of minds, and minds are in the head, then a naturalized account of intentionality and of mind must be in terms of one of the natural sciences appropriate to what goes on inside heads. That is, a naturalized account of intentionality must be in biological or neurophysiological or physical terms. Or else in terms of information-processing or language-using or symbol-munching machines. Or else in terms of a behaviouristic psychology or in terms of neuropsychology or cognitive science.

But why should we refuse to give the (by now more honorific than descriptive) titles 'natural' and 'naturalized' to consciousness as experienced directly from the point of view of the person or organism that is conscious? If certain organisms have the ability to have subjective conscious experiences, and if the theory of the evolution of species, in roughly the way Darwin described it, is true, then consciousness must have evolved and must be as natural as anything else that has evolved.[1] If conscious sensory experiences cannot be adequately explained in biological or neurophysiological or physical or functional or information-processing terms, then so much the worse for those explanatory systems. Such inadequacy becomes an argument for yet another special science or special explanatory system, not grounds for calling into question the reality or naturalism of consciousness.

Consciousness is also part of our folk psychology. So if, as has happened very frequently in recent decades, you begin your philosophy of mind from a standpoint of what is sanctioned by our folk

---

[1] See Steven Rose (1976, ch. 6) for a modern attempt to make sense of when and why consciousness evolved.

psychology, then you should not leave out consciousness. For we, ordinary people, are just as ready to give an explanation for our ordinary behaviour in terms of conscious sensory experiences as we are to give an explanation in terms of our folk psychological categories of knowledge, belief, desire, hope, want, intent, and so on. 'I left the seminar because I felt queasy' is as acceptable a reason as 'I left the seminar because I knew I had a meeting at three o'clock'. On the other hand, as will become clearer in Chapter 8, I do not think that an account of consciousness should be of the same kind as an account of knowledge, belief, desire, and the other propositional attitudes. Not the least reason for this is that consciousness is not dispositional but occurrent, and its content is not necessarily propositional.

ANOTHER WAY TO TAKE THE 'BOGEY' OUT OF CONSCIOUSNESS

In the previous section, I pointed out that it is uncontroversial to consider consciousness as a product of the evolution of species. That being so, it seems reasonable to conclude that human consciousness is a feature of our biology. However, it seems that consciousness arises sometimes from brain processing and sometimes not. Or, more accurately, it arises sometimes from some varieties of cell network activity but not from others. Neurophysiologically speaking, consciousness seems to be something that from time to time *arises out of* and *is maintained by* certain sorts of brain processing. Put bluntly, it seems most natural to describe consciousness as a product of brain processing rather than as a segment of it. What is more, consciousness is clearly a different form of the physical from the brain processes from which it arises. This should not worry us. After all, such 'dualities of form' already exist in regard to the physical. At a micro level we have accepted matter and energy as two distinct forms of the physical. So another duality of form, at a higher level of activity, between neurophysiological events and conscious sensory experiences should not cause us undue anxiety. So this is not a *substance* dualism that I am advocating but a *mode* dualism. I am suggesting that we look upon consciousness and brain states as two distinct 'higher-level' modes of the physical.

Now it has been suggested to me that I should not, or need not, explain the physical nature of consciousness in terms of such a higher-level duality of physical forms.[2] For an alternative, less dualist, picture may preserve all that I want to preserve about consciousness—namely, that it is physical, that is knowable in a direct, knowledge-by-acquaintance way, that its contents have qualia, and that it can give rise to a new sort of intentionality—yet avoid the taint of excessive dualism.

This less dualist version would be explained as follows. Certain analogue brain records or processes—one would speculate that they would be at a high level of summation or, in general, at a highly processed level of brain activity—would exhibit a 'duality of *access* to the physical' (i.e. two 'ways in' to knowledge of one and the same mode or sort of physical state) rather than a duality of physical *modes*. That is, it might be the case that such analogue brain records and processes would be accessible *both* via a subjective 'knowledge by acquaintance' *and*, at least at some time in the future, via neurophysiological investigation. Our subjective, intimate *knowledge by acquaintance* of these high-level analogue brain records or processes *would be* our conscious sensory experiences, replete with qualia and the subjective point of view. Our scientific *neurophysiological knowledge*, on the other hand, would be our objective point of view about the same processes. By correlating the two, at least at a particular time and in regard to a particular person, we would have *knowledge that* this particular analogue brain record or process is the one we know subjectively as a sensory experience of such-and-such quality. This latter knowledge would be achieved, at least partly, presumably, by correlating the result of the subjective, knowledge-by-acquaintance way in to this high-level, summatory analogue brain process with the result of the neurophysiologist's observation of what is happening in the brain at the very same time. To put it over-simplistically, one way of doing this might be by probing or prodding the brain in various electrochemical ways, and under laboratory conditions, such that we would then be able to correlate a particular high-level, analogue brain record (in its guise of transitory network activity of a particular sort, if this were feasible) with the also transitory sensory experience prompted by the

---

[2] I owe the suggestion about a 'duality of access' thesis entirely to Jack Copeland of the University of Canterbury, New Zealand, though any mangling of his idea is entirely due to me. His suggestion arose during one of a series of most helpful discussions with him about intentionality.

same probing and prodding. In some such way, we might eventually be able to state that a particular analogue brain record or process known by neurophysiological investigation at a particular time is the very same one that the subject in whose head resides such a record or process knows in a conscious subjective way at that same time.

This way of explaining the physical nature of conscious sensory experiences has the satisfying feel of something that has been trimmed and tidied up with Ockham's Razor. If you can do away with a duality of physical modes, or 'stuffs', by substituting for it a duality of access to just one and the same sort of physical mode, or stuff, then, theoretically speaking, you ought to. For you should not multiply modes, or stuffs, beyond necessity. Thus certain token analogue brain records are one and the same thing as certain token sensory experiences.[3]

I do not know which of these views to take. My inclination is still towards the earlier view of treating consciousness as a physical *product* of the brain's physical processing, though in a different mode of the physical from that of brain processing itself. My tentative reasons are as follows. Theoretical neatness isn't everything. And neurophysiologists themselves seem to speak of consciousness as arising out of neuronal activity and as a product of neuronal activity. Admittedly this may only mean that neurophysiologists are not interested in the niceties of a distinction between a duality of physical modes versus a duality of access to the physical. More worrying is the thought that, ultimately, it might not make much sense to speak of correlating two forms of access. For correlating a subjective access with an objective, or 'scientific', access, so as to lay open for all to see that there is a double access to one and the same physical analogue brain process, seems only to be possible in regard to token–token correlations. For, from the point of view of what is actually happening at the level of brain functioning, there does not seem to be anything like a stable analogue brain record or processing pattern, say pattern 235, which is always activated in the same way, cell for cell, whenever I have a sensory experience of, say, a red tomato. What the brain does seems to be very labile and shifting and transient, at least when compared with the stability of

---

[3] In regard to the distinction between 'type–type' and 'token–token' correlations and identities, the reader should refer to Ch. 5 n. 2.

our sensory experiences as reported by the subject of them. So such momentary token–token correlations will never really satisfy serious 'correlators' and so serious 'dual accessors'.

Finally I am not too sure whether, in regard to intentionality, much of importance hangs upon my taking the duality of physical modes path rather than the duality of physical access pathway. So for the moment, at least, I shall hang on to my inclination towards the former.

NATIVISTS, EMPIRICISTS, AND EVOLUTIONISTS

My immediate problem here is to explain how an organism with conscious sensory experiences can find a way of associating these sensory experiences with the environment which gave rise to them. In short, how do we ever come to *know* that our sensory experiences are *of the world outside* and so employ them as guides for making our way in the world?

There are two traditional answers or solutions to this problem. The first of these, the nativist solution, says that we are born with innate categories or concepts, and that included among these is something like a concept of 'outsideness' or objectivity, in terms of which even a newborn infant must interpret its sensory experiences. The second of these solutions, the empiricist one, says that we acquire this sense of the objectivity or 'outsideness' of our sensory experiences along with the having of our first sensory experiences. Sensory experiences arrive hallmarked with 'from the outside' on them or, rather, as part of their qualia or phenomenal content.

My 'bottom-up' strategy as regards intentionality clearly leads me to reject the nativist solution. For, in modern terms, and in the context of naturalizing intentionality, the nativist account means going the way of brain representations, or languages of the brain, or 'mentalese', or their cousins or in-laws. As I endeavoured to argue in a detailed way in the previous chapter, a foetus in the womb, or a newborn infant, or a fully grown human (or a dog or frog for that matter), in so far as it has a brain, possesses the intentionality that all brains possess. I described such intentionality in terms of analogue transformations which give rise to analogue impressions or records which carry information. However, since analogue brain records are not maps or representations of any sort, they neither receive nor stand in need of interpretation. They embody information without representation. They do not fall foul of the problem of how a brain might interpret its own representations. The 'aboutness' of such brain records is the same aboutness as that possessed by any other naturally occurring, causally produced analogue record or impress, such as a footprint.

It follows from that account that, initially, all sensory experiences or sensory outputs possess a similar level of intentionality as do the analogue brain records which are the covariant causes of those sensory outputs. That is, it follows—as effect follows cause (in this case in the form of yet another analogue transformation process)— that sensory experiences themselves are also analogue records. They are not, of course, analogue impresses or records in wet sand or in the electrochemical activations of cell networks. They are analogue records in the physical mode, or stuff, we call 'consciousness', which, I suggested, is best construed as a result, or product, of our brain's processing.

Our ordinary term for these product analogue records, 'sensory experiences', seems as good as any. For if, as I have argued, our brains are made up of analogue systems (albeit with the occasional deployment of 'thresholds' or binary 'gates' that may make some analogue records more determinate), then the end-points or products of the workings of any such systems—including the sensory ones of sight, hearing, taste, and so on—unless we have independent grounds for positing a shift to representations proper, must also be analogue impresses or records. The outputs, or products, of, say, our organs for hearing and tasting, when they are functioning properly, are best construed as sensory experience records which mirror in a causally covariant analogue way what has come into the system, whether this be mediated by sound-waves (as in the case of hearing) or chemicals (as in the case of taste). This seems to make sense. Sensory experiences of green reflect in an analogue way features of the environment as delivered by light-waves reflected back from those features and stimulating our visual system. Sensory experiences of red reflect in an analogue way different features of the environment, though still mediated by light-waves being reflected back from those features and striking our visual systems.

In short, for what seems to me to be good reasons, my account has turned its face firmly against the nativist position. Now I have also come to think that the orthodox empiricist solution must be false as well, though I have to confess, somewhat shamefacedly, that I had accepted a modern version of that story for some time. It went something like this.

Let us take it, as some developmental psychologists aver, that it is a fact that the earliest sensory experiences, even of a foetus, are experienced by the experiencer as from the outside. If the nativist picture is untrue, then it can only mean that the 'otherness', or 'coming-from-the-outside-ness', of sensory experiences must be part of their qualia. For there is nowhere else to look.

Another way of putting this is to say that, in explaining how we come to think of our sensations and perceptions as 'of the world', the empiricist says that we must be able to do so without reference to anything other than these sensory experiences themselves. It must be the case that the one 'housing' the sensory information, that is, the one 'giving a home' in consciousness to the analogue record which any sensory experience is, im-mediately (without mediation) experiences the 'aboutness' of that information, even if only in the most embryonic way. In turn, this immediate experience must be part of the phenomenological content, or qualia, of the experience itself, for it cannot be found anywhere else.

The above, it now seems to me, amounts to just a modern version of the seventeenth- and eighteenth-century empiricist account of how sense impressions differ from ideas. The former were held to be stronger and more vivacious and more vivid and of greater intensity than ideas. That is, their status, as being 'from the outside', as being received impressions or object-imposed sensory impresses, had to be part of their qualia.

I think that both the old and the modern versions suffer the same fate. Such phenomenological qualities as vivacity or intensity or vividness cannot really tell us that what is in conscious sensory experience is 'from the outside' rather than from memory or imagination. It is no improvement to add, as does the modern version, that, in some unexplained way the knowledge that sensory experiences are caused by objects or events 'outside' is not an inference from vividness or vivacity or intensity but is itself a phenomenal quality. That just seems less philosophically honest than the old version. It seems like sleight of hand. If you cannot infer the 'outsideness' from other qualia, then say it is itself a quale, and so no inference is required.

So what can be done? Where can I go now? My solution is that there is a *tertium quid*, there is a third possibility. The path, I believe, again lies in terms of evolution. Indeed this is a place where I think the biologizers should be heard.

In more detail, the answer lies in seeing that, of course, something must be innate, if sensory experiences are to be successful in guiding our way in the world 'outside'. But for that to happen, you do not need innate *concepts* or *hypotheses* or *representations* or *languages* or anything like that. They are more than you need. All you need, in terms of innateness or predispositions or 'hard-wiring', is that a foetus or newborn infant, or for that matter a frog or gnat, *act in the appropriate way* when it receives stimulation to its sensory systems from the environment; that is, that a foetus or infant act in response to a sensory experience in a way appropriate to its being *truly* a sensory experience. All you need is, that the foetus or infant act in a way that reflects the fact that sensory experiences are usually the result of some stimulation to the sensory system by something in the external environment. But the foetus or infant or frog *does not need to know this* in the sense of having a concept about it. The first actions of a foetus, such as turning its head towards a sound, or the first actions of a newborn infant in turning towards the light are probably as automatic and tropic, behaviourally speaking, as the actions of a snail retreating back into its shell when you touch its slimy antennae with your finger.

I am not denying that it is on the basis of this sensory-experience-leading-automatically-to-behaviour-directed-to-the-source-of-the-sensory-experience, that is, on the basis of an input-directing-output tropic 'loop', that our eventual concepts of 'object' and 'outside' are formed. *But the actions come first, the conceptualization comes after*, probably a long time after, when we have learned some language. If a frog can get by without concepts, then a foetus, and probably an infant, can. An infant probably has no concept of 'outsideness' or objectivity; then again, it probably has no concept of 'not outside' or 'wholly internal' either. Who needs such excess baggage, if you can travel without it? Who needs such baggage if your simple sensory experiences and behaviour appropriate to them delivers all you need in the external world, though you do not know about externality and internality?

This way of dealing with the old nativist versus empiricist confrontation seems to me to be in keeping with my bottom-up strategy. With a bottom-up strategy the rule should be 'Push everything as high up as possible'. With a top-down strategy the rule seems to be 'Push everything down as far as possible', that is, pack as much as you can into brain-level processing; that way you do not have to explain much at the other, higher levels. If the brain is already a language user, then explaining how someone with a brain is a language user is a push-over.

To recapitulate, the first step, the 'loop', is innate and placed in us, in our biology, by evolution and shaped in us by our individual maturation. Conceptualization, on the other hand, is up to language. We share these basic, innate, biologically embedded, behaviour-appropriate-to-sensory-experience 'loops'—though not the exact same ones, for evolution changes things as well as carries them forward—with most, if not all, of the other organisms. But that is no scandal. That is just how things are. Primitive sensorimotor responses go all the way down the (non-plant) organism branches of the evolutionary tree.[4]

In the rest of this chapter I want to make out, in detail, a case that a new level of intentionality, or more accurately new levels of intentionality, arise on the back of this loop, and can do so without recourse to concepts of any sort (including those of objectivity and externality). For in the next sections I am going to investigate the possibility that it is the ability of the subject of sensory experiences to associate, in a single tranche of awareness, a sensory experience, first with behaviour (picked out in a sensory way), then with other sensory experiences, that produces new layers of intentionality. Towards the end of this chapter I shall argue that one of these new levels of intentionality, in so far as it becomes entangled with conventions, might be seen as the precursor of the intentionality of language.

I shall endeavour to put some factual flesh on my abstract outline of the nature of these new levels of intentionality (that go beyond the level of intentionality shared by all analogue records) by borrowing unashamedly from the work of developmental psychologists.[5]

---

[4] I have wondered whether Colin McGinn (1991, ch. 2) might not be an adherent of something like the account I have just sketched in. I should add that, while I have come to differ from McGinn on this issue, I have found the above chapter of great help and very stimulating.

[5] I have depended heavily, in regard to work in developmental psychology, on Mandler (1990), Maurer and Maurer (1990), Slater (1990), Bower (1982), Piaget (1955, 1977, 1980), Cohen (1979), Kagan (1972, 1979), Luria (1976), and Bühler (1930).

As I mentioned at the beginning of this chapter, I do this as a heuristic device which may prevent me from inventing capacities we do not have. My examples, thereby being truer to the facts, will be less liable to spoil my bottom-up strategy. However, I must admit that, after reading at some length in developmental psychology, I became rapidly convinced that it is a subject in which there is still a great deal of disagreement. In consequence, it is very hard to give an uncontroversial overview of any stage of child development. One definite thing that did seem to emerge was that, since Piaget, there has been a concerted movement in the direction of placing the cognitive skills of infants at ever earlier points. Another was that developmental psychologists are now very wary of carving out Piagetian stages or phases defined in temporal terms. So my examples of the nature of early sensory experiences, and of early behavioural performances, taken from developmental psychology, will be hedged in with such locutions as 'almost certainly', 'maybe', 'there is something like agreement that' and 'perhaps'.

THE LAYERED INTENTIONALITY OF BEHAVIOURISTICALLY INTERPRETED PRIMITIVE SENSORY EXPERIENCES

If I am to make good my case that, while the brain has only low-grade, uninterpreted, analogue record intentionality, higher grades of intentionality begin with sensory experiences, then I am confronted by another very fundamental problem. For if I hold, as I do, that our sensory experiences are also no more than analogue records of certain features of the world around about us, then it looks as if the intentionality of sensory experiences must remain locked in at the same ground level of intentionality as that of the brain's analogue processing. In this section and the following, I will try to show how, through an association with behaviour or with other sensory experiences in more complex memory-enriched sensory experiences, base-level sensory experiences become the building-blocks for higher levels of intentionality.

In this section I want to argue that we make the first step up the intentionality ladder, or move a step along the intentionality continuum towards the sophisticated end, when we consider cases where a sensory experience is inductively combined with behaviour by the person having the sensory experience rather than merely 'wired in' biologically to the behaviour. I am going to suggest that, while it is too early and inappropriate a stage to speak of the interpretation of content and so of representations which stand in need of interpretation, I believe that something which is a forerunner of interpretation is going on. But let me again put this in terms of a concrete example.

First let me sketch in some general background about human development. It can be said that there is something like agreement among developmental psychologists that a foetus in the womb, at least by the last few months of pregnancy, will begin to receive some stimulation of some of its sensory organs. Of these senses, hearing is probably the most developed because the most stimulated at this stage. Even while floating in the uterus's amniotic fluid, the foetus is surrounded by a variety of sounds, though these are damped and dampened in various ways. For a foetus lives in a pool in the midst of its mother's vital organs. It is surrounded by the throbbing of the heart as it pumps blood around its mother's body, by the squelches and gurgles of her digestive system and of the peristaltic action of her intestines, and by the breathy heavings of that twin bellows we call the lungs. In a muffled way, almost certainly (though no one can be sure) the foetus hears the sounds of its mother's voice and footsteps as they vibrate internally in the bones and cavities and fluids of her body. Finally the foetus may hear some of the sounds from the environment, such as from events in the room or street or wherever its mother happens to be.

At least towards the end of pregnancy, during the last two or three months, a foetus also probably experiences some feelings and some tastes. The foetus can and does move its limbs about and bump into the walls of the uterus and feel some of the outside pressures on its mother's stomach. There will be embryonic and not very fine-tuned feelings from all of these sources. The foetus will also take into its mouth some of the amniotic fluid and so its taste buds, though not well developed, are likely to receive some stimulation from that source. However, since the cerebral cortex is not well developed (in regard, for example, to memory), there may be few lasting impressions from any of these sensory events. Most of the impressions that do occur may be very fleeting.

Let my particular working example be that of a foetus in the womb that hears a dampened throbbing sound, like 'gluph duph, gluph duph'. This is my attempt to give a muffled foetal version of the traditional medical lecturer's 'glub dup' account of the sound of heartbeats. In this case the heartbeats are the mother's. Moreover, the 'gluph duph' sound should be taken to refer specifically to a heartbeat which is quicker than normal, say caused by the mother's movements or other exertions. (For, of course, while she is still alive, the mother's heart is always beating.) Now this sound in the foetus's ear will exhibit the first, analogue record, level of intentionality in so far as it has a causal link with the input of pressure waves in the amniotic fluid caused by the mother's heartbeat, and in so far as its auditory system is working normally. That is 'gluph duph' is analogically true of or true to some properties of the pressure waves and so in turn to their source.

However—and this is where the second level of intentionality begins (that is, the first step up occurs)—the sound of 'gluph duph' may lead, at least eventually, to the foetus reacting in a certain way whenever it hears the sound. Let us say that the foetus 'swims' in the amniotic fluid, or at least changes its position, so that its head is towards the upper side of the womb closest to where its mother's heart is beating faster than normal. Moreover, after a trial-and-error period, it does that whenever it hears 'gluph duph'. Let us suppose that it does so because it obtains some sort of comfort (or, at least, some dissipation of the discomfort of being moved about as a result of its mother's exertions) by getting closer to the source of the increased rhythmic pressure waves in the amniotic fluid.

Now consider an occasion in the life of the same foetus when its mother, while lying down on a couch, absent-mindedly drums her fingers on the lower part of her stomach near the lower end of the womb. The foetus hears this drumming as 'gluph duph' or as something approximating reasonably closely to this. As soon as it hears this *faux* version of the sound, let us say that it had been asleep, the foetus migrates in the usual way to the upper corner of the womb where its mother's beating heart is located.

If it is fair to say that our sensory systems are there to help us find our way in the world, and that this directional role is part of their evolutionarily proper function, then the foetus has got it wrong in the second case. It has been fooled. The embryonic mapping function it learned for 'gluph duph' has misled it this time. It has *misinterpreted* the sound in that, on hearing it, it went to the usual spot in the upper corner of the womb nearest to its mother's heart. Because it makes sense to employ an attenuated usage of the term 'misinterpret' in this context, and to apply it to the subject of the behaviour, so it makes sense to employ the word 'interpret' in the same context, albeit, again, in an attenuated sense of the word.

Of course, as adults, we engage in and may need to engage quite frequently in a sophisticated and non-attenuated version of the interpretation of sounds. If you are a soldier, it is important to know where the sound of gunfire is coming from, to give it a direction, not just to know that it was 'from the outside' and so not a figment of your imagination. This directional ability gains further employment with the onset of language. It is important from the point of view of communication to know who it was that spoke, that is from what direction you are being spoken to.

However, I do not want to get ahead of myself at this stage. For my basic point in this section was that even to learn to turn one's head towards a sound, or in some other behaviouristic way to manifest a learned response to a sound, is to add a new layer to the intentionality of sensory experiences. But how can this be explained at the 'nitty-gritty' level, without reference to concepts?

To return to our example, what registers 'on the inside', so to speak, in the foetus's head, is not easy to construe. But I do not think that anything like concepts need be brought in. For concepts are not the only way to 'hold in mind' things which can be used for guiding action in the future. Things can be held in perceptual memory, and used as a guide for future action. Though we can only guess at what goes on in the mind of a foetus or newborn infant, the following may be a plausible, non-conceptual scenario.

Movements, of the head or limbs, involve proprioceptive feelings, that is feelings (conscious registerings) of the movements of the muscles required to move the head or limb. If a foetus moves in a certain direction, then *ipso facto* that movement involves feelings. If the scenario is that the foetus has moved closer to the source of a sound, its mother's increased heartbeats, then here, with the felt movement, we have a second sensory something. If moving towards the sound brought comfort, then this can be construed as a third sensory something. The latter may amount in this context to a feeling of sensuous pleasure, associated with the feel of the rhythmic pressure waves resulting in the amniotic fluid from the heartbeats.

Now if the foetus comes to associate in memory the sound of the heartbeats with the proprioceptive feelings which accompany its movements, and with the ensuing feelings of bodily pleasure, then the foetus has set up a simple, inductively induced, sensory experience *conjunction*. A conjunction of sensory experiences 'made fast' in memory is not a concept. But it is doing a similar task to a concept. Its being held in *memory* provides the glue that holds together the pieces of the action-guiding 'loop'. This conjunction of sensory experiences can then be cued for use by the input segment of the loop. When the foetus again hears an increased level and frequency of the sound of its mother's heartbeats, then, prompted by memory, it may move about till it brings itself closer to the pleasurable (at least in the sense of comforting) heartbeats. Its memory for the proprioceptive feelings which accompanied the successful movements last time will probably be the intermediate link in the memory loop between the conjoined memories of the initial sound and of the ensuing comfort.

From the outside, from the point of view of an observer, it is still the old biological loop sound plus movement. From the inside, however, in the arena of sensory experiences, things have changed. Things have become much more complicated. Via the growth of memory, the 'insider', or subjective, conscious version of the loop has taken over. The loop has passed from being purely innate and biological to being grasped in sensory experience. It has come out of its purely biological closet. It has entered a new arena. A new sphere and type of intentionality have appeared.

THE INTENTIONALITY OF AN INFANT'S ASSOCIATED SENSORY EXPERIENCES

In the last section I argued that, when we investigated the earliest deliberate movements of a foetus, and took into account 'the conscious and so subjective point of view', a new and richer layer of intentionality showed itself; that is, a layer richer than the 'aboutness' of pure brain analogue records which carry information about the environment (or, for that matter, the analogue records of *isolated* sensory experiences). This richer layer involved one sensory experience, via memory, acquiring a behavioural accretion, and in that sense only being 'interpreted' by the foetus, whose head 'housed' the sensory experience, in a behaviouristic way. Of course, it is possible that a foetus could have evolved such a primitive perception-to-appropriate-response loop in a non-conscious, purely biological way. Some animals lower down the evolutionary tree may indeed operate in this way, perhaps most if not all the time, and most creatures probably operate via such non-conscious loops some of the time. We call the latter subliminally triggered reflexes. But the point is that, whether we like it or not, we humans have evolved so that, for much of the time, and for better or for worse, we have to respond via conscious perception. No one, at least certainly not I, is saying that evolutionary developments are *ipso facto* better than other possible developments, or necessarily constitute 'progress'.

Now, in this section, I want to introduce a case of sensory experience intentionality, where the person who has the sensory experiences is not involved in a behavioural response. The loop, in a sense, is simpler. It involves one sensory experience being given significance by its being associated with another through some learning process. Yet, as we shall see, from the point of view of the possibilities opened up, it is a much more important form of intentionality.

I will illustrate this in terms of infancy this time. Choosing an example from infancy may help to offset any objections of the form 'You have attributed to a foetus powers that some developmental psychologists say they just do not have' or 'Putting it in the context of a foetus stretches credulity'. In addition, I take my examples from infancy because it is easier in that context to graft on, in a gradual or developmental way, some subsequent points about slightly more advanced forms of sensory experience intentionality.

Initially, in this section, I want to suggest that the association-of-sensory-experiences intentionality must involve both the ability to separate off one sensory experience from another, and then the ability to combine them and operate them in parallel. This latter ability must involve some 'reason' for selecting these experiences, rather than other ones, for putting together. In this section, I want to argue also that even this sort of complex sensory experience intentionality does not involve representations.

But before getting on to discuss some examples in detail, let me once again dip into developmental psychology in order to sketch an outline of the sensory life of early infancy.

As soon as a baby emerges from the womb into the world of separate existence, its senses are suddenly flooded with stimulation. In particular the baby experiences light for the first time, and sight gradually emerges as the dominant sense. Even though a newborn baby's visual system is immature, it reacts to light. The newborn baby will squint as it is dazzled by even ordinary levels of room lighting. On the other hand, the other senses are also subject to a massive bombardment of stimulation. For a newborn baby not only experiences a wider spectrum of temperatures than it did in the womb, it is also the subject of greater amounts and different types of movement and feeling. It is picked up and hugged and felt and prodded and tickled. As regards sound it hears voices and other sounds 'in the raw' for the first time, that is no longer from within the protection of the womb and its submerged world.

As, roughly speaking, there can be no maturation without stimulation, a baby develops continually and with great speed as a result of the bombardment of the senses which has greeted its emergence from the birth canal. In fact, as regards the newborn baby's own experiences, it seems initially to have sensations and not much more, for it is not yet able to make anything out of its sensations except in a fairly primitive behaviouristic way. We have seen that an infant is probably born with the capacity to separate itself from the world, at least behaviourally or in action. On the other hand the newborn baby's sensory experience might still be described as being somewhat like (to use Hume's description) 'a bundle of sensations'. This 'bundle of sensations' should not be confused with a *mélange*, however, for the newborn baby probably can separate reasonably clearly one sort of sensation from another.

Somewhat paradoxically, not merely does an infant sharpen its ability to separate its sensations, it also gains the ability to operate its sensory systems together or in parallel. This ability, of course, has many uses . For example, it enables an infant to begin to engage in finely tuned purposeful behaviour. For merely to move a hand to grasp something (which, recall, was a massive leap forward in the evolution of the primates) requires eyes to work in tandem in order to see in proper focus both the object and one's hand, and one's hand in relation to the object. Grasping an object also needs these visual experiences to work in tandem with a proprioceptive system to feel the tension and movement of one's own muscles in order to control the grasping movement, and with a sense of touch to know when one has contacted the object or bumped into some obstacle, and a sense of balance to maintain a body posture throughout the operation of grasping an object with one's hand.

In terms of a different, simpler example, I want to argue that this growing ability to operate its senses in tandem or in parallel enables an infant to attain to the intentionality of imbuing one sensory experience with the significance of another sensory experience. For with the ability to operate sensory systems in parallel there comes in addition, via an ever stronger memory, the ability to link or associate sensory experiences in a quite secure and long-term way. Let us say that an infant has a present (occurrent) visual experience of a coloured something (it is of a blue bowl, seen initially from the side, as its mother is bringing it over from the kitchen work-surface to the infant's high chair). This visual experience recalls a second sensory experience, a taste (it is, in fact, the taste of the same sweet baby food that the infant's mother has placed in the bowl every day for the last three weeks . For the mother has won a month's supply of Cow and Gate apple and banana purée in her local supermarket's free draw). In the infant's consciousness, the sight of the blue bowl carries with it, more or less instantaneously, in a *Gestalt*, the taste of apple and banana purée.

Of course the infant does not see the blue bowl 'as a bowl' or taste the food 'as apple and banana', much less as 'Cow and Gate apple and banana purée', for it has no language and so has no concepts.[6] It cannot see things in that sophisticated, language-based, adult way. But it can associate sensory experiences, and so enrich the one with the significance of the other. We should probably say, also, that the infant cannot anticipate the taste of apple and banana whenever it sees the blue bowl, for anticipating probably only applies, strictly speaking, to the ability to represent to oneself a future state of affairs. This an infant clearly cannot do. But one sensory experience regularly calling up another, via memory, does seem to be on the same continuum as the later sophisticated propositional attitude called 'anticipating'.

On the other hand the infant would suffer what we adults call disappointment, if, say, its mother, in a fit of absent-mindedness, put the blue bowl down in front of the child without having remembered to put the apple and banana purée in it. The child puts its fingers in the bowl and then puts its finger in its mouth. No taste,

---

[6] It would take me too far afield to argue for the 'no language, no (proper) concepts' axiom. It is certainly a common view to hold. For example, in Flew (1984) 'Concept 1' is defined as 'That which a person has when he understands or is able to use some portion of his language'. 'Concept 2' is even more linguistically circumscribed, being defined in terms of predicate expressions.

except that of finger, follows. The child wails. The mother realizes what has happened, and so on. In some primitive sense of these terms, the child can be said to have been misled by its visual experience of the blue bowl or to have misinterpreted its visual experience of the blue bowl.

It would be wrong to explain or interpret this phase of sensory experience intentionality, just because it is now in the context of infancy, in terms of representations of any sort. The visual experience is not a representation or symbol of the taste to which it is habitually linked. There is nothing conventional about the link between the two, because there is nothing public about it, and so nothing agreed about it. There is, for example, no forum in which the link could be corrected or adjusted by someone else. It is not even a private representation, for there is no episode of 'Let the one be symbol for the other', on the part of the infant. The visual experience is not a representation of anything. The visual experience is just itself, a visual experience. It is imbued with meaning for an infant only in the very primitive sense that, via the power of association and then recall, it has been hooked up with another experience, in this case a taste. If you hanker after some jargon, then in this context an infant's visual experience is more like a 'concatenation of presentations' than a 'representation of one thing by another'. Or, if you prefer something with a more literary flavour, it is 'a Proustian association'. It is the taste of the madeleine calling up instantaneously another sensory experience with which it has become inextricably linked. It is one sensory experience cueing the recall of and so a renewed presentation of another previously contiguous sensory experience. This cueing is automatic or purely causal. Depressing the pedal of a piano dampens the sounds generated by the vibrating wires of the piano. My knowing this does not make the sight of the pedal into a representation of the sound of a damped chord. It may, on the other hand, by simple association always call to mind the sound of some particular damped chord, though, in an adult, this is unlikely.

To return to our earlier example, some sort of selection must have gone on. Otherwise why is the visual experience of the blue bowl linked with the taste of apple and banana, rather than with the sight of the cat? For the cat always comes around at any feeding-time, no matter who is involved, in the hope of picking up a tasty snack. The answer, I presume, must be in terms of the first link involving a distinct and strong pleasure for the infant, while the second does not do so, at least not to the same extent. So the link or chain between the visual experiences is fashioned by an ensuing state of pleasure. Eating the apple and banana is very pleasant, at least if you are very young and very hungry. Seeing the cat, although also a pleasant thing, does not quite compete. Habituation is a function of pleasure in this case, not mere association.

The important point is that it does seem very plausible that the linking of the sight and taste is made possible by a link at the same sensory level. For a baby's consumption of its food is likely to be sensory, if not sensual as well. While it is not really our concern here, it is interesting to speculate that such links, via the medium of pleasure, and in consequence ensuing desire, may amount to the primitive beginnings of our value systems.

INTENTIONALITY GOES PUBLIC: THE WAY FORWARD

I have called this section 'Intentionality Goes Public'. Perhaps I should have given it the title 'Intentionality Goes Fully Public', for, of course, even the intentionality built upon the association of sensory experiences had some public aspect to it. For quite often the sensory experiences involved would have been perceptual ones of publicly observable objects or events. However, it was not essential to that level of intentionality either that the sensory experiences be of publicly witnessable objects or events, or that the sensory experiences be shared. This new level of intentionality is different precisely because it is based on an association or link which must be public and shared.

Let me put this another way. So far in this chapter I have discussed a number of ways of filling in the basic 'aboutness' relation which involve sensory experiences. The first involved a very primitive sensory experience (a sound heard in the womb) being given significance and so content by becoming associated or conjoined with a sensory experience of a behavioural response (the proprioceptive feelings of a movement in a particular direction in the womb) and a sensory experience of some upshot of that movement (a feeling of bodily pleasure). The second involved the association of two sensory experiences by an infant. It was an infant's version of the Proustian taste of the madeleine calling up from memory some other associated experience. While both these ways of filling in the aboutness relation were on the same level, namely the first level up from brain-level intentionality, they were importantly different. For the second way laid the groundwork for a new level of intentionality.

Now, in this section, I will outline a new, third level of intentionality. Just as what I called 'sensory experience intentionality' involved a jump up from purely brain-level intentionality, so this first form of public, and conventionally governed, intentionality involves a distinct jump up from merely sensory experience intentionality. It is also important in another way. It is the bridge between prelinguistic and linguistic intentionality, though this level itself remains prelinguistic.

This new, third level of intentionality, at least in its completed form, involves the aboutness relation being filled in, on the one hand, by a learned, shared, conventional activity, a deliberately uttered sound, and, on the other, by some shared, publicly witnessable perceptual experience or group of perceptual experiences. That is the reason why this new level of intentionality might be said to be the bridge between clear cases of prelinguistic intentionality and clear cases of sophisticated adult intentionality involving the use of language, concepts, and thought. Put more starkly, this level of intentionality might be viewed as the beginning of the end of infancy. For, of course, the word 'infant' means 'non-speaker', and is derived from the Latin 'in' meaning 'not', and 'fans' which is the present participle of the verb 'fari' meaning 'to speak'.

The cases I have in mind are ones where an infant first witnesses its mother, or someone else, deliberately conjoining a deliberately uttered sound with some indicated and publicly witnessable and so shareable object or event; and where the child is then coached or coaxed into imitating this conjoining of deliberately uttered noise and shared public event, or else the child is smart enough to learn to do this by itself.

Some non-human animals also seem to have learned to do this. For a zoologist might witness the following scene. One monkey is heard to make a barking sound, like 'Rark! Rark!' Another monkey, on hearing that sound, is seen to run high up into a nearby tree. It repeats the cry of 'Rark! Rark!' made by the first monkey. Other monkeys now join it up the tree or up a nearby tree. Some moments later a leopard appears. The sound 'Rark! Rark!' has communicated something to other monkeys in so far as it has been linked in some way with 'leopard approaches' or, at least, with something more amorphous which might be described as 'moving-object-of-a-certain-size-and-shape-that-inspires-fear approaches'.

Now it is time to try to elucidate this new level of intentionality in the context of human infancy. The sounds 'Bye-bye!', said by Mummy, may eventually be associated in the infant's mind with the sight of Daddy going out the door in the morning or, more strictly, with the visual experience of a large shape, with a certain smell, and making certain familiar noises, moving in a certain direction. Next, spontaneously or as the result of coaching, the infant may take to joining in the chorus of 'Byebyeing' in the morning. Even if its version is a fairly poor imitation, and comes out as 'Ba-ba!'

The *first significant step forward* is taken here, when the infant is witness to a conjunction of experiences where *the conjunction is dictated by someone else.* The infant is witness to and so shares in a sound being constantly and deliberately conjoined by someone with a sight (or a shared auditory experience being deliberately linked by someone with a shared set of visual experiences). The *second significant step* here is that the infant gives up the role of being just the passive recipient of or captive witness to this associ-ation of sensory experiences. It *takes on the active role of being a producer* in respect to one of these experiences. It joins in the task of deliberately making noises at such a time and in such a context, where the noises are deliberately and frequently juxtaposed in space and time with, and so linked to, the shared visual experiences. The infant produces a sound which, though the infant itself does not know it, is a kind of proto-speech. It has become an utterer of sounds with significance, even if its performance in that role is crude. The *third significant step* here is that the process of learning to conjoin a deliberately uttered noise with a shared public sensory experience has a *conventional slant* to it. The noise is one that the infant finds already in use in its circumscribed speech community. Furthermore, the infant's 'Ba-ba!' is done in imitation of the sounds which are already in use. It is done, say, in imitation of the mother's or grandmother's or child-minder's 'Bye-bye!' What is more, these attempts at imitation are subject to correction. So the infant's 'Ba-ba!' is a conventional act because it involves imitating a sound which is already in use for communication in that circumscribed speech community where the imitation has been produced in a coached-and-corrected and so rule-governed way.

However, I think that there is *yet another significant step* being made here by the infant. I think that the infant is genuinely engaging in *an act of communication.* In some embryonic way these 'Ba-ba!' sounds have been uttered in order to have significance for another person. The utterance is coached so as to be reasonably clearly articulated and out loud. Part of the process of learning is learning to get it right. Another part of the process is learning that it is a noise that is directed to another person, and is aimed at being given 'uptake' by that person. Thus, when the sound is uttered, not merely in the right way, but also at the right time and in the right context, it receives a response. Someone replies with a series of 'Bye-byes!' It may also elicit warm approval: applause and hugs and smiles, or in general positive reinforcement.

The infant can in fact communicate useful information with its proto-speech. Let us say that the mother is in the lounge, the father is just emerging into the hallway from the bedroom, and the infant is crawling along the hallway. On witnessing its father doing all the things he does when he gets ready to leave the house by the front door, the infant utters the sounds 'Ba-ba!' The infant's mother comes from the lounge, notes that in fact her husband is about to leave the house, and says to him, 'I didn't know you were going out today. I thought you said you were staying at home to work on your speech to the Rotary Club.' The mother has learned something she did not know.

I think that at this level of intentionality there is a different and more complex sense of 'getting it wrong' or 'misinterpreting' at work. The process of getting it wrong has also become active and public and part of the learning process itself. Now it is not simply a case of an infant being fooled or misled. It is a case of an infant mis-signifying or actively making a mistake, and being corrected, and then having another shot at it. There is a deeper sense of getting it wrong on offer because there is a deeper sense of getting it right involved. Because the intentionality involved is complex, the 'getting it right' is comparatively sophisticated, and it can go wrong in more than one way. To take some examples: In the early stages of learning to link the uttering of 'Ba-ba!' to Daddy's disappearing out the front door, the child might utter these sounds when Daddy comes in the door at night. Initially and mistakenly the child has linked the sounds to the act of someone coming through the door in either direction. But even when the child has more or less learned that

'Bye-bye!' is for departures only, it can still get it wrong. For it can misread the signs of departure. Daddy has put his coat on but he is not leaving the house. He is simply cold because the central heating has failed. Then the child can get it wrong in the reverse direction so to speak. It can interpret someone else's 'Bye-bye!' incorrectly. Because the person concerned had a Belfast accent, the child might not recognize 'Baye-baye!' as a version of 'Bye-bye!', and so might not respond in the usual way with its own 'Ba-ba!'

However, I do not think that the infant's use of such sounds as 'Ba-ba!', in imitation of its mother's use of 'Bye-bye!', amounts to the employment of words. For it is only at a later stage in a child's development that it can be said to use the sounds in a way which demonstrates that *it understands them as words*. This stage is probably signalled by a child's correct use of the uttered sounds 'Ba-ba!' not merely when its father leaves the house in the morning but also when the visitor leaves in the afternoon and grandmother leaves in the evening. I think that this is so even if it has got to the stage of getting it right on most occasions when Daddy leaves the house. It seems still to be a stage short of the real thing. Because its words, such as 'Ba-ba!', are still used in a partly personal and private way, as meaning something like 'Noise for when Daddy leaves the house' (when this is shorn of any conceptual contents involving the concepts of fatherhood, departure, and domicile).

Whether the sounds 'Ba-ba!', as uttered by the child, are representations or not I find difficult to decide. Certainly, being on the way to becoming words, these sounds are on the way to becoming linguistic symbols and so linguistic representations. My own inclination is to say that, while the child's sounds 'Ba-ba!' are not yet linguistic representations, they might deserve the status of a more primitive sort of representation. For example, we might think of the utterance 'Ba-ba!' as in some sense 'standing for' Daddy's departure if the child utters it *some time before* Daddy departs in the morning. That is, the sounds 'Ba-ba!' have some sort of separated or independent life, so that it could be said that they have achieved the status of standing proxy for something not merely beyond themselves but absent. Let us say that it is a bank holiday, and Daddy does not have to go to work. Not knowing about bank holidays, the child starts uttering the sounds 'Ba-ba!' while Daddy is still in bed, trying to have a sleep-in. Here the child seems to be using the sounds 'Ba-ba!' to signify something which is not merely beyond or separable from itself but something not even immediately conjoined to it in space-time. The uttered sound is doing something like standing public proxy for a Daddy-departure.[7]

In attempting to put some analytical structure on to this important phase, when intentionality first goes public, I did make use of the notion of imitation. I spoke of an infant imitating the sound made by its mother when she said 'Bye-bye!' Quite likely such an infant would also be involved in imitating the hand-waving that often goes along with saying 'Bye-bye!' In addition, such an infant would be involved in imitating the timing of an adult employing the sounds 'Bye-bye!' The infant learns not merely how to say 'Bye-bye!' but when to say it and in what context. So, you might now say, is not imitation, or mimesis, to use an older term, a form of representation?

My response is that only some sorts of imitation involve representation. Or, to beg the question momentarily, only representational imitation involves representation. Thus, if I produce, with a palette of oil paints, a mimetic version on canvas of what I now see out the window, then I am producing in two dimensions a representation of the real three-dimensional thing. However, if I copy your hand-waving in the sense that I wave farewell back to you as you depart, then I am reproducing in the same dimensions, and with more or less the same materials, and with more or less the same purpose, more or less the same motions. There is no real waving goodbye or original production of 'Bye-bye!' of which these are only representations. All genuine wavings goodbye and sayings goodbye are equally real. Just as one glass made by a factory from the same mould is as genuine as another glass made from the same mould, so my waving goodbye or saying goodbye is as genuine as any other

---

[7] The literature of developmental psychology sometimes refers to these 'proto-concepts' or 'preconceptual conceptual equivalents' as 'image schemas'. Thus Mandler writes 'that image schemas—notions derived from spatial structure, such as trajectory, up–down container, part–whole, end-of-path, and link—form the foundation of the conceptual capacity [of an infant]. These authors suggest that image schemas are derived from preconceptual perceptual structures, forming the core of many of our concepts of objects and events and of their metaphorical extensions to abstract realms. They demonstrate in great detail how many of our most complex concepts are grounded in such primitive notions. I would characterize image schemas as simplified redescriptions of sensorimotor schemas' (1990: 242). In particular, Mandler refers to the work of Lakoff (1987) and Johnson (1987). On the other hand, this material should be balanced with material which suggests that an infant's 'concepts' may be more innate and less dependent upon sensorimotor trial-and-error learning than we think. See Spelke *et al.* (1992).

product from the same conventional linguistic mould. Because an infant's version of a wave or of saying goodbye comes out imperfectly compared to our adult versions does not make it into a representation. It is like a glass with a flaw in it. Real and genuine but imperfect. Besides, in linguistic communications, we have a much greater tolerance towards imperfections than do glass manufacturers. We put up with a foreigner's saying 'Baiye-baiye!', 'Bawbaw!', and 'Beh-beh!' Given that the accompanying hand-wave is reasonable, and the context right, it does not really matter much.

SOME BRIDGING REMARKS

In Chapter 6 I attempted to make sense of the hidden world of brain-level intentionality. In this chapter I attempted, first, to make sense of the move from the world of brain-level, analogue record intentionality to the world of sensory experience intentionality. As a crucial step in this move, I argued that one had to make sense of how it is that we come to experience our sensory experiences as 'coming from the outside'. I argued that this could be achieved without falling into either the traditional nativist accounts or into the traditional empiricist accounts. I suggested that there was a third alternative, an evolutionary-cum-biological account. Then, by means of examples taken from the life of a foetus and of an infant, I tried to tease out and to explain the role of the various factors involved in sensory experience intentionality. Finally, again drawing examples from early infancy, I attempted to explain the important bridging step from a human's prelinguistic life to a linguistic life; that is, the stage of intentionality when it becomes public and conventional.

These stages are a philosopher's stages, of course, not those of a developmental psychologist, though they draw, with gratitude, upon the work of developmental psychology. They are a philosopher's stages because they are generated solely as an analytic or explanatory aid. They are an attempt to separate things off from one another and in so doing to make matters clearer, philosophically speaking. They are not an attempt to carve out stages in the maturation of an individual foetus or infant, psychologically speaking. In real life, two or more of my stages or phases may be indistinguishable to the developmental psychologist. Or else, because of my particular narrow interests, which *ipso facto* take no account of developments in other aspects of an infant's life, they may be quite useless from the point of view of developmental psychology.

In this chapter, as part of my overall bottom-up strategy of showing how one can get from analogue record, brain-level intentionality to the sophisticated intentionality of the propositional attitudes, I have tried to show that consciousness, in the form of sensory experiences, is the essential bridge or link. In the last section of this chapter, I drew attention to a particularly important plank of this bridge, namely the point at which intentionality went fully public. That discussion will also serve as a bridge to the next chapter. For in that chapter I shall discuss the intentionality of the propositional attitudes. For these attitudes are individuated and attributed only by linguistically endowed, reasonably adult humans, and in all sorts of ways are shot through with language and concepts. But I shall argue that our propositional attitudes are not just features of language. I shall argue that they are real, macro, intentional features of persons, but ones which are reducible neither to brain-level intentionality nor to the subjective, semi-private intentionality of sensory experiences.

8

An Adult's-Eye View of Intentionality

PUTTING PROPOSITIONAL ATTITUDES IN THEIR PLACE

In Chapter 6 I suggested that one reason why the problem of intentionality has proved so intractable might be that the would-be problem solvers have assumed that intentionality is to be found in just one place (or, at least, that real intentionality is). In consequence, a lot of recent discussion of intentionality has started where I think it should end. For, in seeking to give an adequate account of intentionality, very often recent philosophers have sought to give such an account via a consideration of what they assumed were the core cases of intentionality, namely beliefs and desires and, to a lesser extent, other cognate intentional acts such as hoping, wanting, wishing, and so on. In making this choice they focused in turn on the time-honoured workaday expressions for our beliefs, desires, hopes, and other cognate cognitive and appetitive states. Thus the problem of intentionality came to be accepted as the problem of giving an adequate account of those mental acts which we describe by means of such expressions as 'He believes that it is now raining', 'She wants to open the window', and 'He hopes that the train will be on time'.

Some believed that the typical grammatical features of such everyday expressions (namely, a verb drawn from our large vocabulary for describing cognitive and appetitive mental acts, and either a that-clause or an infinitive phrase governed by the verb) gave vital clues to the nature of human intentionality. These grammatical commonplaces were believed to mirror the real psychological facts whereby humans take in information through their sensory systems and then, with faculty-like modules, operate over the information in such a way that this new information can be combined with old, and conclusions drawn, or decisions taken to act in the light of the conclusions. The that-clauses and the infinitive phrases of our everyday psychological descriptions represented information taken in by our sensory systems and then processed into capsule form. The cognitive and appetitive verbs in the same descriptions represented our mental acts of taking up various attitudes to the resulting information bytes or capsules. These allegedly real psychological facts, mirrored by the grammatical features of our propositional-attitude expressions, were then variously placed in the brain (the most popular location) or in the world of phenomenological experiences or in some, far from obvious but nevertheless real, intermediary domain. Alternatively, some philosophers, who started from the same place in their endeavours to give an adequate account of the intentionality of mind, despaired of there being any real psychological facts mirrored by the grammar of our ordinary propositional-attitude talk, and suggested that all there was to intentionality were certain grammatical features and a certain quotidian usefulness for expressions with such features.

In Chapter 6 I argued that we should start from a different point if we were to give an adequate account of intentionality. To put it another way, if, instead of beginning with this ancient and by now rather stale diet of our adult linguistic expressions for our beliefs and desires and the other propositional attitudes, we sampled items from a different menu, we would have a much healthier view of intentionality. For what I recommended in that chapter was that we should start where intentionality itself begins. We should employ a 'bottom-up' strategy. We should start first with the foundational, non-propositional, analogue intentionality of the brain, then move to a consideration of a foetus's or infant's first conscious intentional episodes, for both of these pre-date anything we feel inclined to describe as language-based, propositional-attitude intentionality. For the brain's information-processing analogue record intentionality is the necessary first step. It is the stage at which information from outside is brought into the human organism.

In Chapter 7 I argued that the basis of the equally important next steps or levels was the creation of a forum for processing that foundational, purely analogue information into something more complex. This forum, I suggested, is one of the brain's own products, consciousness. For in consciousness are to be found the products of the brain's processing of inputs to the sensory systems, namely our sensory experience analogue records. I then argued that these sensory experiences, whose action-guiding powers can be explained in a way that avoids the nativist–empiricist dispute, are the first step in the ascent to sophisticated, language-based intentionality. By being combined in various ways, with behaviour and with other sensory experiences, these purely analogue sensory experiences begin the long climb upwards to real representational intentionality.

Now, in this chapter, I want to discuss this top-level, sophisticated, representational intentionality which is connected, in an intimate but highly layered and complex way, with our propositional-attitude talk. However, I am not going to say that this sort of intentionality is just a feature of language, nor am I going to say that it can be reduced to states or processes of human brains, nor am I going to say that it is just a feature of consciousness. How can this be?

THE INTENTIONALITY OF THE LINGUISTIC VEHICLE OF OUR PROPOSITIONAL ATTITUDES

In this section I want to get out of the way, though not pass over, the four types of intentionality associated with our attribution of the propositional attitudes to one another *in so far as such attributions involve linguistic expressions*. These types of intentionality are real but they are not the deepest level of intentionality which I believe is to be found in connection with the propositional attitudes. The intentionality I will be discussing in this section is a combination of the intentionality of language itself, the intentionality of the peculiar expressions we have generated for attributing the propositional attitudes to ourselves and others, and the intentionality which, though generated by the grammar of our propositional-attitude expressions, goes beyond purely linguistic intentionality.

The Intentionality of Linguistic Symbols

Our ordinary intentional talk—our attribution to ourselves and others of the propositional attitudes ('I believe that . . .', 'She hopes that . . .', 'They desire that . . .')—in the first instance, is intentional in the way that any linguistic *representation* or *symbol* is. For the canonical expression of the propositional attitudes is the linguistic attribution of them to ourselves and others. A representation or symbol is intentional in a rule-governed way. I cannot apply the word 'dog' or the symbol '$' just in any old way I like. It is not up to me, an individual, to give it meaning. I share in the meaning it has in the community I am in. If I misuse the word or symbol, sooner or later I will be corrected either verbally or in some other behavioural way. Though there may not be an agreed definition of 'dog' and '$', there are agreed limitations on their use. There may not be rules about their use to which I could refer, but their use is nevertheless rule-governed. Their use is governed in a more oblique way, by the response of the speech community in which I employ those words or symbols. So their meaning, their 'aboutness', is not arbitrary but conventional.

The Intentionality of the Grammatical Forms Employed in our Attributions of the Propositional Attitudes

There is another, still comparatively minor and linguistic, sense in which the propositional attitudes are intentional. This might be called a grammatical form of intentionality. For the usual grammatical form of our propositional attitude attributions is that of a verb that governs or operates over either a propositional expression of some content (a that-clause) or an infinitival one (a to-phrase). Thus we say 'He believes *that* so-and-so' or 'She hopes *to* such-and-such'. What follows the 'that' and the 'to' (the *so-and-so* and the *such-and-such*) are what gives a content to and so completes the attitude. It does not make sense to say 'He believes' in the way it makes sense to say 'Elvis lives' (excepting where 'He believes' is elliptical for 'He believes in God'). The description 'He believes' is essentially incomplete as an expression. It is content-hungry. We have to say *what* he believes. We have to say something such as 'He believes that it will rain tomorrow' or 'He believes Elvis is still alive and hiding in Tennessee', or at least give some other filling for the 'content gap' in the linguistic expression of our propositional attitudes. Thus, we might put it, the very language we use to express our attributions of the propositional attitudes to ourselves and others is a language of contents and of attitudinizing over them. This in turn means that our beliefs and other propositional attitudes are held to be essentially 'about' something and so intentional in that grammatical sense as well.

The Intentionality Arising out of Content Expressions which Have no Referents

However, there is more to this grammatical form of intentionality. It shades off into what might be called two aspects of *logical* or *sense and reference* intentionality, for there is an intimate logical and semantic link between the governing verb and the particular expression that has been chosen as the description of the content. The first of these two sorts of sense and reference intentionality is connected with the content–object distinction. For it can happen either that the content of a propositional-attitude expression no longer exists or that it never existed, yet the propositional attitude remains intact.

I might believe that the former President of the United States, Lyndon Johnson, is still alive and in retirement in Texas. In fact, he is dead. But my belief is perfectly genuine. For the contents of beliefs are independent of their having a referent in the world of space-time.

The contents of beliefs and other propositional attitudes are also independent of their referents ever having existed in the world of space-time. I might believe that Homer was a great poet. But it may be the case, as some scholars say, that there never was a single person who was a poet in ancient Greece, wrote the *Iliad* and the *Odyssey*, and bore the name Homer.

The contents of beliefs are even independent of whether or not the believer knows they have no referent in space-time. He can believe, perfectly legitimately, that Estella was cruel to Pip, while either knowing or not knowing that Estella and Pip have no other 'existence' than as characters in the novel *Great Expectations*.

This independence of content from object gives the contents of our propositional attitudes the status of having an 'aboutness' which is 'inesse' (or 'existing in') and so internal to the propositional attitudes themselves. That is, the aboutness is internal to the attitudes themselves which underlie the expressions of the propositional attitudes. This is the first level of propositional-attitude intentionality which has crept beyond being a purely linguistic feature of the expressions of those attitudes. The next sort of intentionality shares in that characteristic.

The Intentionality Arising out of the Interplay of the Sense and Reference of Content Expressions

This variety of sense and reference intentionality is tied more closely to the sense and reference distinction itself, though it still arises out of the fact that the contents of our propositional-attitude expressions are individuated in terms of their sense rather than in terms of any objects or events to which they might refer.

When we say 'She believes that the man in the corner has a roving eye', then we are saying that what she believes is *only that which is captured by* and so *meant by* (in the sense of being patent in terms of the usual 'face value' sense and reference of) the expression 'the man in the corner has a roving eye'. We must not extend the content of her belief beyond that. We ourselves may know a lot more about the person picked out by the descriptive phrase 'the man in the corner with the roving eye'. We may know that he is the President of Global Financial Services and has been married three times. However, from this, it does not follow that *she* believes that the President of Global Financial Services has a roving eye or that the man who has been married three times has a roving eye. For she may not know what we know. If we have grounds for saying of anyone 'She believes that p', then it does not follow (it is not logically legitimate) that we can substitute for p, in the expression 'She believes that p', any expression, say q, which has the same referent but a different sense.

THE PERSPECTIVAL INTENTIONALITY OF OUR PROPOSITIONAL ATTITUDES

In this section I want to take a further, more determined step away from associating the intentionality of our propositional attitudes merely with linguistic or quasi-linguistic features. For I think that there are a number of ways in which our propositional attitudes are intentional in a deep, non-linguistic way. The first of these ways I will call 'perspectival intentionality' for reasons which will become obvious soon enough. I choose to deal with it first, because it is closely allied to, and seems to underlie, what I have just discussed under the label of 'sense and reference intentionality'. It also seems to have priority in another sense, namely that this sort of intentionality clearly grows out of the previous, sensory experience stage of intentionality.

Oftentimes our core cognitive propositional attitudes, namely of knowledge and belief, are clearly built on a necessarily limited perceptual foundation. For our perceptual grasps of the world around us are *ipso facto* on the basis of limited, slanted, perspectival 'input'. We only confront the world, its objects, and events as contained and *limited by the senses* we have, and so by the particular views or perspectives or slants or viewpoints which the context and our perceptual powers allow us.

Even in the crudest form of this, we are limited to a front view of someone or a side view or a back view. We cannot, usually, have all three. So my belief that she was unmarked by the accident may result from my seeing her head-on, and not being able to see the bald patch and big scar at the back of her head. So I might exhibit these limitations very clearly when I come to manufacture second-order beliefs about that woman. I might, for example, come to believe that the person who was luckily unscarred by the accident was the one who got top marks for the last essay. At the departmental meeting, however, it might be announced that the woman who was severely scarred by an accident got top marks for the last essay. I might dispute this and only then learn that my belief about who was top in the last essay, and the Head of Department's belief about the same matter, in fact 'home in on' the same object or target.

This perspectival aspect of our knowledge and beliefs can arise in less crude ways, and in ways which do not depend on a slanted sensory viewpoint giving rise to false beliefs. It can arise in regard to the perspectivity of our *conceptual* grasps of things. For, in a real sense, our conceptual knowledge is just as perspectival as our sensory knowledge. I might grasp something under one sort of conceptual scheme or description but fail to realize that another conceptual categorizing, which someone else employs, is an equally valid conceptual grasp of that person or thing. So I might not be able to put one conceptual grasp and another together, in order to generate a more rounded state of knowledge. I know Fred quite well and know that he is a former fighter pilot. You also know him quite well, but in a different context. You know him as the last man, except for his assassin, to see Trotsky alive. So I am quite excited when you tell me that, on Sunday, when I come to lunch, you will introduce me to the last person, except for his assassin, to see Trotsky alive.

When I come to lunch, and you introduce me, with a great flourish, and with proprietorial pride, to old Fred, I am bitterly disappointed. Neither my grasp of Fred (as a former fighter pilot) nor yours (as the last person, excepting his assassin, to see Trotsky alive) are based on immediate sensory knowledge by acquaintance of what was expressed in the descriptions under which our beliefs were formed. Nevertheless, our beliefs are still firmly circumscribed, and so perspectival in that sense. What is more, they can both be true. When we get knowledge 'about' anything, it is always about a bit of that thing. At times a good bit, but still always just a bit.

Part of the full understanding of our *other* propositional-attitude expressions, that is, those other than the core cognitive ones of knowledge and belief, will involve realizing that they are attributed on top of or on the basis of an assumed or presumed cognitive content. They are built on top of knowledge or belief. Thus to love or hate, or to desire or have an aversion for, or to hope for or despair about, and so on, is to take up an attitude to someone or something *as known or believed to be so-and-so*; that is, as known or believed *under a certain limited slant or description*. I love Mary Lou as the most generous person I have ever met. You know that she has starved her children, thrown her aged and paralytic mother on to the street, and then sold all her mother's possessions so as to keep herself in the manner in which she would like to grow accustomed. I love Mary Lou because I know of her generosity towards me, but know little or nothing more about her. Indeed my love might cease if it were less perspectival and slanted. Perhaps a lot more of our numerous, second-level, propositional attitudes would suffer a similar fate if we were omniscient.

THE DISPOSITIONAL INTENTIONALITY OF OUR PROPOSITIONAL ATTITUDES

I will call this, the deepest sort of intentionality associated with the propositional attitudes, 'dispositional intentionality'. I give it this title because it involves realizing both that our propositional-attitude attributions are dispositional attributions, and that, ultimately, dispositional attributions are to be understood as the recognition of the existence of what I shall call 'whole-person intentionality' or 'holistic aboutness'. To put this another way, when we observe, or learn of, or at least guess at the 'environmental input' to a human (that is, what he or she sees or hears or . . . in general, notices, albeit in a perspectival way) and then note the 'behavioural output' (that is, what that same person does, or, in general, how he or she responds), we go on to summate or round up the results of this observation in a conceptual-cum-linguistic way. We try to make sense of that person in terms of whole conceptual segments or parcels of such input and output. We try to take an overview and describe what we think that the observed person was 'about', rationally and conceptually speaking, when producing such outputs in the light of such inputs. We say 'He believes in God' or 'She hopes to be an architect' or 'He fears death' or 'She is afraid of enclosed spaces'. We are describing what whole tracts of that person's life *mean* to us sophisticated, concept-using observers.

In the context of brain-level intentionality, we saw that the basic intentional relation '*x* is about *y*' involved *x* being an analogue brain record, while *y* was the causally covariant source of that analogue record in the environment. In the context of infant sensory experience intentionality, we saw either that both the *x* and *y* were both sensory experiences or that *x* was a sensory experience while *y* was a piece of behaviour, including quasi-linguistic behaviour. With regard to the intentionality of linguistic or other representational systems, we saw that the *x* was some symbol or representation, and that *y* was some object or event or activity in the world, or perhaps some concept, picked out by the symbol or representation. Now, with dispositional, propositional-attitude-expressed intentionality, the *x* is the *person as a whole* who has been observed to perceive, or is presumed to have perceived, certain aspects of his or her environment (i.e. has a certain sensory input) and who has been observed to act or react, or to have failed to act or react, in a certain way (i.e. has a certain behavioural output). On the other hand, *y* is the reality underlying the linguistically and conceptually expressed dispositional interpretation of what that person was 'up to' or 'about', when responding in just those ways in just those contexts or environments. With our talk of the propositional attitudes we are saying what whole persons are about.

I have called *y* the 'reality underlying the dispositional interpretation'. I might just as easily have called it the 'reality underlying a conceptualization of what a person is about'. For the 'interpretation' is also the conceptualization of what we think non-infant humans (and sometimes infant humans) are doing. For, in a charitable way, perhaps, we assume that, in what humans are doing, they do not merely act purposively and deliberately, but they also act rationally. All this we express in a very sophisticated and precise and highly conceptualized vocabulary. This vocabulary, in turn, is nothing other than our talk about beliefs, desires, hopes, wants, and all the other items in our propositional-attitude linguistic storehouse.

DISPOSITIONS AND OCCURRENCES, AND SOME RELATED DISTINCTIONS

I have just suggested that underlying our propositional-attitude attributions is the deepest sort of intentionality which arises in connection with the propositional attitudes. I referred to this intentionality as the reality underlying the dispositional interpretation of what that person was 'up to' or 'about'. To make sense of these claims, I need to say something about the nature of dispositions and dispositional attributions.

I will begin on this task by bringing forward a well-known and well-used philosophical distinction. The distinction I have in mind is the *occurrence–disposition* attribution distinction.[1] I can attribute to someone or something that he (or she or it) is occurrently undergoing or engaging in something, or currently exhibiting some ability or capacity. Contrariwise, I can attribute a disposition to someone or something; that is, I can say that he (or she or it) is not now acting or reacting in a particular way, but that he (or she or it) is prone or liable or disposed to act or react in a particular way, if certain specifiable circumstances occur in the future. Both kinds of attribution, occurrent and dispositional, are considered in this section as literal attributions, not metaphorical ones (though, as we shall see later, there are metaphorical versions).

If I say that this cow is walking about, or is now chewing grass, I am making an occurrent attribution. For I am saying of this cow that, here and now, such-and-such is occurring. On the other hand, if I say that the cow is nervous, I may only be making a dispositional attribution in regard to it. I may only be saying what the cow is liable or prone to do, if certain circumstances occur. From observation of

---

[1] For further discussion of the nature of dispositional attributions, see William Lyons (1980, ch. 4).

the cow over a number of weeks, I may form the opinion that she is nervous, because whenever any other cow comes near her, she jumps up, bellows, looks agitated, then runs off in a skittish way. She is not now jumping up, bellowing, looking agitated, or running away in a skittish manner, but is quietly chewing her cud. Nevertheless, she is still nervous. If I say that the same cow is also a haemophiliac, I am attributing a proneness or capacity or disposition which may *never* have been activated or displayed in any way so far, and may never be so in the future. The vet may tell me that to be a haemophiliac is to possess blood which lacks the clotting agent that helps to stem blood flow from a wound. After examining my cow he may tell me that it lacks that clotting agent and so is a haemophiliac. He is making a dispositional attribution and a literal attribution. But this particular disposition (to bleed without the blood being able to congeal) may never be activated or displayed in an occurrent way. My cow may never yet have been wounded and may die without ever having been so. Or the vet may have given the cow medicine that counteracts its haemophilia.

Sometimes the occurrent–dispositional distinction is glossed by means of another distinction, the *categorical–hypothetical* distinction. For to attribute a disposition to someone or something is to state, at least by implication, what would happen or fail to happen *if* certain specifiable circumstances obtain. In that sense a dispositional attribution is a hypothetical claim. It is alleging that such-and-such will happen *if* . . . Occurrent attributions, however, attribute actions, reactions, and inhibitions, and so on, with no *ifs* or *buts* about it. That is, such attributions are categorical. A claim is being made about some present occurrence.

Of course, dispositional attributions are closely connected with occurrent categorical attributions, not just contrasted with them. For a dispositional attribution could be described as a hypothetical attribution of a categorically occurrent something or other, or a series of them. A dispositional attribution could be described as saying *what would occur* or is likely to happen, occurrently and categorically, if certain background conditions and environmental conditions ever obtained.

Dispositional attributions are also either *determinate* or *determinable* ones. To attribute a determinable disposition is to attribute a disposition or proneness to act or react in a particular determinate way. Being a cigarette smoker is a determinate and so single-track disposition. You can only be truly described as a cigarette smoker if you are prone or liable to do something very definite and circumscribed, namely smoke cigarettes. On the other hand, being thought to be vain is to be the subject of an attribution of a merely determinable and so multi-track disposition. It is not clear, just by attributing vanity to some person, exactly what that person is liable to do. Some vain people may spend a lot of time in front of a mirror. Others may always want to be photographed in a certain light and from a certain direction. Others may refuse to venture out of doors unless they are replete with make-up, styled hair, and a costume they have not worn previously. And so on. There is no telling exactly what a vain person might do or refuse to do, or in what way they might act or react, but we have a rough idea.

SOME DISTINCTIONS IN REGARD TO THE 'CATEGORICAL BASE' OF DISPOSITIONS

Dispositions are not just hypothetical, lawlike generalizations produced on the basis of noting behavioural output in the light of contextual-cum-perceptual input. There is an internal factor, or a lack of some factor, at work. This factor, or absence of factor, is sometimes called the non-dispositional 'categorical' basis of dispositions. Thus the categorical basis of haemophilia is the absence of a clotting agent. The categorical basis of fragility in Venetian glass, that is of its disposition to break when let fall from even a moderate height or when tapped even lightly, will be its physico-chemical (probably crystalline) molecular structure.

The dispositions picked out by propositional attitudes must also have a categorical base, otherwise they would not be dispositions. Just as there must be something or other (even if it is 'an absence') in a haemophiliac that makes that person different from a non-sufferer from haemophilia, similarly there must be something in a person who believes in God which is absent in the case of someone who does not.

However, things are much more complicated than that. And I want to explain these complications in terms of two new distinctions about the categorical bases for dispositions.

Single versus Multiple Categorical Bases for Dispositions

Let us say that a simple type of sea anenome, call it the 'Sea Zombie', is rather 'behaviourally challenged', even by sea anenome standards. It just opens up like a flower and then closes. It opens up when the right sort of nutrient is present in the sea around it; it closes when it isn't. It can do nothing else. It just sits there, on its rock, patiently waiting to perform its simple role.

Let us say, also, that the internal causal condition for this opening up, when suitable external environmental conditions obtain, is a single simple array of seven interconnected nerve-cells. Indeed any and every Sea Zombie will be found to have this same cell arrangement which plays exactly the same role of opening and shutting its flower-like food absorption apparatus. The disposition of the Sea Zombie to open its apparatus in conditions C, and to close them in conditions C^*, has a single, identifiable, internal, categorical base.

Let us now take the case of a 2-year-old infant's action of picking up a spoon. We observers, from the outside, describe this as a single action, and so the disposition to do it as a single determinate disposition to grasp spoons. Here the categorical base is most unlikely to be simple or single in number. For to grasp something, even for an infant, will involve the activation of a whole series of systems. It will involve the infant's capacity to focus its eyes on the spoon, the infant's capacity to move its arm, the infant's awareness of the movement via its proprioceptive feelings, the infant's awareness of where to place its arm in space, the infant's capacity to close its fingers in a grasping movement, the infant's capacity to feel when it has grasped something, and so on and on. What, on the surface, had been described as a single disposition to do so-and-so, is seen, now, after a look inside and underneath, to involve the causal mediation of a large number of categorical bases for what, in reality, are a large number of dispositions, all working in the right order and in a co-operative way.

What has been described, from the outside, or observer's point-of-view, as a single disposition to grasp spoons has turned out not to have a single categorical base but a multiple one.

Stable versus Fluid and Unstable Categorical Bases for Dispositions

Let us say that the categorical base for the opening and closing of the Sea Zombie's feeding apparatus is quite stable. That is, when the Sea Zombie opens and closes its feeding apparatus on Monday, and then again on Tuesday, and yet again on Wednesday, the seven exact same cells, in just the exact same configuration, and in just exactly the same co-operative way, are active. We might even find that all Sea Zombies, not just the one we are observing, have a similar set of seven cells arranged and operative in exactly the same way. Such a categorical base would be a stable one.

Now it may turn out that, after investigation, we find that the categorical basis for the opening and closing of an elephant's mouth is an arrangement of cells. But, in this case, we might find out, to keep it simple, that on Tuesday the set of cells which causally engineered the opening of the elephant's mouth was different from the set of cells that performed the same function on Monday. Not merely were there seven cells in operation on Tuesday but seventeen in operation on Monday, it was also discovered that the seven in use on Tuesday only overlapped as regards two cells with those in use on Monday. What is more, this fluid use of cells was common to all elephants in regard to the opening and closing of their mouths. By merely knowing that some elephant had opened or closed its mouth, you could not predict which set of cells, or how many cells, had been in operation.

Such a categorical base would be described as fluid and unstable. Furthermore, the unity and stability implied by our outer, macro description of some elephant as closing its mouth, is not mirrored by what is happening at the micro level of the internal causal activity of its categorical neural base. The macro level of description is thus not always a good guide as to what is happening at the micro level. Our maxim here might be Goethe's saying '"State" is a foolish word, because nothing stands still and everything is in motion' (letter from Goethe, 23 November 1812, quoted in Reed 1984: 53).

PROPOSITIONAL-ATTITUDE ATTRIBUTIONS AS ATTRIBUTIONS OF MULTIPLE, AND FLUID AND UNSTABLE-BASED, DETERMINABLE DISPOSITIONS

By means of a few examples I want, now, to make it clear that the attribution of propositional attitudes is the attribution of not merely determinable rather than determinate dispositions, but of determinable dispositions with multiple and unstable bases.

When we attribute a propositional attitude to someone we know the sort of thing that counts as evidence for and the manifestation of that attitude, but we do not imply thereby that there is just one precise activity that must occur in the defining circumstances. Even a quite precise and clearly defined propositional attitude, such as, for example, a hope that it will not rain tomorrow afternoon between three and four o'clock, is a determinable disposition. For my expression of the belief that you have this hope will not be an indication to someone else of exactly what you may have done or said (which were my grounds for attributing to you this hope), nor will it be an indicator of what exactly you will do in the future (when the specified circumstances, namely between three and four o'clock tomorrow, come to pass). You may, of course, have said to me, 'I hope that it will not rain between three and four o'clock tomorrow'. However, you may not have said anything to me or to anyone else. But I, and the other schoolteachers at Ballysaggart Primary School, may have seen you look at the weather forecast for tomorrow in the local newspaper, and then heard you announce that the prize-giving ceremony would take place outdoors, in the school grounds, between three and four tomorrow afternoon.

When it is five past three tomorrow afternoon, and the rain pours down, again there is nothing definite (or determinate) that you must do as a manifestation that you had indeed hoped that it would not rain between three and four. On the other hand there is a wide set of things from which your behaviour is likely to be drawn. You might say something like 'Damn! It's raining. I was hoping it wouldn't', or just say 'Damn' and then announce that the prize-giving will now take place in the assembly hall. If you are of a stoical temperament, however, you may just look heavenwards, smile to yourself, and make the announcement about the change of venue in a slightly world-weary voice. If you are from the opposite end of the personality spectrum, you might throw a tantrum, drop everything, go home, take to the gin bottle, and make out a rough copy of your resignation letter to the Department of Education.

To take another example, when I say of the vicar that he believes in God, I am not claiming that he is going about mumbling to himself 'I believe in God', or that he has in his stream of conscious experiences an item which could be labelled 'believing in God'. I should not be claiming either of these things because, among other reasons, I can legitimately attribute a belief in God to the vicar, when he is asleep or when he is absorbed by the television broadcast of the women's tennis final at Wimbledon, and even if he has never ever said the words 'I believe in God' to himself or to anyone else. Certainly the vicar, on a suitable occasion, perhaps when provoked by the village atheist, will display his belief in God for all to see. He may then say, with vehemence, 'I believe in God', or go down on his knees whenever the village atheist passes by, and in a stage whisper beg God to forgive the atheist his unbelief. But he may do neither of these things, but do something else which is revelatory of belief in God.

Because propositional attitudes, such as a hope that it will not rain tomorrow afternoon between three and four o'clock and a belief that God exists, are determinable or multi-track dispositions, it is unlikely that the underlying categorical bases for propositional-attitude dispositions are going to turn out to be single or stable. This unlikelihood is increased when we reflect that the brain has literally billions of cells and more than enough to get by with, even if we never ever used the same cell twice. What is more, since the brain is the product of bit-by-bit evolution, and not the result of some single design or production process, it has not been engineered for simplicity or neatness. A human can do things, from the point of view of the brain, in a number of ways and frequently does. So it seems that, in regard to our propositional attitudes, the simplicity of our expressions of them is not mirrored at the micro level. Hoping or believing, for example, are never going to be reducible to some single, stable, neuronal something-or-other.

On the other hand, it does not follow from this that our beliefs and hopes and desires and intentions, and other propositional attitudes, are reducible to the surface reality of their linguistic expressions. Indeed this is not the case. Our propositional attitudes are real pronenesses of ours to act or react, or fail to act or react, in various ways. It is the purpose of our rich, heavily conceptual, and so culturally shaped, adult vocabulary of the propositional attitudes to reduce the multiplicity and variety of the resulting human behaviour to manageable proportions. At a macro level, with our cultural and conceptual, and so linguistic, 'eye', we discern, and so parcel up and label, whole segments from this multiplicity of human actions and reactions. In so doing we are using our skills of conceptual ordering to reduce the potential chaos of this teeming multiplicity and variety into something neat, usable, and useful; into something of use for the important task of explaining and predicting and so making sense of one another. The results we call our common-sense, or folk, psychology. The acquisition of this folk psychology, in turn, provides us with the means of ordering our own lives better. We not merely learn to make sense of what other people do, we make what we ourselves do seem more sensible as well.

THE CAUSE–GROUNDS–NATURE DISTINCTION IN REGARD TO A PROPOSITIONAL ATTITUDE SUCH AS A BELIEF

In the last few sections, I have been focusing a great deal on the expressions of our propositional attitudes, and how we come to attribute them to one another, and how they are attributions of a very complex and unstable sort of determinable disposition. It is now time to speak more ontologically and make absolutely clear what my view is about the reality underlying our linguistic expressions of the propositional attitudes. For I have said that this is the deepest sort of intentionality associated with the propositional attitudes. I called it the 'aboutness' of whole persons, as distinct from their brains or conscious experiences. I will endeavour to do this in terms of a distinction between the *cause of a belief* (that is, the way a belief might be generated), the *grounds on account of which we come to attribute beliefs* (that is, the grounds or evidence on the basis of which we attribute a belief to ourselves or others), and the *nature of beliefs* (that is, exactly what beliefs are).

The Cause of a Belief

The cause of a belief can be practically anything, from hypnosis, via a blow to the head, to the most sophisticated deductions of the finest informal logician. The cause of a belief is anything that can give rise to or generate a belief. Such causes, of course, need not be known to the person to whom the subsequent attribution of a belief is made. Even when the believer thinks that he (or she) knows the cause, he may be mistaken. For the subject has no privileged access to the cause of his own belief.

My belief that earthworms are dangerous may have arisen because of a childhood trauma. I was playing with earthworms when the nasty man who lived next door did something terrible to me. I now have a phobia about earthworms, but I have no idea how it arose. I have long ago repressed what knowledge I had of the cause of it. That is why I am undergoing therapy with my local psycho-analyst or psychotherapist.

But I might never have known the cause of my belief that earth-worms are dangerous. I may have a pathological fear of them be-cause they resemble snakes, in shape if not in size, but I have never been aware of this connection. It has embedded itself in me, surrep-titiously, so to speak. It has crept up on me unawares.

Then again I might be a rather poor amateur zoologist who has not studied his textbooks very carefully, and so quite openly, from a mere scrutiny of a few pictures of earthworms, and after noting their likeness to certain very small and very dangerous South American grass snakes, come by simple and fallacious reasoning to the conclusion that earthworms are highly dangerous.

It is this very fact, that beliefs can be caused in a myriad of ways, only one of which is by means of careful observation and careful reasoning, that makes the belief-based mental disorders so hard to cure. To get rid of the disordered belief, such as a paranoid one, or to get rid of the disordered belief which in turn has given rise to a disordered evaluation which, say, is at the heart of some affective disorder, such as a phobia, then one has to try and work out how these disordered beliefs were caused, and only then try and undo the damage.

The Grounds on Account of which we Attribute Beliefs

We attribute beliefs to others 'from the outside', in much the same way as we attribute other dispositions. We make these attributions on the basis of evidence. In the case of beliefs, it will mainly be contextual and behavioural clues. Sometimes the clues are more circumstantial than immediate.

I might attribute to my wife a belief that I, her husband, am an inconsiderate person, because of certain things she has said and done in the past. On the other hand, none of these things may include the uttering of a sentence such as 'You are an inconsiderate person' to me, or the uttering of a sentence like 'My husband is an inconsiderate person' to some third person. My wife may never even have said to herself, in her head, 'My husband is an inconsid-erate person.' No such linguistic expression of the propositional attitude as applied to me may exist or have existed anywhere or at any time. The evidence upon which I base my attribution to my wife, of a belief that I am an inconsiderate person, may be much more amorphous and indeterminate. She may, for example, have once said of Mr Bentley, who lives next door, on hearing that he was late home one night when he said he would be home early, that he was an inconsiderate man. Again I might know that she adores my father, who is known in his neighbourhood as Mr Clockwork, because of his extreme punctuality, and hear her talk about him as a most considerate husband. The evidence may be quite circumstantial.

Now there is an asymmetry in regard to the grounds on the basis of which others attribute beliefs to you, and the grounds on the basis of which you attribute beliefs to yourself. On the other hand, this asymmetry is not one of direct, internal, causal link to beliefs on your part, while I and others have only circumstantial grounds for attributing beliefs to you. Rather it is that you have a direct internal route to *one sort of evidence* which others cannot directly tap into. You are the possessor, the only possessor, of your internal conscious life. So you are the only one who has *knowledge by acquaintance* of any conscious deliberations or ruminations or day-dreams or wishful thinkings or plans of action which go on in your head. Only you, in other words, have access to your very own interior life.

But this 'special access' should not be misunderstood. It is only access to a different sort of evidence for a belief, not direct access to a belief. According to my account a belief is not the sort of thing to which you can have direct access anyway. It is not 'in the head'. Indeed it is not an occurrent something or other at all. It is a disposition, which in turn is what is picked out by a very complex, macro, from-the-outside, summatory type of factual claim about the actions and reactions of oneself or others, in a certain context or contexts, according to the conventions of folk psychology, and over time. This will be clearer if we reflect that our own attributions to ourselves, on the basis of our own interior lives, can be mistaken and can be corrected by others. We have no privileged access to our own beliefs, only to *one sort of evidence* for them, albeit a powerful sort.

But let us see this point by means of examples. I might believe that I am a very liberal person. In my 'heart of hearts', that is, in my conscious ruminations about myself and my life, and my social conscience, I might think of myself as being without any racism about any race whatsoever. In the sixties I might have marched with the civil rights marchers, and worn civil rights badges, and joined civil rights societies. Nowadays, whenever I think on these matters, I say to myself, in my own head, in my own language, and with my own vocabulary, 'Whatever else I am, at least I am not a racist.'

Nevertheless, I might be mistaken about this belief of mine. I might be racist (I might, for example, believe in the inferiority of black people) and not realize this. Though others might. They may notice that, nowadays, thirty years after the great civil rights marches, I always criticize the performance of black baseball players but rarely do so in regard to white baseball players. They may notice that, as I travel about New York, I always speak of black neighbourhoods as 'run down' and 'unsavoury', but never use these adjectives of white neighbourhoods no matter how run down and unsavoury they are. And so on and so forth. Even when the grounds are pointed out to me, I may refuse to see them. I may refuse to acknowledge what the evidence points to. For, in my interior life, which safeguards my self-concept, it is unthinkable.

Of course, it could be the case that I am in possession of the *only* evidence available about some belief of mine. I may never have spoken to anyone about my views about my great-uncle, who died many years ago. And there may be no one alive who can recall what I said or did in my great-uncle's presence. In short, there have been no publicly available clues as to my beliefs about my great-uncle. So I might attribute to myself a belief that my great-uncle was a most patient and kindly man, solely on the basis of what, in the privacy of my own ruminations, on this particular day, I think I am recalling about my great-uncle. I might, then, for the first time ever, say, out loud, publicly, 'I believe my great-uncle was a kind and patient man.' No one can have grounds for contradicting me. But I could still be mistaken about my own belief. For privileged access to some evidence is not privileged access to all possible and relevant evidence. For unforeseen circumstances could arise which reveal in me a different attitude to my uncle, a different disposition. A sudden mention of his name a month later, in a certain context, might make me blurt out and so make manifest evidence of a completely different attitude to him. I might be caught unawares and say, 'He was really a mean old bugger who put on a saintly air.'

To say that the attribution of a propositional attitude to oneself can be wrong is not to say that self-attribution and other-person attributions are on an equal footing. For it follows from the point I am emphasizing—that saying to oneself in one's head, or saying about oneself out loud, that 'I believe that so-and-so' or 'I hope that such-and-such' are just attributions (although, if correct, also expressions)—that there is *some privilege for the self* in regard to self-attributions. For my interior life is only open to me, and this interior life—of my conscious experiences or states—is one source of evidence for making a correct attribution to oneself of propositional attitudes. If I think a lot about the wickedness of humans but never say so out loud, then I am in a better position to describe myself as believing in the inherent wickedness of humans, or as being a misanthropist, than are others.

To sum up, privilege in this context merely means possessing the sole right of access to one sort of evidence, one's own conscious states. There is no privileged access to the truth about our own propositional attitudes. Furthermore, our sole access to one sort of evidence, our own conscious states, must be balanced by our tendency to be biased in favour of ourselves. For the fact that most often we like to think of ourselves in a good light (and it is arguable that it is psychologically dangerous to do otherwise; see Lyons 1986: 142 ff.) will mean that we engage in a certain amount of bias in favour of ourselves. We are more likely, for example, to attribute considerateness to ourselves than inconsiderateness, and more likely to attribute to ourselves a belief in the equality of all races than the opposite, because that is how nowadays most people would like to think of themselves.

There is an additional aspect to this sole right of access which we have to our own conscious states. Since we all have the capacity to remember, and since we are in our own company all the time, and so observe our own external overt behaviour more often than others do (though perhaps, again, less objectively and perceptively), we will have a particularly large storehouse of evidence as a basis for making some attribution to ourself of a propositional attitude. If asked by some pollster in the street whether or not you believe in an afterlife, you may not be able to answer the question immediately. You may have to run through your memory, trying to recall what sort of opinion you may have expressed to your friends when you last listened together to a debate on the radio about the possibility of life after death, and trying to recall what you said when your daughter asked you whether heaven and hell existed, and so on.

On a number of occasions, certainly, you will be in a better position than others to make such a review of your past actions and utterances, and so be in a better position to attribute a particular propositional attitude to yourself. But there will also be a number of occasions when this will not be true. If you are an adolescent girl, who is mooning about the house all day, unable to concentrate on anything, displaying a sudden loss of appetite and an unwillingness to go anywhere with your friends, your mother might realize before you do that you are in love with the boy next door.

To take another example. If you are one of the many suspects in a country house where there has been a murder, you may sincerely reply to PC Plod or Patrolman Pigro's question by saying that you believed you were alone in the library at the time, and your statement might be taken at face value. However, Hercule Poirot or Lieutenant Columbo, who are more observant than the common run of mankind, and the common run of policemen, and better at interpreting the significance of what they observe, and so better at employing our folk psychology to make attributions of propositional attitudes, may say otherwise. Poirot or Columbo may point out that you must not have believed that you were alone in the library, because the butler, who was passing the open door of the library, heard you belch and say 'Excuse me' and saw you raise your hand to your mouth. As Hercule Poirot might explain to you, 'Non, non Monsieur. You must not have believed you were alone in the library. For not even an English gentleman says "Excuse me", and raises his hand to his mouth, when he belches in private.'

What a Belief Is

A belief is a disposition. It is the whole parcel of perceptual input, of inner states or processes, and their output in terms of behavioural, linguistic, facial, gestural, and any other manifestations. But dispositions are not their manifestations—or even their behavioural manifestations in the light of input—for to say that would be to fall back into behaviourism. Nor are dispositions their inner categorical or structural-cum-causal basis either, for to say that would be to reduce them to brain states or processes, and we would be back with crude reductionism. Besides, such type–type reductionism is out, because there is likely to be a host of micro analogue records in the brain in regard to any one particular macro-attributed propositional attitude. To take our previous example, of a vicar who believes in

God: There will be a different analogue record underlying his speech act 'I believe in God', or his kneeling down as the village atheist passes by, or his holding services every Sunday, or his comforting the dying with the words 'God will take you to his bosom, my child'. Yet they are the behavioural grounds for (and perhaps the only manifestation of) the vicar's belief in God.

But there are other reasons for thinking that a reduction to brain states or processes, of the determinable dispositions which are the reality underlying our propositional attitudes, does not make sense. This reason is that, even if we could isolate a separate brain ana-logue record for each of the different behavioural and linguistic and gestural episodes which were and are the evidence for attributing a belief in God to the vicar, these analogue records themselves are not stable. The brain is labile and shifting as regards how it produces output. To keep it simple, though it would not be neat and simple, let us say that brain pattern 231 is responsible for moving the muscles which enabled the vicar to kneel down last night, and brain pattern 772 for his praying to himself, while brain pattern 334 is respons-ible for the vicar saying today, 'I believe in God', in answer to the question 'Do you believe in God?' However, tomorrow it might be brain pattern 269 which brings about the vicar's kneeling down, 785 his praying silently, and 488 his saying, 'I believe in God'. For propositional-attitude attributions are made at a very high level. They are overall or summary-like attributions. They attribute a dis-position about a medley of dispositions, underlying which are a myriad shifting patterns of brain activation. It makes no sense at all to look for particular brain processes, or structures, or representa-tions, or quasi-linguistic instructions, as *the real belief* which under-lies the outer manifestations. Even to look for such things is to miss the point.

One source of the urge to place the propositional attitudes in our brains in a literal, categorical, and concrete way may be the fact that, of course, as adults we do sometimes form sentences in our heads, or out loud, which do attribute beliefs or desires or hopes to ourselves. I might say to my wife, 'I hope it does not rain tomor-row,' or, while I am travelling to work on the bus, I might say to myself, in my head, 'I hope it does not rain tomorrow.' I might be learning Italian, and so say it to myself in my head in Italian. Or I might try to say it in Russian. But no matter in what language, or whether out loud or in the privacy of my own skull, my expression in sentence form of the proposition 'I hope it does not rain tomorrow' is not a hope. For hopes are no more hope sentences than they are hope gestures or hopeful glances. Hopes are no more a particular linguistic description of the hopes than Independence Day is the sentence in my diary that says 'Independence Day is the Fourth of July'. Certainly my hope that it will not rain tomorrow makes it more likely that I will utter the sentence 'I hope it will not rain tomorrow' rather than the sentence 'I hope it will rain tomorrow'. But so what. It will also make it more likely that I will be happier if it does not rain rather than does rain tomorrow, and more likely than not that I will be interested in this evening's weather forecast for tomorrow. A disposition is not merely not to be identified with a particular bit in the brain which may have a causal role in regard to some manifestation of it, it is not to be identified with any one particular consequence or manifestation either. A propositional-attitude disposition is the whole package deal of being disposed over time to actions and reactions of a certain sort in certain specifiable circumstances, which strikes someone who is trying to make sense of it all that there is a rationale there. Your habits of doing x and y and z and m and n and o are to be summed up as a fear or a hope or a belief or a wish. Or perhaps they do not make much sense to anyone. They do not form any evidence for any attitude.

LITERAL AND METAPHORICAL ATTRIBUTIONS OF THE PROPOSITIONAL ATTITUDES TO OURSELVES AND OTHERS

We can make *literal* attributions of propositional attitudes or *metaphorical* ones. I might say, about my cat, when she looks up at me with wide-open eyes and steady gaze and with ears erect, 'She is wondering why I am so late tonight.' Of course the cat is doing no such thing. My attribution to my cat of the propositional attitude of wondering is metaphorical. For a start, the cat has no concepts. So she has no concept of lateness and so cannot wonder why I am late. Let me take another example of a metaphorical attribution. I might fail to start my car in the morning and complain that 'She's annoyed at me for leaving her in the garage all week.' Again, literally, this is nonsense. Cars cannot get annoyed.

On the other hand such metaphorical attributions are not just a looseness or failure to be exact on my part. They are not nonsense.

My anthropomorphizing attitudes to my cat and car, my drawing them into my life by making them recipients of my folk psychological intentional attitudes, is a way of drawing them into my understanding and so, thereby, bringing them closer to me affectively speaking. It is easier to like or love (and hate) what you understand.

However, it is only in regard to humans that we make literal attributions of the propositional or intentional attitudes. When I say, 'She is annoyed that I am so late,' about my wife, I am making a shrewd and informed guess at the source of my wife's unsmiling face and sharp conversational tones. She may not have formed in her head, or anywhere else, the sentence 'I am annoyed that my husband is so late home on my night off,' any more than the cat had, but the attribution still fits my wife in a way that it can never fit the cat. For, in regard to my wife, it is a plausible attribution to say that she is annoyed and to attribute this to her literally. To attribute it literally is to say that she has the conscious states, and says and does just the sort of things, a person who is annoyed at someone's being late is liable to have, say, and do. For, in regard to my wife, my attribution to her of annoyance is made on the basis of evident facts about her appearance and behaviour (her countenance, her voice, her gestures, her actions), and the context (which, in this instance, involves reference to previous events and other propositional attitudes—I had said I would be home before seven o'clock, she probably knows it is now well after eight o'clock, the dinner the cook prepared for seven o'clock is liable now to be dried up and close to inedible). More importantly, there is also the more general background of my knowing that my wife is a rational human with conceptual skills sufficient to justify my implied attribution to her of a capacity to understand such things as lateness, promising, and so on. Thus my attribution of annoyance to my wife is a literal attribution of a propositional attitude because it is an attribution of a propositional attitude which, according to the folk psychology shared by her and me, is appropriate to just such a person in just such circumstances.

THE PROPOSITIONAL-ATTITUDE EXPRESSIONS AS DESCRIPTIVE, PREDICTIVE, AND BEHAVIOUR-GUIDING

In this section I want to argue that our talk about propositional attitudes has at least three important, and importantly different, roles.

These roles I refer to as the macro interpretive-cum-descriptive, and the pragmatic-predictive, and the behaviour-guiding.

The Macro Descriptive-cum-Interpretive Role

When we describe someone as 'believing that so-and-so' or 'desiring that such-and-such', we are parcelling up aspects of a human by saying that he or she is disposed to exhibit certain sorts of behaviour (including verbal behaviour) in certain sorts of circumstances *and* interpreting these parcels according to a conventionally accepted common-sense way of doing so. The level of description which we adopt when we employ these propositional-attitude expressions about ourselves and others is at such a high level that it makes no sense to reduce it to any other level such as the neurophysiological or the biological. If we find it useful, as we do, to observe and interpret and describe humans at the level of taking whole parcels of perceptual input and behavioural output as 'the unit' of observation and interpretation, then to talk of reducing such explanations can only amount to giving up talk about humans at this macro parcelling level. The only justification for doing so would be if we found we could no longer operate with it, or if we found that, while we could still use it, it was less useful for our ordinary psychological purposes than other ways of explaining humans which employed different units of explanation.

But this, presumably, would also apply to other forms of macro description that we use. When an economist talks about an increase in the money supply being one of the causes of inflation, then he is describing a real cause and a real effect. But it would not make much sense to reduce that level of description to, say, the level of physics and chemistry. Not merely does it not make sense, it does not seem feasible. The economist's description 'There was growth in the money supply by 5 per cent over the last month' is usually made on the basis of such observations as that there was an increase in the amount of borrowing from banks and other financial institutions, and an increase in the amount of money printed by the central bank. Now it is hardly feasible to try then to reduce the myriad individual operations of borrowing money, in many different ways, from many different persons and institutions, to the level of cause and effect at the level of electrons and protons and neutrons and such subatomic particles. Yet our failure to be able to do that does not cast doubt on the efficacy or reality of the macro explanations of economists in terms of inflation, money supply, and so on. Why should we think that matters are different in regard to the macro explanations of our propositional-attitude talk? Why should we worry about the seeming impossibility, even incomprehensibility, of reducing such talk to a lower level?

The Pragmatic-Predictive Role

We also use our propositional-attitude descriptions to predict the behaviour of others. If we were not able, in a reasonably neat and quick way, to predict what our fellow humans were likely to do at least a great deal of the time, we would be ridden with anxiety and fear, because we would be ignorant about our fellow humans and find them alarmingly unpredictable.

Learning how to interpret humans in terms of the propositional attitudes is, literally, gaining a new guidebook by which we better negotiate our way around our social world. But let me illustrate this claim by means of a fanciful account of how the very first folk psychology of propositional-attitude terms might have developed among the first groups of *Homo sapiens*. Let us imagine a rather psychologically and philosophically shrewd ancestor at a meeting of the tribal leaders who are reviewing a rather disastrous wild-boar hunt that was held the previous day. Let us call this ancestor Sharpoo. Sharpoo stands up and says 'Look, we need to do more than cry out that Muggoo, the leader of the hunt, ran away rather than stood his ground when the wild boar ran towards him, because a running mood fell upon him yesterday. That's just not a helpful comment. It does not help us to decide whether we should replace Muggoo as leader of the hunt or not. We need some account of Muggoo, or for that matter of people in general, which will enable us to predict what they will do. We need to know what Muggoo is likely to do next time he is head of the hunting party. I suggest we invent a richer and subtler account of what we think goes on between our ears which leads us to behave in one way rather than another. Instead of just a one-category psychology of moods which are retrospectively labelled according to the behaviour they give rise to—that is, running moods, sleeping moods, crying moods, and so on—we need to divide the in-the-head precursors of human action into two sorts, at least, namely what we can be supposed to know or believe about the world and ourselves, and what we would like to do in the world or desire the world to be like. If we wanted to, later on we could extend these two basic categories, by splitting up each one into a variety of subcategories.

'If you reflect on this, I believe you will see its value. I myself have been learning things about Muggoo. In terms of my suggested categories, I have found out something about his beliefs and desires which will help us see what he is likely to do in the future. I have discovered that, owing to his upbringing in the mountains, among the mountain people, Muggoo believes that wild boar are in fact supernatural beings such that, if you are bitten by them, then you will go to hell. In short, Muggoo ran away because he believed he would be bitten by the wild boar and did not want to go to hell. I suggest that he is likely to run away again, in much the same manner, if retained as leader of the hunt. Since I do not believe that wild boar are demons, may I nominate myself for the post of leader of the hunt?'[2] At which point Sharpoo sits down to wild applause and, by acclamation, is elected leader of the hunt. Contrary to his wishes, so he says, over the years he has gained the reputation of being able to see into human souls.

Let me give another illustration of the predictive role of a propositional-attitude description. This one non-fictional. In a recent article in the *New Yorker*, the neurologist Oliver Sacks described his visit to a woman, Temple Grandin, who, though employed as an Assistant Professor in an Animal Sciences Department, had suffered all her life from autism. Autism is generally described as a disease that seems to involve a strange and engulfing mental aloneness and aloofness (as the etymology of the word—from the Greek word for 'self'—implies). It also involves, very often, a need to engage in repetitive and stereotyped movements, which seem to an observer like elaborate rituals. Among other things, those suffering from autism seem to fail to make eye contact with other humans, to display a poverty of facial expressions, and to chatter in a manner which is often disengaged from the context. But the exact manifestation of the disease does, of course, vary from patient to patient.

---

[2] I have, of course, cheated a little in giving this account. For even in the process of explaining why a non-propositional-attitude folk psychology is too crude to be useful, Sharpoo is forced to use propositional-attitude verbs like 'decide', 'think', 'predict', and so on. Strictly speaking, Sharpoo's speech should read more like 'Saying Muggoo was in running mood, not good. Better to say . . .'. But after a few sentences of that, I'd have no readers. Besides, it is rather difficult to talk about humans without employing the propositional attitudes.

Oliver Sacks writes in his article that one of the things he learned, from speaking to Temple Grandin, was that she had difficulty in interpreting and so in predicting the actions and reactions of others. She had to do it in a primitive, almost purely perceptual, way. In the context of our present discussion, we could say that she seemed unable to understand or take part in our folk psychological explanations in terms of beliefs and desires and the other propositional attitudes. But let us hear Oliver Sacks himself:

> She [Temple Grandin] was bewildered, she said, by Romeo and Juliet [when she read or witnessed the play] ('I never knew what they were up to'), and with 'Hamlet' she got lost with the back-and-forth of the play. Though she ascribed these problems to 'sequencing difficulties', they seemed to arise from her failure to empathize with the characters, to follow the intricate play of motive and intention. She said that she could understand 'simple, strong, universal' emotions but was stumped by more complex emotions and the games people play. 'Much of the time,' she said, 'I feel like an anthropologist on Mars.'
>
> She was at pains to keep her own life simple, she said, and to make everything very clear and explicit. She had built up a vast library of experiences over the years, she went on. They were like a library of videotapes, which she could play in her mind and inspect at any time—'videos' of how people behaved in different circumstances. She would play these over and over again, and learn, by degrees, to correlate what she saw, so that she could then predict how people in similar circumstances might act. (Sacks 1994)

In other words, Temple Grandin had to do in her time-consuming, non-conceptual, 'videotape' way what we are able to achieve more quickly and more efficiently with our clever, sophisticated, linguistic-cum-conceptual set of propositional attitudes and the other parts of our folk psychology.

The Behaviour-Guiding Role

What is more, this description and interpretation is not just confined to specialist interpreters in the way, say, that a psychoanalyst's is, but is also the chief driving force behind the very actions and reactions of ordinary people which are being parcelled up and interpreted. I not merely explain and describe my neighbour's actions and reactions in terms of beliefs and desires and hopes and intentions, and so on, I myself also act and react in accordance with the beliefs, desires, hopes, intentions, which I have attributed to myself. I order my life in accordance with my folk propositional-attitude understanding of myself and others. Indeed part of the force of describing these propositional-attitude explanations as 'common sense' or as 'folk psychology' is to underline the fact that such explanations pervade the thinking of everyone who shares the same culture. Such explanations are not merely the stuff of our explanations in regard to others, they are also the very stuff of our own self-concepts and the terms in which we make plans for the future and guide our actions in the present.

As adults, at least most of the time, we think before we act or react, and thinking for an adult is in terms of the concepts expressed in a natural language. I really did go to the cinema last night because I believed that Charlotte Rampling was in the movie. In fact she was not. It was Debra Winger. And when I went to the clinic last week it was because I believed I might have TB. In fact I did not. I only had a hangover. Irrespective of the truth or falsity of our beliefs, about ourselves or others, and irrespective of the truth or falsity of our purported knowledge of our own beliefs, very often what we represent to ourselves as our own beliefs are what guide our behaviour.

The above may be rather confusing. We need, first, to make a distinction between the beliefs a person has and the beliefs a person thinks she has. For both of these will influence her actions, even though they may on occasion be at variance with one another. For example, Sue may believe that, as the shopkeeper claimed, her son is indeed guilty of stealing the can of Coca-Cola from the corner shop. But she may be unable to acknowledge that belief. In her conscious ruminations she may only be able to attribute to herself, and so to express, the belief that her son could never be guilty of such an act as stealing from a shop.

Her belief that her son was guilty of stealing (attributed to her, let us say, by a clever psychologist) influences her actions and reactions. It keeps her awake at night. It makes her tearful during the day. It makes her want to tell her neighbour about various acts of honesty which her son has performed. Her attribution to herself of a belief that her son could never be guilty of stealing (repeatedly expressed to herself in her own stream of ruminative consciousness) leads her to tell the policeman that her son had no need to steal any can of Coca-Cola as there were three cans already in the fridge at home, and leads her to harbour very angry feelings towards the shopkeeper who reported to the police that her son had stolen a can of Coke.

Of course, very often (perhaps most often) our beliefs and our attributions to ourselves of beliefs will coincide. If they didn't, we would be very mixed up psychologically and reveal this in very anomalous behaviour. Eventually we would be led away quietly to some institution for rehabilitation. In terms of our example above, the mother is most likely both to believe, and to know that she believes, that her son is guilty of stealing, though she may not be prepared (or even able) to admit this to anyone else. In consequence she may say that she believes that her son is not guilty of stealing but believe otherwise and know that she believes otherwise. Nevertheless, even her saying that she believes her son is not guilty may also influence her behaviour. For the sake of 'keeping up a front' and of helping her son come to terms with what he has done, she may feel that she has to support him by acting as if he was not guilty.

This means that we should extend the twofold distinction (between believing and attributing to oneself a belief) into a threefold one. We need to distinguish between Sue *believing* that *p*, Sue *attributing to herself a belief* that *p*, and Sue *saying to someone that she believes* that *p*. All three are defined in terms of the categories of our folk psychology and all three can lead to actions and reactions of various sorts. Our folk psychology explains our behaviour and guides our behaviour, and so influences our life, at a number of potentially confusing levels.

THE PROPOSITIONAL ATTITUDES AS FOLK PSYCHOLOGY

Arguably the richest (the most conceptually sophisticated) segment of any natural language is that which philosophers have labelled its 'folk psychology'. Some have used this term pejoratively, putting folk psychology on a par with folk medicine as being a kind of obsolete and so backward science. I do not use the term pejoratively, for I do not see it as failed or inadequate science that will give way to a better, because more sophisticated or up-to-date, science. In giving propositional-attitude explanations we are not challenging physics or biology or neurophysiology or even professional academic psychology (for one could imagine academic psychologists, in the manner of psychoanalysts, carving up humans and their actions and reactions in a completely different way than does our folk psychology).

Our propositional-attitude talk is, then, far more important talk than some have allowed. For a start it is our way of changing from infancy to adulthood mentally. Among the things a child learns, gradually and slowly, once it has begun to speak, is the common-sense, or folk, psychology of its own culture expressed, most often, in terms of the propositional attitudes. By adulthood it has learned how to talk with great variety and subtlety about the actions and reactions of itself and others in terms of an interwoven tapestry of propositional attitudes, that is in terms of beliefs, desires, hopes, wants, loves, hates, intentions, decisions, questions, thoughts, doubts, fears, and so on. That is, the child has learned how to explain, predict, exonerate, comfort, condone, command, commiserate, decide, detest, defend, and so on, in terms of this rich tapestry of propositional attitudes. 'I told her she was dying of cancer because I believed she would want to know'. 'He believed that it was all right to conceal the truth because the public would not have understood what he was trying to do.' 'She believes that, if he believes that the allied forces have moral objections to using biological weapons or toxic gas, he will use them himself if the war begins to go against him.' 'If she was a better person, she would not want to be promoted in these circumstances.' 'If I really wanted to make money, and knew about the realities of academic life, I would not have become a philosopher.'

A culture develops and perfects its common-sense, or folk, psychology as a way of enriching the communication and especially the understanding of persons in that culture. On the other hand, it is not easy to employ our folk psychology in the understanding of persons in a very different culture. To be plunged into contact with a tribe which has never previously been in contact with Western people would be for a Western visitor to be plunged into confusion. One can imagine an anthropology student visiting Womp Womp Island in order to gather material for his dissertation. He seems to be having difficulties, which he voices in a letter home. Let me quote an extract: 'I asked myself whether he was laughing? Or was he just nervous? Or what? All I had done was ask him for some water? And why did that woman last week giggle when her friend's leg was gored by a wild pig? Don't these people care about one another? Oh yeah. Let me tell you this one. The other day I saw one of the men putting palm fronds with food on them at the foot of a tree. Do they think that trees can eat? Boy, oh boy, are these guys peculiar. By the way, I'm thinking of taking up physics when I get back.'

If the anthropology student had been more patient, he might have come to an understanding of their folk psychology. If he had learned that the palm trees are believed by the Womp Womp people to be inhabited by arboreal spirits that need constant placation by means of offerings of things which are held by the Womp Womp people to be valuable, he would have understood the point of putting food on palm fronds at the foot of the palm trees. If he had known that what we call a giggle is the sound emitted by the Womp Womp women when they are in deep shock, he would have understood the incident about the wild pig. If he had known that the Womp Womp believe that requests should only be made by a person who has a higher social rating, or 'face' value, than the person of whom the request is made, he would have realized that his requesting water from the chief's son was a *faux pas* of great magnitude. Even to begin to understand another culture, not merely do we need to know what particular beliefs and desires, hopes and needs, and so on, a community has, but also we need to know how to link these attitudes to their facial expressions, gestures, body movements, cries, behaviour, and utterances. We need to know how and when to apply 'He believes so-and-so' and 'She desires such-and-such' and 'He is hoping for so-and-so' and 'She is intending to do such-and-such'.

To return to the matter of an individual human's gradual addition of sophisticated, folk psychological, intentionality to his or her original infant intentionality, it should be made clear that this development is not mirrored by developments in the brain. The human brain is more or less completely matured by the time a child is 3 or 4 years old. Further psychological development after this age is in terms of learning about itself and others, and the interplay between the two in terms of the culture's vehicle for achieving this understanding, its common-sense, or folk, psychology. This in turn is only possible for those with speech or some other way of forming and learning concepts. For our psychological development after infancy, in the second great phase (or series of great phases) of intentionality, lies in great part in this remarkable ability of humans to invent conceptual classifications which enable them to make attributions to one another of propositional attitudes. Just as our ancestors may have been instructed how to employ propositional attitudes by a Sharpoo, so with time and learning we modern humans advance from a purely descriptive utterance, such as 'She is crying', to an intentional attribution, 'She is crying because she is sad'. As we grow older we learn how to thicken these psychological descriptions by linking them to context and to content and to other attributions. We advance to 'She is crying because she is sad, because her friend has just died, because she loved her friend and because she realized her friend did not want to die as she was so young and so full of plans for the rest of her life', and so on.

We could go on, indefinitely, thickening our account of why someone is crying (or, for that matter, laughing or running or staring, or whatever). While a child gradually acquires the ability to do this, this ability has nothing to do with a newly developed keenness of the eye or sharpness of the ear or sensitivity of the nose or tongue. Nor is it a gain in brain power in the neurophysiological sense. The ability that enables the child to develop from knowing someone is crying to knowing that she is crying because she is sad, because her friend has just died, because she loved her friend and realized she did not want to die, because she was so young and full of plans, is in great part a conceptual ability. For primarily it is a reflection of a person's gradual acquisition and employment of the armful of concepts that the prelinguistic child cannot yet acquire. Concepts are not sensory experiences, nor are they brain analogues. Concepts are inculcated into our mental life (into that part of our life where awareness of one thing leads us into an awareness of another thing beyond itself) as part of our understanding of the representations of linguistic utterances. Our infant acquisition of sensory knowledge about the world and ourselves, which never ceases until our senses cease to receive stimulation with damage or death, is overlaid after infancy by a conceptual acquisition of information about the world and ourselves. Indeed, in adult life, our conceptual life comes to dominate the former and interfere with it. The sensory world comes to be interpreted in terms of our conceptual understanding of it and, if our concepts and their application are crude, our sensory world comes to be distorted by our conceptual understanding. Literally speaking, our conceptual information is always dependent to some degree on our sensory systems for the simple reason that conceptual information (linguistically based and described information) comes to us, into our head, via (usually) our sight or hearing of written or spoken sentences in some natural language or some other symbolic system.

Once a human has language, he or she has two ways of gaining information. This is why humans are so sophisticated in comparison with other animals. While other animals may employ a language-like communication (mating-cries, warning-signals, expressions of emotion), they do not, because they cannot, communicate in terms of concepts. So animals other than humans neither have nor have any possibility of a folk psychology, because they cannot form concepts of belief, desire, hope, wish, intention, decision, and so on.

BIBLIOGRAPHY

ALSTON, WILLIAM (1983), Review of Fred Dretske, *Knowledge and the Flow of Information, Philosophical Review*, 92.

AQUINAS, ST THOMAS (1970), *Summa Theologiae* (*c.*1265–73), gen. ed. Thomas Gilby (London, Blackfriars, in conjunction with Eyre & Spottiswoode and McGraw-Hill).

AQUILA, RICHARD E. (1977), *Intentionality: A Study of Mental Acts* (University Park, Pennsylvania State University Press).

ARMSTRONG, DAVID M. (1968), *A Materialist Theory of the Mind*, International Library of Philosophy and Scientific Method (London, Routledge & Kegan Paul).

—— (1973), *Belief, Truth and Knowledge* (Cambridge University Press).

AUGUSTINE (1983), *Confessions* (400), trans. E. M. Blaiklock (London, Hodder & Stoughton).

AYER, ALFRED JULES (1946), *Language, Truth and Logic* (1936) (New York, Dover).

—— (ed.) (1959), *Logical Positivism* (New York, Collier Macmillan–Free Press).

BECHTEL, WILLIAM (1987), 'Connectionism and the Philosophy of Mind: An Overview', *Southern Journal of Philosophy*, 26, supp.

—— (1988), *Philosophy of Mind: An Overview for Cognitive Science* (Hillsdale, NJ, Lawrence Erlbaum).

BELL, DAVID (1991), *Husserl*, The Arguments of the Philosophers, ed. T. Honderich (London, Routledge & Kegan Paul).

BIGELOW, JOHN (1983), Review of Brian Loar, *Mind and Meaning, Australasian Journal of Philosophy*, 61.

BILGRAMI, AKEEL (1989), 'Realism without Internalism: A Critique of Searle on Intentionality', *Journal of Philosophy*, 86/2.

—— (1992), *Belief and Meaning: The Unity and Locality of Mental Content* (Oxford, Basil Blackwell).

BLACKBURN, SIMON (1984), *Spreading the Word: Groundings in the Philosophy of Language* (Oxford, Clarendon Press).

BLAKEMORE, COLIN (1977), *Mechanics of the Mind*, BBC Reith Lectures 1976 (Cambridge University Press).

—— and GREENFIELD, SUSAN (eds.) (1989), *Mindwaves: Thoughts on Intelligence, Identity and Consciousness* (Oxford, Basil Blackwell).

BLOCK, NED (1978), 'Troubles with Functionalism', in C. Wade Savage (ed.), *Perception and Cognition: Issues in the Foundations of Psychology*, Minnesota Studies in the Philosophy of Science, ix (Minneapolis, University of Minnesota Press).

BLOCK, NED (1980), 'What is Functionalism?', in N. Block (ed.), *Readings in Philosophy of Psychology* (Cambridge, Mass., Harvard University Press), i.

—— (1986), 'An Advertisement for a Semantics for Psychology', in Peter A. French, Theodore E. Uehling, Jr., and Howard K. Wettstein (eds.), *Studies in the Philosophy of Mind*, Midwest Studies in Philosophy, x (Minneapolis, University of Minnesota Press).

BODEN, MARGARET (1979), *Piaget*, Modern Masters (London, Fontana–Collins).

BOER, STEVEN E. (1985), Critical Review of Brian Loar, *Mind and Meaning, Nous*, 19.

BOGHOSSIAN, PAUL A. (1990), 'The Status of Content', *Philosophical Review*, 99.

BOWER, T. C. R. (1982), *Development in Infancy*, 2nd edn. (New York, W. H. Freeman).

BRADFORD, H. F. (1987), 'Neurotransmitters and Neuromodulators', in Gregory (1987).

BRENTANO, FRANZ (1966), *The True and the Evident* (1930), ed. Oskar Kraus, Eng. edn. ed. R. M. Chisholm, trans. R. M. Chisholm, I. Politzer, and K. R. Fischer (London, Routledge & Kegan Paul).

—— (1973), *Psychology from an Empirical Standpoint* (1874), ed. Oskar Kraus, English edn. ed. Linda L. McAlister, trans. A. C. Rancurello, D. B. Terrell, and L. L. McAlister (London, Routledge & Kegan Paul).

—— (1981), *Sensory and Noetic Consciousness: Psychology from an Empirical Standpoint III* (1929), ed. O. Kraus and Linda McAlister, trans. M. Schättle and L. McAlister (London, Routledge & Kegan Paul).

BROADBENT, DONALD (1958), *Perception and Communication* (Oxford, Pergamon).

BRODAL, PER (1992), *The Central Nervous System: Structure and Function* (Oxford University Press).

BÜHLER, KARL (1930), *The Mental Development of the Child: A Summary of Modern Psychological Theory* (1919), trans. from 5th German edn. by Oscar Oeser (New York, Harcourt Brace).

BURGE, TYLER (1979), 'Individualism and the Mental', in Peter A. French, Theodore E. Uehling, Jr., and Howard K. Wettstein (eds.), *Studies in Metaphysics*, Midwest Studies in Philosophy, iv (Minneapolis, University of Minnesota Press).

—— (1992), 'Philosophy of Language and Mind 1950–1990', *Philosophical Review*, 101.

CARNAP, RUDOLF (1937), *The Logical Syntax of Language* (1934), trans. A. Smeaton (London, Kegan Paul, Trench, Trubner).

—— (1955), 'Meaning and Synonomy in Natural Language', *Philosophical Studies*, 6.

—— (1959a), 'Psychology in Physical Language' (1931), in Ayer (1959).
—— (1959b), 'The Elimination of Metaphysics through Logical Analysis of Language' (1932), in Ayer (1959).
—— (1963), 'Intellectual Autobiography', in Schilpp (1963).
CARRUTHERS, PETER (1986), *Introducing Persons: Theories and Arguments in the Philosophy of Mind* (London, Routledge).
—— (1992), *Human Knowledge and Human Nature: A New Introduction to an Ancient Debate* (Oxford University Press).
CHISHOLM, RODERICK M. (1957), *Perceiving: A Philosophical Study* (Ithaca, NY, Cornell University Press).
—— (1958), 'Sentences about Believing', app. to H. Feigl, M. Scriven, and G. Maxwell (eds.), in *Concepts, Theories, and the Mind–Body Problem*, Minnesota Studies in the Philosophy of Science, ii (Minneapolis, University of Minnesota Press).
—— (1967a), 'Franz Brentano', in Edwards (1967), i.
—— (1967b), 'Intentionality', in Edwards (1967), iv.
—— and SELLARS, WILFRID (1958), 'Chisholm–Sellars Correspondence on Intentionality', app. to H. Feigl, M. Scriven, and G. Maxwell (eds.), *Concepts, Theories, and the Mind–Body Problem*, Minnesota Studies in the Philosophy of Science, ii (Minneapolis, University of Minnesota Press).
CHOMSKY, NOAM (1959), Review of B. F. Skinner, *Verbal Behaviour*, in *Language*, 35.
—— (1968), *Language and Mind* (New York, Harcourt, Brace & World).
—— (1980), 'Rules and Representation', *Behavioral and Brain Sciences*, 3.
CHURCHLAND, PATRICIA SMITH (1986), *Neurophilosophy: Toward a Unified Science of the Mind–Brain* (Cambridge, Mass., MIT Press).
—— and SEJNOWSKI, TERRENCE J. (1990), 'Neural Representation and Neural Computation', in Tomberlin (1990).
CHURCHLAND, PAUL (1979), *Scientific Realism and the Plasticity of Mind*, Cambridge Studies in Philosophy (Cambridge University Press).
—— (1981), 'Eliminative Materialism and the Propositional Attitudes', *Journal of Philosophy*, 78.
—— (1984), *Matter and Consciousness: A Contemporary Introduction to the Philosophy of Mind* (Cambridge, Mass., MIT Press).
CLARK, ANDY (1988a), 'Thoughts, Sentences and Cognitive Science', *Philosophical Psychology*, 1.
—— (1988b), *Microcognition: Philosophy, Cognitive Science, and Parallel Distributed Processing* (Cambridge, Mass., MIT Press).
—— (1990), Review of Fred Dretske, *Explaining Behavior*, in *Philosophical Quarterly*, 40.
—— (1993), *Associative Engines: Connectionism, Concepts, and Representational Change* (Cambridge, Mass., MIT Press).

COHEN, LESLIE B. (1979), 'Our Developing Knowledge of Infant Perception and Cognition', *American Psychologist*, 34/10.

COMTE, AUGUSTE (1830–42), *Cours de philosophie positive*, 6 vols. (Paris, Bachelier).

CRAIK, K. J. W. (1943), *The Nature of Explanation* (Cambridge University Press).

CRICK, FRANCIS (1989), 'The Recent Excitement about Neural Networks', *Nature*, 337.

CUMMINS, ROBERT (1983), *The Nature of Psychological Explanation* (Cambridge, Mass., MIT Press).

—— (1989), 'The Role of Representation in Connectionist Explanations of Cognitive Capacities', Paper delivered to the Second Mind and Language Workshop, Birkbeck College, July.

DALGARNO, MELVIN, and MATTHEWS, ERIC (eds.) (1989), *The Philosophy of Thomas Reid*, Philosophical Studies no. 42 (Dordrecht, Kluwer).

DARWIN, CHARLES (1881), *The Descent of Man and Selection in Relation to Sex* (1871), 2nd edn. (London, John Murray).

—— (1972), *The Origin of Species* (1859), intro. L. Harrison Matthews, Everyman (London, Dent).

DAVIDSON, DONALD (1980), *Essays on Actions and Events* (Oxford, Clarendon Press).

—— (1990), 'Representation and Interpretation', in Mohyeldin Said *et al.* (1990).

DELBRÜCK, MAX (1986), *Mind from Matter? An Essay on Evolutionary Epistemology*, ed. G. S. Stent, E. P. Fischer, S. W. Golomb, D. Presti, and H. Seiler (Oxford, Blackwell Scientific Publications).

DENNETT, DANIEL C. (1978), *Brainstorms: Philosophical Essays on Mind and Psychology* (Brighton, Harvester).

—— (1983a), 'Styles of Mental Representation', *Proceedings of the Aristotelian Society*, 83.

—— (1983b), 'Intentional Systems in Cognitive Ethology: The "Panglossian Paradigm" Defended', *Behavioral and Brain Sciences*, 6.

—— (1986), *Content and Consciousness* (1969), International Library of Philosophy and Scientific Method (London, Routledge & Kegan Paul).

—— (1987), *The Intentional Stance* (Cambridge, Mass., MIT Press).

DOWLING, JOHN E. (1992), *Neurons and Networks: An Introduction to Neuroscience* (Cambridge, Mass., Belnap).

DRETSKE, FRED (1969), *Seeing and Knowing* (University of Chicago Press).

—— (1981), *Knowledge and the Flow of Information* (Cambridge, Mass., MIT Press).

—— (1986), 'Misrepresentation', in R. Bogdan (ed.), *Belief* (Oxford, Clarendon Press).

—— (1988), *Explaining Behavior: Reasons in a World of Causes* (Cambridge, Mass., MIT Press).

ECCLES, JOHN C. (1973), *The Understanding of the Brain* (London, McGraw-Hill).

—— (1989), *Evolution of the Brain: Creation of the Self* (London, Routledge).

EDELMAN, GERALD (1978), 'Group Selection and Phasic Reentrant Signalling: A Theory of Higher Brain Function', in G. M. Edelman and V. B. Mountcastle (eds.), *The Mindful Brain: Cortical Organization and the Group-Selective Theory of Higher Brain Function* (Cambridge, Mass., MIT Press).

—— (1985), 'Neural Darwinism: Population Thinking and Higher Brain Function', in Michael Shafto (ed.), *How we Know*, Proceedings of the Nobel Conference, 10 (San Francisco, Harper & Row).

—— (1989), *The Remembered Present: A Biological Theory of Consciousness* (New York, Basic Books).

—— (1992), *Bright Air, Brilliant Fire: On the Matter of the Mind* (New York, Basic Books).

EDWARDS, PAUL (ed.) (1967), *The Encyclopedia of Philosophy*, 8 vols. (New York, Collier Macmillan–Free Press).

EMMERICH, WALTER (1968), 'Personality Development and Concepts of Structure', *Child Development*, 39.

FIELD, HARTRY (1977), 'Logic, Meaning and Conceptual Role', *Journal of Philosophy*, 74.

—— (1981), 'Mental Representation', in N. Block (ed.), *Readings in Philosophy of Psychology* (Cambridge, Mass., Harvard University Press), ii.

FLANAGAN, OWEN (1991), *The Science of the Mind*, 2nd edn. (Cambridge, Mass., MIT Press).

FLEW, ANTONY (ed.) (1984), *A Dictionary of Philosophy*, 2nd rev. edn. (London, Pan Books).

FODOR, JERRY A. (1976), *The Language of Thought* (Brighton, Harvester).

—— (1981*a*), 'Propositional Attitudes', in N. Block (ed.), *Readings in Philosophy of Psychology* (Cambridge, Mass., Harvard University Press); repr. from *Monist*, 61 (1978).

—— (1981*b*), *Representations: Philosophical Essays on the Foundations of Cognitive Science* (Cambridge, Mass., MIT Press).

—— (1983*a*), 'Imagery and the Language of Thought: Dialogue with Jerome Fodor', in Miller (1983).

—— (1983*b*), *The Modularity of Mind: An Essay on Faculty Psychology* (Cambridge, Mass., MIT Press).

—— (1984), 'Semantics, Wisconsin Style', *Synthese*, 59.

—— (1985), 'Fodor's Guide to Mental Representation: The Intelligent Auntie's Vade-Mecum', *Mind*, 94.

—— (1987), *Psychosemantics: The Problem of Meaning in the Philosophy of Mind*, Explorations in Cognitive Science (Cambridge, Mass., MIT Press).

250   *Bibliography*

FODOR, JERRY A. (1989), 'Problems of Content in the Philosophy of Mind,' Donnellan Lectures delivered at Trinity College Dublin.

—— (1990), *A Theory of Content and Other Essays* (Cambridge, Mass., MIT Press).

GAZZANIGA, MICHAEL S. (1989), 'Organisation of the Human Brain', *Science*, 245.

GEACH, P. T. (1957), *Mental Acts: Their Content and their Objects*, Studies in Philosophical Psychology (London, Routledge & Kegan Paul).

GESCHWIND, NORMAN (1972), 'Language and the Brain', *Scientific American*, 226/4.

—— (1978), 'Specializations of the Human Brain', *Scientific American*, 241/3.

—— (1981), 'Neurological Knowledge and Complex Behaviours', in Donald A. Norman (ed.), *Perspectives on Cognitive Science* (New Jersey, Ablex–Lawrence Erlbaum).

GODFREY-SMITH, PETER (1988), Review of Ruth Garrett Millikan's *Language, Thought and Other Biological Categories, Australasian Journal of Philosophy*, 66.

GREGORY, RICHARD L. (ed.) (1987), *The Oxford Companion to the Mind* (Oxford University Press).

GRICE, H. P. (1952), 'Meaning', *Philosophical Review*, 66.

—— (1968), 'Utterer's Meaning, Sentence-Meaning, and Word-Meaning', *Foundations of Language*, 4.

GRIMM, ROBERT H., and MERRILL, DANIEL D. (eds.) (1988), *Contents of Thought*, Arizona Colloquium in Cognition (Phoenix, University of Arizona Press).

GUNDERSON, KEITH (ed.) (1975), *Language, Mind and Knowledge*, Minnesota Studies in the Philosophy of Science, vi (Minneapolis, University of Minnesota Press).

GUTTENPLAN, SAMUEL (ed.) (1975), *Mind and Language*, Wolfson College Lectures 1974 (Oxford, Clarendon Press).

HAHN, LEWIS EDWIN, and SCHILPP, PAUL ARTHUR (eds.) (1986), *The Philosophy of W. V. Quine*, Library of Living Philosophers, xviii (La Saue, Ill., Open Court).

HALDANE, JOHN (1988), 'Psychoanalysis, Cognitive Psychology and Self-Consciousness', in P. Clarke and C. Wright (eds.), *Mind, Psychoanalysis and Science* (Oxford, Basil Blackwell).

—— (1989a), 'Reid, Scholasticism and Current Philosophy of Mind', in Dalgarno and Matthews (1989).

—— (1989b), 'Brentano's Problem', in *Grazer philosophische Studien*, 35.

—— (1989c), 'Naturalism and the Problem of Intentionality', *Inquiry*, 32.

HAMLYN, D. W. (1971), *The Theory of Knowledge*, Modern Introductions to Philosophy (London, Macmillan).

HARMAN, GILBERT (1973), *Thought* (Princeton University Press).

—— (1974), 'Meaning and Semantics', in M. K. Munitz and P. K. Unger (eds.), *Semantics and Philosophy* (New York University Press).

—— (1975), 'Language, Thought and Communication', in Gunderson (1975).

—— (1987), '(Nonsolipsistic) Conceptual Role Semantics', in Ernest LePore (ed.), *New Directions in Semantics*, Cognitive Science no. 2 (New York, Academic Press); this is an expanded version of 'Conceptual Role Semantics', *Notre Dame Journal of Formal Logic*, 23 (1982), which was repr. in Peacocke (1993), i.

—— (1990), 'The Intrinsic Quality of Experience', in Tomberlin (1990).

HARRIS, ROY (1989), 'The Grammar in your Head', in Blakemore and Greenfield (1989).

HAUGELAND, JOHN (1990), 'The Intentionality All-Stars', in Tomberlin (1990).

HEIL, JOHN (1991), 'Perceptual Experience', in McLaughlin (1991*a*).

HELMHOLTZ, H. (1873), *Popular Lectures in Scientific Subjects*, trans. E. Atkinson, intro. J. Tyndale (London, Longmans, Green).

HOLLINGDALE, S. H., and TOOTILL, G. C. (1975), *Electronic Computers* (1965), 2nd edn. (Harmondsworth, Penguin).

HOOKWAY, CHRISTOPHER (1988), *Quine: Language, Experience and Reality* (Cambridge, Polity Press).

HUMPHREY, GEORGE (1951), *Thinking: An Introduction to its Experimental Psychology* (London and New York, Methuen–Wiley).

HUNDERT, EDWARD (1989), 'Can Neuroscience Contribute to Philosophy?', in Blakemore and Greenfield (1989).

HUSSERL, EDMUND (1931), *Ideas: General Introduction to Pure Phenomenology* (1913), trans. W. P. Boyce Gibson (London, George Allen & Unwin).

—— (1960), 'Phenomenology' (1929), trans. C. V. Solomon, in Roderick M. Chisholm (ed.), *Realism and the Background of Phenomenology* (New York, Free Press).

JAMES, WILLIAM (1950), *The Principles of Psychology* (1890), 2 vols. (New York, Dover).

JACKSON, JOHN HUGHLINGS (1958), *Selected Writings of John Hughlings Jackson*, ed. J. Taylor, G. Holmes, and F. M. R. Walshe, 2 vols. (London, Staples).

JERISON, HARRY J. (1976), 'Paleoneurology and the Evolution of Mind', *Scientific American*, 234/1.

JOHNSON, M. (1987), *The Body in the Mind: The Bodily Basis of Meaning, Imagination, and Reason* (University of Chicago Press).

JOHNSON-LAIRD, P. N. (1983), *Mental Models: Towards a Cognitive Science of Language, Inference and Consciousness* (Cambridge University Press).

KAGAN, JEROME (1972), 'Do Infants Think?', *Scientific American*, 226/3.
—— (1979), *The Growth of the Child: Reflections on Human Development* (Brighton, Harvester Press).
KENNY, ANTHONY (ed.) (1969), *Aquinas: A Collection of Critical Essays*, Modern Studies in Philosophy (London, Macmillan).
—— (1984), 'Intentionality: Aquinas and Wittgenstein', in *The Legacy of Wittgenstein* (Oxford, Basil Blackwell).
KÖHLER, WOLFGANG (1947), *Gestalt Psychology: An Introduction to New Concepts in Modern Psychology* (New York, Mentor).
—— (1973), *The Mentality of Apes* (2nd edn. 1927), trans. Ella Winter (London, Routledge & Kegan Paul).
KREBS, JOHN (1989), 'The Evolution of Animal Signals', in Blakemore and Greenfield (1989).
KRISTOFFERSON, A. B. (1975), 'Attention', in H. J. Eysenck, W. J. Arnold, and R. Meili (eds.), *Encyclopedia of Psychology* (London, Fontana), i.

LAKOFF, G. (1987), *Women, Fire and Dangerous Things: What Categories Reveal about the Mind* (University of Chicago Press).
LEWIN, ROGER (1987), *Bones of Contention: Controversies in the Search for Human Origins* (New York, Simon & Schuster).
—— (1989), *Human Evolution: An Illustrated Introduction*, 2nd edn. (Oxford, Blackwell Scientific).
LOAR, BRIAN (1981), *Mind and Meaning*, Cambridge Studies in Philosophy (Cambridge University Press).
—— (1988), 'Social Content and Psychological Content', in Grimm and Merrill (1988).
—— (1990), 'Phenomenal States', in Tomberlin (1990).
LOEWER, BARRY (1982), Review of Fred Dretske, *Knowledge and the Flow of Information, Philosophy of Science*, 49.
—— and REY, GEORGES (eds.) (1991), *Meaning in Mind: Fodor and his Critics* (Oxford, Blackwell).
LOPTSON, PETER (1986), Critical Notice of Brian Loar, *Mind and Meaning, Canadian Journal of Philosophy*, 16.
LURIA, A. R. (1976), *Cognitive Development: Its Cultural and Social Foundations* (1974), ed. Michael Cole, trans. M. Lopez-Morillas and L. Solotaroff (Cambridge, Mass., Harvard University Press).
—— (1987), 'Speech and Brain Processes,' in Gregory (1987).
LYCAN, WILLIAM G. (1980), 'Form, Function and Feel', *Journal of Philosophy*, 78.

—— (1984), Review of Brian Loar, *Mind and Meaning, Philosophical Review*, 93.

—— (1990*a*), 'Phenomenal states', in Tomberlin (1990).

—— (ed.) (1990*b*), *Mind and Cognition: A Reader* (Oxford, Basil Blackwell).

LYONS, JOHN (1977), *Chomsky* (1970), Modern Masters Series (London, Fontana–Collins).

LYONS, WILLIAM (1980), *Gilbert Ryle: An Introduction to his Philosophy* (Brighton and Totowa, NJ, Harvester and Humanities Presses).

—— (1986), *The Disappearance of Introspection* (Cambridge, Mass., MIT Press).

—— (1990), 'Intentionality and Modern Philosophical Psychology, I. The Modern Reduction of Intentionality', *Philosophical Psychology*, 3.

—— (1991), 'Intentionality and Modern Philosophical Psychology, II. The Return to Representation', *Philosophical Psychology*, 4.

—— (1992), 'Intentionality and Modern Philosophical Psychology, III. The Appeal to Teleology', *Philosophical Psychology*, 5.

—— (1995), 'Introduction: Philosophy of Mind in the Twentieth Century', in W. Lyons (ed.), *Modern Philosophy of Mind* (London and Rutland, Vt., Everyman, Dent and Tuttle).

MCALISTER, LINDA L. (ed.) (1976), *The Philosophy of Brentano* (London, Duckworth).

—— (1982), *The Development of Franz Brentano's Ethics*, Elementa, Schriften zur Philosophie und ihrer Problemgeschichte, xxvii (Amsterdam, Editions Rodopi).

MCGINN, COLIN (1988), 'Using Common Sense', Review of Jerry Fodor's *Psychosemantics*, in *Nature*, 331 (Jan.).

—— (1989*a*), 'Can we Solve the Mind–Body Problem?', *Mind*, 98.

—— (1989*b*), *Mental Content* (Oxford, Basil Blackwell).

—— (1991), *The Problem of Consciousness: Essays towards a Resolution* (Oxford, Basil Blackwell).

MACKAY, DONALD (1987), 'Information Theory', in Gregory (1987).

MCLAUGHLIN, BRIAN (ed.) (1991*a*), *Dretske and his Critics* (Oxford, Basil Blackwell).

—— (1991*b*), Review of Dretske, *Explaining Behavior, Philosophical Review*, 100.

MALONEY, J. CHRISTOPHER (1985), Review of Fred Dretske, *Knowledge and the Flow of Information, Nous*, 19.

MANDLER, JEAN M. (1990), 'A New Perspective on Cognitive Development in Infancy', *American Scientist*, 78.

MARENBON, JOHN (1987), *Later Medieval Philosophy (1150–1350): An Introduction* (London, Routledge & Kegan Paul).

MARTIN, NORMAN M. (1967), 'Rudolph Carnap', in Edwards (1967), ii.

MAURER, DAPHNE, and MAURER, CHARLES (1990), *The World of the Newborn* (Harmondsworth, Penguin).

MELTZOFF, ANDREW N., and MOORE, M. KEITH (1992), 'Early Imitation within a Functional Framework: The Importance of Personal Identity, Movement, and Development', *Infant Behavior and Development*, 15.

MEYERS, R. G. (1989), Review of Fred Dretske, *Explaining Behavior*, *Review of Metaphysics*, 42.

MILLER, JONATHAN (ed.) (1983), *States of Mind: Conversations with Psychological Investigators* (London, BBC).

MILLIKAN, RUTH GARRETT (1984), *Language, Thought, and Other Biological Categories: New Foundations for Realism* (Cambridge, Mass., MIT Press).

—— (1986), 'Thoughts without Laws: Cognitive Science without Content', *Philosophical Review*, 95.

—— (1989*a*), 'Biosemantics', *Journal of Philosophy*, 86.

—— (1989*b*), 'In Defense of Proper Functions', *Philosophy of Science*, 61.

—— (1989*c*), 'An Ambiguity in the Notion "Function"', *Biology and Philosophy*, 4.

—— (1990), 'Truth Rules, Hoverflies, and the Kripke–Wittgenstein Paradox', *Philosophical Review*, 99.

—— (1991), 'Speaking up for Darwin', in Loewer and Rey (1991).

MOHYELDIN SAID, K. A., NEWTON-SMITH, W. H., VIALE, R., and WILKES, K. V. (eds.) (1990), *Modelling the Mind* (Oxford, Clarendon Press).

NAGEL, THOMAS (1986), *The View from Nowhere* (Oxford University Press).

—— (1993), 'The Mind Wins!', Review of John Searle, *The Rediscovery of the Mind, New York Review of Books* (4 Mar.).

NATHAN, PETER W. (1987), 'Nervous System', in Gregory (1987).

PANSKY, B., ALLEN, D. J., and BUDD, G. C. (1988), *Review of Neuroscience*, 2nd edn. (New York: Macmillan).

PAPINEAU, DAVID (1987), *Reality and Representation* (Oxford, Basil Blackwell).

PEACOCKE, CHRISTOPHER (1992), *A Study of Concepts* (Cambridge, Mass., MIT Press).

—— (ed.) (1993), *Understanding and Sense*, International Research Library of Philosophy, 2 vols. (Aldershot, Dartmouth).

PEARCE, JOHN M. (1987), *Introduction to Animal Cognition* (Hillsdale, NJ, Lawrence Erlbaum).

PIAGET, JEAN (1955), *The Child's Construction of Reality*, trans. M. Cook (London, Routledge & Kegan Paul).

—— (1977), *The Origin of Intelligence in the Child* (1936), trans. Margaret Cook (Harmondsworth, Penguin).

—— (1980), *Six Psychological Studies*, ed. David Elkind, trans. Anita Tenzer (Brighton, Harvester).

PILBEAM, DAVID (1984), 'The Descent of Hominoids and Hominids', *Scientific American*, 250/3.

PUTNAM, HILARY (1975*a*), 'The Meaning of "Meaning" ', in K. Gunderson (ed.), *Language, Mind and Knowledge*, Minnesota Studies in the Philosophy of Science, vii (Minneapolis, University of Minnesota Press); repr. in Putnam (1975*b*).

—— (1975*b*), *Mind, Language and Reality* (Cambridge University Press).

—— (1989), *Representation and Reality* (Cambridge, Mass., MIT Press).

QUINE, W. V. O. (1960), *Word and Object* (Cambridge, Mass., MIT Press).

—— (1961), *From a Logical Point of View*, 2nd edn. (Cambridge, Mass., Harvard University Press).

—— (1975*a*), 'Mind and Verbal Dispositions', in Guttenplan (1975).

—— (1975*b*), 'The Nature of Natural Knowledge', in Guttenplan (1975).

—— (1979), 'Facts of the Matter', in Shahan and Swoyer (1979).

—— (1981), *Theories and Things* (Cambridge, Mass., Belnap).

—— (1986), 'Autobiography of W. V. Quine', in Hahn and Schilpp (1986).

—— (1992), *Pursuit of Truth*, rev. edn. (Cambridge, Mass., Harvard University Press).

QUINTON, ANTHONY (1967), 'Knowledge and Belief', in Edwards (1967), iv.

RAMSEY, F. P. (1960*a*), 'Last Papers (1929): B. General Propositions and Causality', in Ramsey (1960*b*).

—— (1960*b*), *The Foundations of Mathematics and Other Logical Essays*, ed. R. B. Braithwaite, preface by G. E. Moore (Paterson, NJ, Littlefield Adams).

RAMSEY, WILLIAM, STICH, STEPHEN, and GARON, JOSEPH (1990), 'Connectionism, Eliminativism and the Future of Folk Psychology', in Tomberlin (1990).

RANCURELLO, ANTOS C. (1968), *A Study of Franz Brentano: His Psychological Standpoint and his Significance in the History of Psychology* (New York, Academic Press).

REED, T. J. (1984), *Goethe*, Past Masters (Oxford University Press).

RICE, MABEL L. (1989), 'Children's Language Acquisition', *American Psychologist*, 44.

RICHARDSON, ALAN, and BOWDEN, JOHN (eds.) (1983), *A New Dictionary of Christian Theology* (London, SCM).

ROSE, STEVEN (1976), *The Conscious Brain*, rev. edn. (Harmondsworth, Penguin).

ROSENBERG, JAY F. (1987), Review of Ruth Garrett Millikan's *Language, Thought, and Other Biological Categories*, *Nous*, 21.

ROSENFIELD, ISRAEL (1988), *The Invention of Memory: A New View of the Brain*, intro. by Oliver Sacks (New York, Basic Books).

ROSENTHAL, DAVID M. (ed.) (1991), *The Nature of Mind* (Oxford University Press).

ROVEE-COLLIER, CAROLYN (1987), 'Learning and Memory in Infancy', in J. D. Osofsky (ed.), *Handbook of Infant Development* (New York, Wiley).

RUSSELL, BERTRAND (1967), *The Problems of Philosophy* (1912), OPUS (Oxford University Press).

RUSSELL, JAMES (ed.) (1987), *Philosophical Perspectives on Developmental Psychology* (Oxford, Basil Blackwell).

RYLE, GILBERT (1949), *The Concept of Mind* (London, Hutchinson).

SACKS, OLIVER (1990), 'Neurology and the Soul', *New York Review of Books*, 37/18.

—— (1994), 'An Anthropologist on Mars: A Neurologist's Notebook', *New Yorker* (27 Dec. 1993–3 Jan.).

SCHIFFER, STEPHEN (1972), *Meaning* (Oxford, Clarendon Press).

SCHILPP, PAUL ARTHUR (ed.) (1963), *The Philosophy of Rudolph Carnap*, Library of Living Philosophers, xi (La Salle, Ill., Open Court).

SCHMITT, RICHARD (1967), 'Edmund Husserl', in Edwards (1967), iv.

SEARLE, JOHN (1980), 'Minds, Brains and Programs', *Behavioural and Brain Sciences*, 3; repr. in D. R. Hofstadter and D. C. Dennett, *The Mind's I: Fantasies and Reflections on Self and Soul* (Brighton, Harvester, 1981).

—— (1983), *Intentionality: An Essay in the Philosophy of Mind* (Cambridge University Press).

—— (1992), *The Rediscovery of the Mind*, Representation and Mind (Cambridge, Mass., MIT Press).

SELLARS, WILFRID (1954), 'Some Reflections on Language Games', *Philosophy of Science*, 21.

—— (1956), 'Empiricism and the Philosophy of Mind', in Herbert Feigl and Michael Scriven (eds.), *The Foundations of Science and the Concepts of Psychology and Psychoanalysis*, Minnesota Studies in the Philosophy of Science, i (Minneapolis, University of Minnesota Press); reprinted in Sellars (1963).

—— (1963), *Science, Perception and Reality* (Atlantic Heights, NJ, Humanities Press).

SHAHAN, ROBERT W., and SWOYER, CHRIS (eds.) (1979), *Essays on the Philosophy of W. V. Quine* (Brighton, Harvester).

SHEEHAN, PETER (1969), 'Aquinas on Intentionality', in Kenny (1969).

SKINNER, B. F. (1957), *Verbal Behavior* (New York, Appleton).

SLATER, ALAN (1990), 'Infant Development: The Origins of Competence', *Psychologist*, 3 (Mar.).

SMITH, BARRY (ed.) (1986), *Foundations of Gestalt Psychology* (Munich, Philosophia Verlag).

SMITH, PETER, and JONES, O. R. (1986), *The Philosophy of Mind: An Introduction* (Cambridge University Press).

SMOOK, R. (1989), Review of Fred Dretske, *Explaining Behavior, Philosophical Books*, 30.

SNOW, C. P. (1967), *Variety of Men* (London, Macmillan).

SNOWDON, P. F. (1988), Review of David Papineau, *Representation and Reality, Mind*, 97.

SPELKE, ELIZABETH, BREINLINGER, KAREN, MACOMBER, JANET, and JACOBSEN, KRISTEN (1992), 'Origins of Knowledge', *Psychological Review*, 99.

STAMPE, DENNIS (1979), 'Towards a Causal Theory of Linguistic Representation', in Peter French, Theodore Uehling, Jr., and Howard Wettstein (eds.), *Contemporary Perspectives in the Philosophy of Language* (Minneapolis, University of Minnesota Press).

STERELNY, KIM (1983), Review of Fred Dretske, *Knowledge and the Flow of Information, Australasian Journal of Philosophy*, 61.

STICH, STEPHEN P. (1981), 'Dennett on Intentional Systems', *Philosophical Topics*, 12.

—— (1983), *From Folk Psychology to Cognitive Science: The Case against Belief* (Cambridge, Mass., MIT Press).

TARSKI, ALFRED (1944), 'The Semantic Conception of Truth and the Foundations of Semantics', *Philosophy and Phenomenological Research*, 4.

—— (1983), 'Der Wahrheitsbegriff in den formalisierten Sprachen' (1935), *Studia Philosophica*, 1; repr. as 'The Concept of Truth in Formalised Languages', trans. J. H. Woodger, in *Logic, Semantics, Metamathematics: Papers from 1923 to 1938*, ed. J. Corcoran, 2nd edn. (Indianapolis, Hackett).

TERRACE, HERBERT (1989), 'Thoughts without Words', in Blakemore and Greenfield (1989).

TIENSON, JOHN (1987), 'An Introduction to Connectionism', *Southern Journal of Philosophy*, 26, supp.

TINBERGEN, NIKOLAAS (1951), *The Study of Instinct* (Oxford, Clarendon Press).

—— (1972), *Social Behaviour in Animals with Special Reference to Vertebrates* (1953), 2nd edn. (London, Chapman and Hall).

TOMBERLIN, JAMES E. (ed.) (1990), *Philosophical Perspectives*, iv: *Action Theory and Philosophy of Mind, 1990* (Atascadero, Calif., Ridgeview).

TREVARTHEN, COLWYN (1974), 'Conversations with a Two-Month-Old', *New Scientist*, 62.

—— (1987), 'Mind in Infancy', in Gregory (1987).

VYGOTSKY, LEV (1978), *Mind in Society: The Development of Higher Psychological Processes*, ed. M. Cole, V. John Steiner, S. Scribner, and E. Souberman (Cambridge, Mass., Harvard University Press).

—— (1986), *Thought and Language* (1934), ed. and trans. Alex Kozulin (Cambridge, Mass., MIT Press).

WASHBURN, SHERWOOD L. (1978), 'The Evolution of Man', *Scientific American*, 239/3.

WILKES, KATHLEEN (1987), 'Describing the Child's Mind,' in Russell (1987).

WILSON, E. O. (1971), *The Insect Societies* (Cambridge, Mass., Belnap).

WITTGENSTEIN, LUDWIG (1958), *Philosophical Investigations* (1953), 2nd edn., trans. G. E. M. Anscombe (Oxford, Basil Blackwell).

WOODFIELD, ANDREW (1987), 'On the Very Idea of Acquiring a Concept', in Russell (1987).

WOODWORTH, ROBERT S., and SCHLOSBERG, HAROLD (1955), *Experimental Psychology*, 3rd edn. (London, Methuen).

WRIGHT, LARRY (1973), 'Functions', *Philosophical Review*, 82.

ZEKI, SEMIR (1993), *A Vision of the Brain* (Oxford, Blackwell Scientific).

INDEX